AMERICAN FRONTIER LIFE

RON TYLER, CAROL CLARK,
LINDA AYRES, WARDER H. CADBURY,
HERMAN J. VIOLA, BERNARD REILLY, JR.
INTRODUCTION BY PETER H. HASSRICK

AMERICAN FRONTIER LIFE

EARLY WESTERN PAINTING AND PRINTS

AMON CARTER MUSEUM · FORT WORTH · TEXAS

BUFFALO BILL HISTORICAL CENTER · CODY · WYOMING

ABBEVILLE PRESS · PUBLISHERS · NEW YORK

PORTLAND HOUSE · NEW YORK

This book was produced in conjunction with the exhibition *American Frontier Life: Early Western Painting and Prints* organized by the Amon Carter Museum and the Buffalo Bill Historical Center, and held at the Buffalo Bill Historical Center, Cody, Wyoming, June 12–September 10, 1987; the Amon Carter Museum, Fort Worth, Texas, October 17, 1987–January 3, 1988; and the Pennsylvania Academy of the Fine Arts, Philadelphia, Pennsylvania, January 28–April 22, 1988.

Editor: Alan Axelrod
Art Director: James Wageman
Copy Editor: Elaine Luthy

Inquiries should be addressed to Abbeville Press, Inc., 488 Madison Avenue, New York 10022.
This 1989 edition published by Portland House, a division of Dilithium Press, Ltd., distributed by Crown Publishers, Inc., 225 Park Avenue South, New York, New York 10003.
Printed and bound in Japan   ISBN 0-517-68786-0
h g f e d c b a

Library of Congress Cataloging-in-Publication Data

American frontier life.

Issued in conjunction with the exhibition American frontier life, organized by the Amon Carter Museum and the Buffalo Bill Historical Center, and held at the center, June 12–Sept. 10, 1987, the Museum, Oct. 17, 1987–Jan. 3, 1988, and the Pennsylvania Academy of the Fine Arts, Jan. 28–Apr. 22, 1988.
Includes index.
1. West (U.S.) in art—Exhibitions. 2. Frontier and pioneer life in art—Exhibitions. 3. Frontier and pioneer life—West (U.S.)—Exhibitions. 4. Indians of North America—Pictorial Works—Exhibitions. 5. Art, American—Exhibitions. 6. Art, Modern—19th Century—United States—Exhibitions. I. Tyler, Ronnie C., 1941–. II. Amon Carter Museum of Western Art. III. Buffalo Bill Historical Center. IV. Pennsylvania Academy of the Fine Arts.
N8214.5.U6A44   1987   760'.0449978   86-28750
ISBN 0-89659-691-5
ISBN 0-89659-693-1 (pbk.)

Front cover and title page: William Tylee Ranney, *Advice on the Prairie*. See fig. 53.
Back cover: Leopold Grozelier, after Charles Wimar, *On the Prairie*. See fig. 118.

CONTENTS

PREFACE

Until recently, there has been little research in the field of western American narrative painting, and this publication seeks to bring to bear new scholarship on the subject. The book presents recent research on nine artists who helped to develop the images of the trapper, flatboatman, pioneer, Indian, and other American "types," and shows the familiar paintings of George Caleb Bingham in context with those of such less well-known artists as William Ranney and Charles Wimar and the relatively unknown works of Charles Deas. The essays demonstrate how the images of these and other artists were related to literature and to the popular prints through which they were transmitted to a wide audience. Narrative painting was especially prevalent in the years 1830 to 1860, when much of the public perception of the West was formed, and the scenes of the familiar—of everyday life—helped the unfamiliar and exotic West become an integral part of America's concept of itself.

The research leading to this publication was made possible by a generous grant from the Luce Fund for Scholarship in American Art, a program of The Henry Luce Foundation, Inc.

We are most grateful to the seven authors who submitted the essays for the book and to Abbeville Press, especially Sharon Gallagher and Alan Axelrod, for this handsome volume.

The exhibition this book documents would not have been possible without the cooperation of the many lenders who are acknowledged in the exhibition checklist, and the staffs of the Amon Carter Museum, the Buffalo Bill Historical Center, and the Pennsylvania Academy of the Fine Arts, as well as the generous support of The Henry Luce Foundation, Inc., Boulevard Mortgage Company, Philadelphia, Mr. and Mrs. Meyer P. Potamkin, and an anonymous donor.

In addition to those mentioned above, we would like to thank the following people who assisted us in the course of the project's many phases: John Abbott, Southern Illinois University at Edwardsville; Nancy K. Anderson, National Gallery of Art; Jean Ashton, The New-York Historical Society; Carol Walker Aten, Vose Galleries of Boston, Inc.; Louisa Bowen, Southern Illinois University at Edwardsville; Kathie Bennewitz, Amon Carter Museum; David Brewster; Donaly Brice, Texas State Archives; James Burke, The Saint Louis Art Museum; Ann Murphy Burroughs, National Academy of Design; John Carbonell; Bruce W. Chambers, Berry-Hill Galleries, Inc.; Elizabeth Cunningham, The Anschutz Collection; Stuart P. Feld, Hirschl & Adler Galleries, Inc.; Abigail Booth Gerdts, National Academy of Design; William H. Goetzmann, University of Texas; Frank Goodyear, Pennsylvania Academy of the Fine Arts; Michael Green, Texas State Archives; Francis Grubar, George Washington University; Charles E. Hanson, Jr., Museum of the Fur Trade, Chadron, Nebraska; Patricia Hendricks, Archer M. Huntington Art Gallery, University of Texas; Sarah Hirsch, The Thomas Gilcrease Institute of American History and Art; Michael Q. Hooks, Archives and Record Division, General Land Office, Austin; Milan Hughston, Amon Carter Museum; David Hunt, Joslyn Art Museum; Ben Huseman, Amon Carter Museum; Elizabeth Johns, University of Maryland; Palmer McCarter, Amon Carter Museum; the late John Francis McDermott; Daniel M. McPike, The Thomas Gilcrease Institute of American History and Art; James H. Maroney, Jr.; Col. Merl M. Moore, Jr.; Elizabeth Ranney Moran; Ranney Moran; Anne Morand, The Thomas Gilcrease Institute of American History and Art; Jane Myers, Amon Carter Museum; Fred Myers, The Thomas Gilcrease Institute of American History and Art; James H. Nottage, Kansas State Historical Society, Topeka; Robert J. Phelan; Mark Pockros; Sue W. Reed, Museum of Fine Arts, Boston; Gary Reynolds, The Newark Museum; Richard Saunders, Middlebury College; Sandra Scheibe, Amon Carter Museum; Julie Schimmel, Gerald Peters Gallery; Wendy Shadwell, The New-York Historical Society; Marilyn Shanewise, Joslyn Art Museum; Michael Shapiro, The Saint Louis Art Museum; Mark Thistlethwaite, Texas Christian University; Esther Thyssen; Martha Utterback, Daughters of the Republic of Texas; Abbot Williams Vose, Vose Galleries of Boston, Inc.; Susan Walther, Huntington Library, Art Gallery and Botanical Gardens; Christopher Kent Wilson, Middlebury College; and Richard P. W. Williams.

Jan Keene Muhlert, Director
Amon Carter Museum

Peter Hassrick, Director
Buffalo Bill Historical Center

Linda Bantel, Director of the Museum
Pennsylvania Academy of the Fine Arts

INTRODUCTION

PETER H. HASSRICK

It is unreasonable to expect that any great interest will be excited abroad in the fruits either of the pen or pencil here, except so far as the subjects are novel, or the execution superlatively great. Tales of frontier and Indian life . . . the adventures of the hunter and the emigrant—correct pictures of what is truly remarkable in our scenery, awaken instant attention in Europe. If our artists or authors, therefore, wish to earn trophies abroad, let them seize upon themes essentially American.

Henry Tuckerman, *Book of the Artists,* 1867

Although not necessarily bent on appealing to European audiences today, this book provides a remarkable opportunity to explore mid-nineteenth-century American painting as it reflects the richness of those frontier themes touted as so "essentially American." Assembled here is a pictorial anthology of western life that mirrors not only the people and activities of this nation's frontier from about 1835 to 1860, but also reviews those images within the context of American aesthetic traditions of the time. Our purpose is to investigate western symbology and iconography as they found a place in paintings and prints of the period and to explore dimensions of native genre and narrative work that advanced the fundamental character of our national artistic tradition. The challenge has been especially rewarding in that this is the first time these paintings and prints have been brought together in an art-historical context.

Stanley, Blackfeet Card Players *(detail, see fig. 3)*

In order to accomplish our goals, we have concentrated on the works of four American nineteenth-century artists who treated western genre and narrative themes extensively. These painters, George Caleb Bingham, Charles Deas, William Ranney, and Arthur Fitzwilliam Tait, are the focus here because they celebrated frontier life as no group of artists before had been able to do. In addition, we have sought to investigate the popularization of frontier pictorial imagery, including a review of the place of painters of Indians—George Catlin, John Mix Stanley, Charles Wimar (fig. 1), Seth Eastman, and Alfred Jacob Miller—within the corpus of American genre and narrative production.

What we have uncovered is fundamentally a narrative tradition, narrative in the sense that the common artistic mission was to tell a story. And the story was a readily appealing one, given the intriguing saga unfolding on the frontier during these artists' lifetimes and their easy identification with that saga.

The four main artists under discussion here were but the heart of a larger group of painters who instilled in the popular American mind of the period a powerful sense of national identity with the frontier and its people. Like the frontier they recorded, their works exuded an aura of freshness and innocence that induced critics to proclaim their purely American flavor. Their themes mirrored the image of America itself. Of Ranney's work, for example, Henry Tuckerman would write, "a more characteristic introduction to *genre* painting in America can hardly be imagined," as Ranney had struck on "a native and promising path" in his views of frontier life. Similarly, of Charles Deas, the same observer would comment that his western paintings displayed a "peculiar 'native American' zest."[1]

What has often been called the "Jacksonian persuasion" was the culmination of a generation of changes following the Second Great Awakening and the reorientation of American values in the early nineteenth century. The great revivals that began at Cane Ridge, Kentucky, in 1801 emphasized a religion of the heart over the old religion of the head and recalled in fervor the first Great Awakening in New England some sixty years earlier. Emotion was more important than mind, a reversal of the authoritative and rational Calvinism that had held sway. In the new religious order, the individual looked for authority in himself and there developed in consequence an almost grass-roots religion, a new mood of egalitarianism, and an emphasis on the perfectibility of the common man.

Politically, this introspective preoccupation with self culminated in the development of a new antiinstitutionalism, a new democratic mood with an expansion of the franchise, and a new emotion-charged style of stump campaigning. This was all accompanied by a great optimism about the future. Intellectually, Americans were overthrowing the classical view of history as cyclical. In its place they were adopting a Christian millennial view, a new version of the familiar New England millennial vision of the seventeenth century. As before, Americans were a chosen people, but this time at the vanguard of "progress" rather than as harbingers of a New Canaan. This translated easily into our Manifest Destiny to take over the American continent; it gave Americans not only the right but the duty to move west.

Two intellectual forces informed the American mind in these early years of the nineteenth century: Romanticism and its adjunct, Transcendentalism. The Romantic movement stressed the differences among peoples and races. Hence, there was a great emphasis politically and socially to discover and accentuate those things that made Americans unique. There followed a rejection of European models and a search for American sources of inspiration in both literature and the visual arts. Especially appealing was the exotic element of America's West, the wilderness and its inhabitants. Combined here were the awe of nature's sublime aspect and the otherworldliness of a people at such physical distance from the borders of civilization. This exotic character of America's frontier most attracted native artists and their growing public.

Transcendentalism emphasized spontaneity. It, too, was in part a response to "grandeur" and devoted greater attention to the individual. There was also a reaction to the Industrial Revolution and the urbanization of Europe and eastern America. Writers and painters began to extol the value of the rural.

After 1800, the United States gradually became a truly continental nation. The states controlled a tremendous western domain. Beginning with the War of 1812, which was fought largely to gain control of the Mississippi Valley, the West and Westerners began to have a political voice. The West was not only a huge territory administered in common by all Americans, it was also the locus of the Indian and of America's greatest asset (in the minds of many artists and writers), the wilderness. Moreover, the egalitarian West and its Daniel Boones seemed to embody the nation's democratic mood. The time was ripe for new visual interpretations set in the West that reflected the individual, the anecdotal, and the egalitarian, as well as America's awakened emotionalism.

Combined with these forces was the growing belief in racial uniqueness, a concept that had a double edge for the Indian. On the one hand, it began to be believed that the Indian was savage by nature rather than by circumstance. To many he thus became irredeemable. On the other hand, as savagery was overtaken by civilization, the Indian would disappear. He was thus to be valued and memorialized as the natural man, a vanishing counterpoint to the evils of civilization. In these postures, the Indian began to fill the chapters and canvases of America's arts and to prevail upon the American popular mind.

By 1830 American literature had begun to advance notions of national identification with western themes. James Fenimore Cooper and Washington Irving, among others in search of American sources of inspiration, had by this time elevated frontier types to the level of national heroes. Popular perceptions of the West and its people afforded exceptionally appealing avenues for literary exploration. As a reviewer of one early Mississippi Valley history remarked, the West was exemplary in almost every aspect:

In the "far west," most things wear a character of higher grandeur and intensity, than on the east side of the mountains. Nature has a deeper and richer dash of poetry in her composition. Her domain is wider and wilder; and if her attire is less trim and symmetrical, it is more opulent in color, and magnificent in drapery. She is enthroned in more queenly pomp and splendour; and the beauty and gorgeousness of her gardens, parks, and pleasure-grounds, not only satisfy the senses, but feast them to satiety.[2]

This store of literary sources became even more abundant as writers began to look beyond the Mississippi River over the expanses of the Great Plains. Here were literary themes ready even for

1. *Charles Wimar,*
The Buffalo Dance, *1860,*
oil on canvas, 24⅞ × 49⅝ in.
The Saint Louis Art
Museum, Gift of Mrs. John
T. Davis

the painter's canvas, as a reviewer of Irving's *Tour on the Prairies* (1834) recounted:

The boundless prairies stretch out illimitably to the fancy, as the eye scans his descriptions. The athletic figures of the riflemen, the gaily arrayed Indians, the heavy buffalo and the graceful deer, pass in strong relief and startling contrast before us. We are stirred by the bustle of the camp at dawn, and soothed by its quiet, or delighted with its picturesque aspect under the shadow of night. . . . Our hearts thrill at the vivid representations of a primitive and excursive existence; we involuntarily yearn, as we read, for the genial activity and the perfect exposure to the influences of nature in all her free magnificence. . . .[3]

Such Edenic subjects were, according to the same enthusiastic reviewer, "susceptible of immediate transfer to the canvas of the painter."

In 1828 Cooper had complained openly about the want of materials for the author of American subjects. The writer was limited by what Cooper termed the "baldness" of American life compared to that of Europe: "There are no annals for the historian; no follies (beyond the most vulgar and commonplace) for the satirist; no manners for the dramatist; no obscure fictions for the writer of romance; no gross and hardy offenses against decorum for the moralist; nor any of the rich artificial auxiliaries of poetry."[4] Fortunately, like the painter Thomas Cole, writers found solace and native inspiration in America's wilderness landscape and historic lore of the Hudson River Valley. There was also much promise in the burgeoning West, and writers and publishers found American audiences eager to read of adventure and exploit on the frontier. There was much with which to identify—the suggestion of paradise beyond known borders, the manifestations of physical growth and maturity for Jacksonian America, and the lure of exotic characters like the Indian and the mountain man. The West was a cornucopia for the imagination.

As the pages of American literature filled with essays on frontier life, so, too, did the canvases of numerous artists. Forays by painters of the 1830s, 1840s, and 1850s into the inviting narrative themes exposed for review by the trapper and the trader, the emigrant and explorer of the West, were often in themselves adventures. Much of what unfolded on the frontier could be considered

2. *Alfred Jacob Miller,* Hunting Wild Horses, *n.d., oil on panel, 13½ × 19 in. Private collection*

3. *John Mix Stanley,*
Blackfeet Card Players, *1869,*
oil on canvas, 28 × 42 in.
John F. Eulich Collection,
Dallas

sources for epic historical paintings, works that focused on such ideals as pioneering, or Manifest Destiny, or progress through civilization, and that found their fullest pictorial expression in Daniel Boone's conquest of the wilderness or the press of wagon trains over the crest of the Rockies.[5]

But much about the frontier was not epic. There were many recorded, factual incidents, not representative of any universal truth or mythology, that were nonetheless worthy of the painter's effort. The buffalo hunt, the capture of wild horses (fig. 2), the camp cook lost on the prairies, and the Indian Medicine Dance are representative subjects. Much was also just everyday, unrecorded occurrences and thus inspired simple genre treatment. A rest on the prairie, voyagers in a canoe, Indians playing cards (fig. 3), and a trapper's wedding provided exemplary genre themes. It is these two areas of interest—depictions that are documentary or sometimes "eyewitness" accounts of specific incidents and those that show everyday genre scenes—on which we concentrate in this volume.

We treat this collective work as "exotic genre" because the locale of the artists' environment was far beyond the reach of the ordinary observer. *Exotic* was also a favorite word in the nineteenth century, loaded with emotional and psychological

13

suggestion. Like the word *sublime,* the term *exotic* connoted picturesqueness through psychological association. The relatively sophisticated eastern and, to some degree, European audiences sported a healthy appetite for what Henry Vyverberg calls "primitivist nostalgia."[6] The frontier satisfied a vital urge for vicarious exploration of a sublime and exotic world.

Traditional genre painting was ranked low on the list of accepted American art forms in the early nineteenth century. Even landscape painting, gradually elevated by the vogue of Thomas Cole and the Hudson River School, had only begun to alter the conventional perception that paintings of nature were somehow inferior to historical paintings. And history painting as a discipline had only recently, within the first quarter of the nineteenth century, been found worthy of the artist's attention. Portraiture had reigned supreme in American pictorial arts, and the interlopers of history, landscape, and genre painting were not as well received.

One of America's first painters known to have "attempted genre with success,"[7] Henry Inman was exemplary in his lament of the artist's plight caused by the limited appetite for genre painting:

The taste of my "customers" . . . is limited chiefly to portraits. They will not commission me to execute Landscapes. . . . I cannot even get a chance to paint a landscape, unless I stick it into a portrait. . . . Why, I should have starved long ago on anything but portraits. . . . People would have their portraits and I must have bread, and I made them pay for their own phizzes just as much as I should have asked them for a phiz of Nature, or a phiz of History. They did it willingly, too, as a general rule and I have many a time received a commission for $300 or $500 for portraits and groups, when the very same persons would not have hung up my "Mumble the Peg" in their parlors.[8]

Considered in his day one of the foremost artistic figures in America, Inman seemed unable to influence public persuasion toward such genre scenes as *Mumble the Peg* (1842; fig. 4). Yet interest in scenes of our national life gradually increased. A good deal of this new appetite was sated by such painters as William Sidney Mount, Francis W. Edmonds, and Jerome Thompson, who portrayed the charms of America's rural and urban communities. At the same time, American thoughts had been drawn westward. Men of letters had settled on Daniel Boone, for example, as the quintessential national hero of the westward movement. Boone, in turn, was the popular precursor of the pioneer, the flatboatman, the woodsman, explorer, and mountain man. Whether plying the uncertain waters of western rivers or trapping beaver in the shadow of the Rocky Mountains, these frontiersmen became emblematic of republican ideals and the emerging democratic man. As Dawn Glanz has written of the trapper, depending on the particular characteristics an artist may have wished to feature, he

could appear as a romantic hero—colorful, individualistic, and even exotic—or as a national hero exemplifying stoic virtues. He could even appear in genre paintings as a kind of democratic hero—that is, as a common man pursuing his profession, a role with which Americans could easily identify. In each of these guises the trapper could also fulfill his role as a mediator between the wilderness and civilization, thus helping to reconcile conflicts between romantic and nationalistic values that existed side by side in American thinking.[9]

The first artists to present themes of frontier life to wide audiences in America and Europe were George Catlin and Alfred Jacob Miller. Catlin's interests were focused on the Indian population in the Far West as inspired by years of firsthand study between 1830 and 1838. His approach combined the art of a portrait painter, the scientific impulse of the Philadelphia intellectual community, and a high sense of personal adventure. The result was an impressive gallery of portraits and scenes of everyday life (fig. 5), many of which carry sufficient anecdotal weight to be considered genre work.

Miller's paintings, the products of a summer excursion to the Rocky Mountains in 1837, fixed equally on the Indian and the trapper. Taken west on an adventurous holiday by Captain William Drummond Stewart, Miller recorded the vibrant frontier life that he witnessed at the heart of the fur-trapping era. Devoid of scientific inclination, Miller brought to visual life literary themes that had been attracting American readers for a decade prior to his sojourn. Where Catlin had concentrated on the Plains Indians, Miller explored pictorially, for the first time, the life, customs, and manners of the mountain man.

Like many other frontiersmen, the trappers represented distant figures, and their way of life, even when ordinary for the circumstances, seemed an exotic existence. These were men and women who lived in a world that lay beyond the limits of established conventions. The artists who explored the pictorial dimensions of the frontier revealed this extraordinary otherworld, saturated with the sounds and sensations, the colors and rhythms of an untrammeled wilderness and unspoiled nature.

In their own day Catlin and Miller were generally recognized more as ethnographic recorders than practitioners of narrative or genre art; this view persists somewhat today. Indeed, with Catlin such an assessment is valid, since he only rarely divorced himself from Indian subject matter. His La Salle series, painted on commission for the French king, Louis Philippe, is the only known nonethnographic western work he produced. Yet in his portraits of Indian life, Catlin was exposing basic, everyday circumstances. As a result, despite the ethnographic focus of Catlin's work, his depictions are fundamentally genre treatments and thus fit comfortably within the parameters of this book.

Miller approached the world of the mountain man in the same way he explored that of the Indian. He was appreciative of both worlds, even though many of his contemporaries viewed him primarily as an Indian painter. His friend and protégé, Frank Mayer, exclaimed that "I have no higher ambition than to place my name near yours as a painter of Indians for I think that your Indian pictures are the best things of the kind yet produced." The art establishment of the day also praised Miller essentially for his Indian subjects. The *Crayon* in June of 1857 acclaimed him not as a genre or historical painter but as the most distinguished of Indian painters, his works being

"among the most valuable records of that interesting people, which Art has preserved. They were painted from sketches made by Mr. Miller during a tour among the wildest tribes at the base of the Rocky Mountains, and at a time when they had not lost their savage virtues or riches. They embrace every variety of subject of Indian life, and are executed with artistic ability."[10]

It is almost solely as ethnographic painters that Miller and Catlin have made their way into modern art-historical thought. In the preface to Hermann Warner Williams's *Mirror to the American Past,* the standard source on American genre painting, these two artists are regarded as inappropriate for inclusion. From Williams's perspective, their work is "basically of ethnographic significance" and, allied with that of later painters John Mix Stanley and Seth Eastman, is classed as "exotic genre." This reference to exotic genre seems more than appropriate when discussing these artists and their western work, and it was a category apart from the type of genre painting with which Williams was concerned. However, when Williams excludes all four because their paintings "rarely show the intermingling of Indian and white cultures," he seems to imply that, without whites as subject matter, there is no genre painting. Elizabeth Johns, who has undertaken an extensive study of American genre painting, emphasizes that a true genre painter must come from within the culture that is depicted. That these eastern artists did not is what marks their work of viewing frontier life, Indian and white alike, as an "exotic genre." They were not from within the culture, yet their lives had crossed paths with the frontier and its people. Emotionally, if not physically, they were sensitive to frontier culture and its potential for aesthetic exploitation. Their work also fits within Williams's further definition of genre painting as "an artist's commentary on a commonplace everyday activity of ordinary people, painted in a realistic manner."[11]

Certainly Miller's imagery was distinct from what is known as the "rustic genre" practiced by contemporaries like Mount. As a follower of Sir David Wilkie, who popularized rustic genre in England during the first quarter of the nineteenth century, Mount had been the initial force behind American genre painting. His "comick" pictures of the early 1830s were intended to reveal America to herself. They were, in their straightforward simplicity, meant to suggest virtuous behavior and convey, as in Mount's *California News* (fig. 6), the optimistic spirit of American life prior to the Civil War. Most contained a wide variety of small, still-life details that helped explain the ordinary incidents in the lives of everyday rural people. Mount's themes of cider making, barn dances, and corn husking "celebrated the yeoman farmer as national symbol and appealed to Jacksonian

6. *William Sidney Mount (1807–68),* California News, *1850, oil on canvas, 21½ × 20¼ in. The Museums at Stony Brook, New York, Gift of Mr. and Mrs. Ward Melville, 1955*

7. *Claude Regnier
(active 1847–53),
after George Caleb Bingham,*
In a Quandry. Mississippi
Raftsmen Playing Cards,
*1852,
lithograph (hand colored),
18¹⁵/₁₆ × 20⅜ in.
Published by Goupil & Co.
Amon Carter Museum, Fort
Worth*

8. *Claude Regnier
(active 1847–53),
after George Caleb Bingham,*
Canvassing for a Vote,
*1852–53,
toned lithograph (hand
colored), 17⅛ × 20⁵/₁₆ in.
Published by M. Knoedler.
Amon Carter Museum, Fort
Worth*

and timeless simplicity. Here is American story-telling in its most lyrical and enduring pictorial form (fig. 7).

Bingham began a celebrated series of riverboat paintings in the mid 1840s with *Fur Traders Descending the Missouri* (1845; fig. 11). This was the first of his paintings to be exhibited at the American Art-Union and is the first of his known extant genre pieces. It was followed over the next six years by a number of riverboat scenes and trapper pictures. In St. Louis the *Daily Missouri Republican* characterized river paintings like *The Jolly Flatboatmen* (1846; fig. 13) as "an entire new field of historic painting," and then went on to praise Bingham for the pure rusticity of his genre views.[13]

A simple, homespun quality pervaded some of Bingham's famous political subjects as well. It can be seen in *Canvassing for a Vote* (1852; fig. 8), a clear testament to American democratization portrayed in the open exchange of ideas among ordinary men. Democracy was touted here, not as the ideal notion that might have been found in history painting of the period, but as "a kind of rough-and-tumble genre" that characterizes Bingham's more formal county election paintings of the early 1850s. As for epic history paintings, American audiences had specific expectations. To be effective, according to one of Bingham's contemporaries, a painting should play down "prosaic feeling" and pass from the actual "to the ideal man; from the tenants of earth to those of a higher sphere: and, in doing this, [embody] conceptions springing out of mundane subjects, in forms of celestial purity."[14]

The purity of Bingham's campaign and election paintings lay precisely in their lack of celestial idealization. They blossomed with objectivity, thus awakening America to a reality that Bingham had experienced firsthand, the real people in the West and the expanding franchise in the new western states. As one recent observer has noted, "until Mark Twain wrote his stories, no other artist left such vivid impressions of the crude and vigorous spirit that in his time animated democracy along the Western hustings."[15]

Although Bingham's specific approach to genre

Americans who saw themselves in this image."[12] Miller's mountain men, though somewhat more removed from established society than Mount's Long Island farmers, were no less a part of that American self-image. Their daily activities, admittedly outside the everyday activities of an Easterner, were nonetheless representative of yeoman toil, part and parcel of harvesting the bounty of the newly awakened continent.

In fact, there is but one painter who might share the mantle of rustic genre in his pictorialization of the American frontier life. His name was George Caleb Bingham, a Missouri portrait painter turned genre artist. In his work is the poetry of life recounted by a master of quiet mood

painting was substantially more rustic in style and interpretation than the other artists treated in this volume, his cause was essentially common with theirs. They all sought a market for work portraying everyday life on the frontier. Their eastern Establishment clientele, enticed by the American frontier novels of Cooper and accounts by Irving, Gregg, and Carson, longed to see what life was like in the West. They longed to have visual imagery of the trapper and pioneer, the Indian and the explorer. Because America was growing, such pictorializations of western life helped to satisfy a thirst for expressions of nationalistic achievement. The frontiersmen were on the cutting edge either as conquerors of what Joshua Taylor has called the "redeemed community,"[16] or escapees to the Eden in the wilderness. In the paintings portraying conquest, the Indians and whites are in contest. Man is pitted against nature or against man, as in Charles Deas's painting, *The Death Struggle* (ca. 1845; fig. 39). In the decade of the 1850s, such histrionics were seen in Charles Wimar's *The Attack on an Emigrant Train* (1856; fig. 90). These dramatic scenes had direct literary precedent. The Wimar painting, for example, was inspired by an incident described in Gabriel Ferry's book, *Impressions de voyages et aventures dans le Mexique, la haute Californie et les régions de l'or,* which had been published in Brussels five years earlier.[17] As historical pieces they verge on the epic and stretch the term *genre* beyond reasonable limits. Given the fact that the artists never witnessed such events, a common prerequisite for a true genre work, the paintings must be regarded as narrative. As such they were avidly appreciated by the public, who viewed the conquest of the wilderness as inevitable.

For those who viewed the frontier as an Eden, rather than an object of conquest, William Ranney and, in some cases, Charles Deas were prepared to answer the call. Both artists had profited from direct exposure to the West. Deas's associates had dubbed him "Rocky Mountains" because he affected the appearance of a mountain man and boasted of numerous direct experiences with Indians of the Far West. Ranney's exploits in the West had resulted in similar associations. His West

Hoboken, New Jersey, studio was likened to the nest of a "bushranger," indicative of Ranney's affinity for the trapper's world. One review of Ranney's works suggested the artist's vision of the pure but ephemeral qualities of nature's western wilds: "Ranney was a faithful student of nature in the direction which his tastes led him. Most of his works were representative of prairie life, consisting of hunting scenes, animals, western character and scenery, faithfully studied, but of which materials he made most interesting pictures. His works have a historical value independent of their artistic merit, when it is considered that civilization is fast sweeping away the original picturesque aspects of pioneer life in the far West" (fig. 9).[18]

As with Deas's and Bingham's work, Ranney's frontier images were transmitted to a broad audience through the medium of popular prints. Most commonly, the work of these artists reached the public through the dissemination of prints by the American Art-Union and other membership organizations. A lucky few even won the original paintings in art-distribution lotteries. The American Art-Union vitally influenced the development of genre painting by supporting and encouraging native art based on themes of American life.[19] The growth of art-unions was impressive; by 1850 these organizations boasted nearly fifty thousand subscribing members.

By 1852, the art-unions were found to be illegal, and the public turned to Currier & Ives for familiar western images. Although that firm had been reproducing popular lithographs since the mid 1830s, it did not venture into frontier subject matter until the 1850s. Its prime supplier of images was Arthur Fitzwilliam Tait, a self-trained English artist who, like Deas, reputedly had been inspired by the paintings in Catlin's Indian gallery and had felt the romantic lure of the West. Ironically, Tait was the only one of our four primary artists who never visited the West, yet his pictures of the trappers and Indians, circulated as sets of lithographs, reached the widest audience of any of the mid-nineteenth-century painters. Two of the most popular sets of prints were *Life on the Prairie* (fig. 76) and a pair called *American Frontier Life* (figs. 77, 78), from which our title is derived.

9. *William Tylee Ranney,*
Halt on the Plains, *1857,*
oil on canvas, 46 × 72 in.
Collection of Mrs. Leonard
F. McCollum (Eleanor
Searle Whitney)

Even more than Wimar and Deas, Tait reveled in the histrionics of frontier life and the conflicts between the forces of civilization and wilderness. Thus most of his paintings and resulting lithographs portray the Indian and the trapper in conflict. His first painting of frontier life lithographed by Currier & Ives, *The Prairie Hunter—One Rubbed Out!* (1852; fig. 69; lithograph, fig. 112), was typical of Tait's taste for violence. More than any of the other artists discussed here, Tait shaped American perceptions of the frontier and its inhabitants. His was the most exotic and dramatic work produced by America's genre painters. The prairies blaze, the foes pursue, and the buffalo charge to their destruction. For Tait, the West was won by conflict and confrontation. And Currier & Ives stood ready to transpose those Tait images into lithographs for avid public consumption.

Probably the most exotic of the themes mid-century painters explored was that of Indian life apart from the white man. A substantial group of artists pursued the Indian as subject precisely to preserve what was seen as their purity of form and their ideal sense of harmony with nature.

George Catlin had initiated that enterprise in the early 1830s and was succeeded by a sincere and dedicated following that included John Mix Stanley and Seth Eastman. Each of the three endeavored to assemble an Indian gallery that portrayed individuals of distinction and celebrated the customs and manners of the native people.

The artistic competition among these painters of Indian life was fierce. Each of the three claimed his cadre of dedicated supporters. The supporters in turn proclaimed the veracity and significance of their favorite painter. First, there was Catlin and his views of American Indian life as praised by the *New York Evening Star* in 1838: "Catlin's Indian Gallery . . . is one of the most remarkable and interesting works that the genius and labor of an individual has created in this age and country. . . . Nothing could redound more to the patriotism, national pride, and honor of our country than the purchase of Congress of this collection of Aboriginal Curiosities, to enrich a National Museum in Washington."[20]

Then there was Stanley, whose views of Indian life were applauded in 1846:

We are well acquainted with the celebrated Catlin Gallery, which attracted so much attention here and in Europe, and which the French Government is now said to be about to purchase. We are familiar, also, with the United States Gallery of Indian Portraits, by Charles King, at Washington, which has been gradually augmenting for many years and is very valuable. But the present collection is superior to them both, not in extent or variety, but the high finish of the paintings; their depth of expression, and the bold and striking air of life and reality with which these wild and singular figures stand out from the canvass.[21]

Finally, there was Eastman, acclaimed in an 1848 issue of the *Daily Missouri Republican:* "Since we have known something of Eastman's pictures, and of Indians, we have ranked him as out of sight the best painter of Indian life the country has produced; a superior artist to Catlin—he has lived and painted for years among the Indians, where Catlin has spent months; his gallery now, is far more complete in all that relates to Indian character, than is Catlin's: and there is in the latter, an effort at effect, as apparent as in the truth of Eastman, to any one who has really seen Indians."[22]

Together, these three painters explored the rich potential for genre subject matter afforded by the Indian cultures they visited. They each produced provocative views of everyday Indian life, yet they each approached it with a slightly different vision. Catlin maintained throughout his work a "resolve to sustain the primitive ideal." The image of the Indian for Catlin was thus one reflective of neo-classical idealization, even in his portrayal of the Indian's simplest daily enterprises. Stanley began his career with similar impulses but, after exposure to the art of the nation's capital in the mid 1850s, softened his interpretation. After 1855, Stanley's Indians became noble rather than heroic. One student of his work, Julie Schimmel, refers to Stanley's portrayal of everyday life as "genre history painting," in which he transforms "ordinary activity into a significant event by imbuing a genre scene with the gravity of a history painting." This is true of the Stanley paintings pictured in this volume.[23]

The third artist, Seth Eastman, found room in his work for idealized rendition and historical genre. He was best known for his unencumbered views of Indian life (fig. 10). His were most often clear, straightforward depictions of what he saw, and the resulting impression was closest to rustic genre work of any of the three.

Combining the efforts of these three Indian painters with the practitioners of rustic genre, exotic genre, and historical narrative brings to light a remarkable cross-section of mid-nineteenth-century American aesthetic expression. The artists were unified by a passion to explore worlds beyond the pale of civilization and by a desire to celebrate the everyday life of frontiersmen and Indians.

Their popularity was undaunted in the years they painted. They thrived on frontier images and on their personal adventures and their unconventional experiences. Later in the century, critics would not be so flattering as contemporaries had been. S.G.W. Benjamin, in his book *Art in America* (1880), concluded that "It is greatly to be regretted that the work of these pioneers in Western genre was not of more artistic value; from a historical point of view, too much importance cannot be attached to the enterprise and courage of men like Catlin, Deas, and Ranney, who, imbued with the spirit of adventure, identified themselves with Indian and border life, and rescued it from oblivion by their art enthusiasm, which, had it been guided by previous training, would have been of even greater value."[24]

Following the Civil War, America's popular

attention was somewhat drawn away from frontier genre themes and turned instead toward a nationalistic identification with the grandeur of the western landscape, portrayed in scenes often devoid of human presence and evocative of universal truths found only in nature where man's intrusion had not been evident. In panoramic western vistas by Albert Bierstadt and Thomas Moran, sublimity and exoticism were God's exclusive province. Even when small Indian figures can be discerned, they are representatives of the greater order of Nature, not of civilization.[25] Perhaps the personal

tragedies of the Civil War had caused American tastes temporarily to turn away from an appreciation of man's role in the West.

Yet in modern times perspectives have swung back substantially. Catlin, Deas, and Ranney, along with their colleagues Bingham, Tait, Wimar, Eastman, can be admired for their technical skills, their sense of artistic mission, their respect for the dignity of humble pursuits, and their ability to breathe pictorial and popular vitality into those things ordinary and adventuresome that embodied American frontier life.

NOTES

1. Henry T. Tuckerman, *Book of the Artists* (New York: G. P. Putnam & Son, 1867), pp. 425, 432.

2. Review of E. H. Flint and L. R. Lincoln, *The History and Geography of the Mississippi Valley* (Cincinnati, 1832) in *American Quarterly Review* 11, no. 22 (June 1832): 289.

3. *American Quarterly Review* 17, no. 34 (June 1835): 533.

4. James Fenimore Cooper, *Notions of the Americans: Picked up by a Travelling Batchelor,* vol. 2 (London: Henry Colburn, 1828), p. 108.

5. Joshua C. Taylor, *America as Art* (New York: Harper & Row, Publishers, 1976), p. 143.

6. Henry Vyverberg, *The Living Tradition: Art, Music, and Ideas in the Western World* (New York: Harcourt, Brace, Jovanovich, 1978), p. 255.

7. "The First Century of the Republic," *Harper's New Monthly Magazine* 54 (April 1876): 700.

8. Quoted in C. Edwards Lester, *The Artists of America* (New York: Baker & Scribner, 1846), p. 43. For a discussion of Inman's place in the American genre tradition, see William H. Gerdts, "Henry Inman: Genre Painter," *American Art Journal* 9, no. 1 (May 1977): 26–48.

9. Dawn Glanz, *How the West Was Drawn: American Art and the Settling of the Frontier* (Ann Arbor, Mich.: UMI Research Press, 1982), p. 30.

10. *Crayon* 4, no. 5 (June 1857): 187. Letter from Mayer to Miller, 5 March 1865, quoted in Marvin C. Ross, ed., *Artists' Letters to Alfred Jacob Miller* (Baltimore: The Walters Art Gallery, 1951), p. 10.

11. Hermann Warner Williams, Jr., *Mirror to the American Past* (Greenwich, Conn.: New York Graphic Society, 1973), pp. 10, 16.

12. See Catherine Hoover, "The Influence of David Wilkie's Prints on the Genre Painting of William Sidney Mount," *American Art Journal* 13, no. 3 (Summer 1981): 5.

13. Quoted in John Francis McDermott, *George Caleb Bingham: River Portraitist* (Norman: University of Oklahoma Press, 1959), p. 185.

14. James Henry, "The Incentives and Aims of Art," *Crayon* 1, no. 4 (24 January 1855): 52. Comment on *Canvassing for a Vote* from William H. Truettner, "The Art of History: American Exploration and Discovery Scenes, 1840–1860," *American Art Journal* 14, no. 1 (Winter 1982): 19.

15. Marshall B. Davidson, "Democracy Delineated," *American Heritage* 31, no. 6 (October–November 1980): 9.

16. Taylor, *America as Art,* p. 144.

17. See John C. Ewers, "Fact and Fiction in the Documentary Art of the American West," in *The Frontier Re-examined,* edited by John Francis McDermott (Urbana: University of Illinois Press, 1967), p. 86.

18. *Crayon* 5, no. 1 (December 1858): 355. Tuckerman, *Book of the Artists,* p. 432, characterized Ranney as a "bushranger."

19. See Jay Cantor, "Prints and the American Art-Union," in *Prints in and of America to 1850,* edited by John D. Morse (Charlottesville: University Press of Virginia, 1970), pp. 297–326.

20. *New York Evening Star,* 1 February 1838, p. 2.

21. *Cincinnati Evening Journal,* 2 February 1846, quoted in Julie Ann Schimmel, "John Mix Stanley and Imagery of the West in Nineteenth-Century American Art" (Ph.D. diss., New York University, 1985), p. 56.

22. *Daily Missouri Republican,* 2 May 1848, p. 5.

23. On Catlin's "primitive ideal," see William H. Truettner, *The Natural Man Observed: A Study of Catlin's Indian Gallery* (Washington, D.C.: Smithsonian Institution Press, 1979), p. 121. On Stanley's combination of genre and history painting, see Schimmel, "Stanley," pp. 188–89.

24. S.G.W. Benjamin, *Art in America* (New York: Harper & Brothers, Publishers, 1880), p. 88.

25. See Barbara Novak, *Nature and Culture: American Landscape and Painting, 1825–1875* (New York: Oxford University Press, 1980), p. 189.

GEORGE CALEB BINGHAM

THE NATIVE TALENT
BY RON TYLER

*I*n 1857 George Caleb Bingham wrote from Düsseldorf to his good friend James S. Rollins: "I have on hand a large picture of 'life on the Mississippi' which will not require a great while to complete, and which promises to be far ahead of any work of that class which I have yet undertaken." Rollins was familiar with Bingham's other flatboatmen pictures, beginning with the well-known *The Jolly Flatboatmen* (1846; fig. 13), and was, no doubt, anxious to see the new picture. Bingham brought *The Jolly Flatboatmen in Port* (fig. 15) home with him, probably in January 1859, and showed it in the Fourth Annual Exhibition of the Washington Art Association, along with three other paintings.[1] It was the culmination of his river series, which began modestly enough in 1838 with what was probably an immature effort entitled *Western Boatmen Ashore* (now lost), the artist's first foray into genre painting after several years as a successful portrait painter. The series was to establish the image of the boatman forever in American history and art.

Born in Virginia, Bingham had moved with his family to the village of Franklin on the banks of the Missouri River between St. Louis and what is today Kansas City. He taught himself to paint and developed an enthusiastic following in Missouri before going east to Philadelphia in 1838 to study the craft further. There he probably visited art exhibitions at Peale's Museum, the Pennsyl-

vania Academy, and various dealers' showrooms and purchased etchings and plaster casts of sculpture for future copying. Perhaps it was a visit to New York—where he could have seen the work of William Sidney Mount, who by then enjoyed a widespread reputation for his scenes of everyday American country life—that inspired Bingham to paint *Western Boatmen Ashore*. He exhibited the painting at the Apollo Gallery (which later became the American Art-Union) in New York, but there is no record of what happened to it. There are apparently no contemporary reviews of the painting, and it probably did not sell. Nor did Bingham immediately continue to paint genre scenes. He returned to his moderately successful portrait career in Washington and Virginia—and in Missouri, where he was soon celebrated as the "NATIVE TALENT."[2]

THE RIVER SERIES

The first hint that Bingham had again taken up the rivermen theme came in 1845 in a newspaper notice that the "Missouri artist" was back in St. Louis with some "fancy sketches" and was now at work on "some paintings which demonstrate the possession of a high order of talent in another line, but to which, we believe, he has not devoted a large share of his time." The newspaper reporter no doubt saw *Fur Traders Descending the Missouri* (1845; fig. 11), one of a pair of western paintings

Bingham, The Jolly Flatboatmen in Port (detail, see fig. 15)

25

that Bingham sent to the American Art-Union in the fall of 1845, and the *The Concealed Enemy* (1845; fig. 12).[3] Originally titled *French Trader and Half-Breed Son, Fur Traders* depicts an old frontiersman lazily paddling his dugout downstream, while his son lounges on the season's catch of furs that almost swamps the crude vessel. Folded in his arms is a rifle, which he has recently used to fell the duck lying in front of him.

Fur Traders is characteristic of Bingham's best work and, in a sense, established two patterns that he followed throughout his career. First, he carefully composed the picture according to principles set forth in popular drawing manuals of the day: the inclined backs of the two figures suggest the apex of a pyramid or triangle, with the boat and river forming the bottom. The paddle, the stick behind the youngster, and the placid layers of water emphasize these lines. On the left the bear cub and its reflection form a vertical line that balances the composition. This is a pattern from which Bingham rarely deviated, and most of his subsequent genre scenes employed some variant of the pyramid, investing them with an almost architectural quality that suggests stability far beyond the ephemeral scene portrayed. Part of the careful composition, no doubt, is due to his working method and technique. His precise study drawings, which in many cases are virtually reproduced in his paintings, combined with his

12. *George Caleb Bingham,*
The Concealed Enemy,
1845, oil on canvas,
29¼ × 36½ in.
Stark Museum of Art,
Orange, Texas

subtle glazes to give his figures a sculptural, deliberate appearance.[4]

Bingham does not merely copy details from models or props, but rather treats each element in the painting as potentially symbolic. A careful analysis of these paintings, which he probably intended as pendants,[5] suggests, for example, that *The Concealed Enemy* represents the demise of savagery in the West, and the *Fur Traders* that region's gradual climb toward civilization. The chained bear cub, a wild animal, has been made into a pet, symbolizing the triumph of civilization. The similarity of poses between the Indian and the trader's son calls attention to the fact that each has a rifle—but intended for distinctly different purposes, one for warfare, the other for hunting. That the trader is gently paddling his dugout downstream toward St. Louis (you can tell from the way the water breaks around the snag) further portends the imminent arrival of civilization. Other aspects of the paintings reinforce the theme of savagery versus civilization: jagged, rocky bluffs of the river versus the placid river itself, the Indian in war paint waiting in ambush versus a dugout almost swamped with the river's produce, the sunset of *The Concealed Enemy* versus the dawn of *Fur Traders*. All these elements convey, in the language and symbols of nineteenth-century aesthetics, the deeper meaning Bingham intended.

Bingham's 1838 experience, when he first came

into contact with the group that became the Art-Union and found inspiration in its desire to encourage "every day scenes of life . . . that illustrate . . . our country; history and its poetry," probably led him to offer the organization *Fur Traders* and *The Concealed Enemy*. Evolved from the Apollo Gallery, the Art-Union had as its primary goal the "promotion of the Fine Arts in the United States." It presented exhibitions, which included borrowed works as well as paintings purchased directly from the artists. The paintings were, in turn, distributed to the membership by lottery. All members received a copy of "a large and costly Original Engraving," which the Art-Union commissioned and distributed each year. These were the first of many sales that Bingham made to the group, and he later acknowledged its support as having been critical in allowing him to move from his moderately successful portrait business to genre and narrative scenes.[6]

In light of a favorable response, the artist was now more at ease with his river pictures and selected two more familiar river types for treatment, the woodboatman and the flatboatman. He produced two splendid pictures, *The Jolly Flatboatmen* (1846; fig. 13) and *Boatmen on the Missouri* (1846; fig. 14), which have proven to be two of Bingham's best and most popular images. *The Jolly Flatboatmen,* the first of the flatboat series, might have drawn on the figures and imagery of the earlier *Western Boatmen Ashore*. In it, Bingham depicted that "singular aquatic race" that Washington Irving had observed during his western trip. The " 'boatmen of the Mississippi,' " Irving wrote, "had grown up from the navigation of the rivers" and "possessed habits, manners, and almost a language, peculiarly their own, and strongly technical." A reporter for the *Daily Missouri Republican* noted, "The western boatmen are a peculiar class in most of their habits, dress and manners. Among them often in the same crew, may be found all the varieties of human character, from the amiable and intelligent to the stern and reckless men. In dress, habit, costume, association, mind, and every other particular, they are an anomaly." The boats themselves were also distinctive, as Timothy Flint recalled: "No form of

water craft was so whimsical, no shape so outlandish." A copy of Bingham's *The Jolly Flatboatmen* was used to illustrate an article by John Banvard that appeared in *Howitt's Journal of Literature and Popular Progress*.

While the reporter for the *St. Louis Weekly Reveille* concluded that "There is an absolute life about them which it is refreshing to look upon," Bingham was, in fact, giving visual expression to distinctly American types that had already emerged in popular literature.[7] Indeed, *The Jolly Flatboatmen* also included nostalgic elements of river activity that had virtually passed from the scene. Even as early as 1838, when Edmund Flagg published the account of his western trip, the flatboat was a "relic of those ancient and primitive species of river-craft which once assumed ascendency over the waters of the West, but which are now superseded by steam."[8]

Another historic element, present in spirit if not in literal fact, is Mike Fink, the king of the riverboatmen. Born probably near Fort Pitt about 1770, Fink had been a hunter and scout before joining the ranks of adventurers who found the river irresistible. He became a legend during his own lifetime, gaining fame for his marksmanship and generally rowdy and irrepressible character, but most of all for his prowess on the river.[9] It would have been impossible for Bingham not to have known of him. The central character in *The Jolly Flatboatmen* does bear a remarkable resemblance to a contemporary description of Mike Fink. Mike, wrote Morgan Neville, who had known him for years,

presented a figure that Salvator [Rosa] would have chosen from a million as a model for his wild and gloomy pencil. His stature was upwards of six feet, his proportions perfectly symmetrical, and exhibiting the evidence of Herculean powers. To a stranger, he would have seemed a complete mulatto. Long exposure to the sun and weather on the lower Ohio and Mississippi had changed his skin; and, but for the fine European cast of his countenance, he might have passed for the principal warrior of some powerful tribe.

13. *George Caleb Bingham,*
The Jolly Flatboatmen,
1846, oil on canvas,
38⅛ × 48½ in.
National Gallery of Art,
Washington, D.C., Lent by
The Pell Family Trust,
Honorable Claiborne Pell,
Trustee

14. *George Caleb Bingham,*
Boatmen on the Missouri,
1846, oil on canvas,
25 × 30 in.
The Fine Arts Museums of
San Francisco, Gift of Mr. &
Mrs. John D. Rockefeller, 3rd

Although at least fifty years of age, his hair was as black as the wing of the raven. Next to his skin he wore a red flannel shirt, covered by a blue capot, ornamented with white fringe.[10]

A close look at some of the literature of the river suggests other possible sources for the flatboat pictures. Both Timothy Flint and Edmund Flagg described scenes that strikingly anticipate *The Jolly Flatboatmen*. Flint, a Harvard-educated missionary who traveled up and down the Mississippi for years, edited the *Western Monthly Review* in Cincinnati from 1827 to 1830 and wrote one of the best travel books about the region.[11] He recalled how alluring the life of the boatman looked to the farm families on the bank as they viewed the keelboats floating down the river:

At this time, there is no visible danger, or call for labor. The boat takes care of itself; and little do the beholders imagine, how different a scene may be presented in half an hour. Meantime, one of the hands scrapes a violin, and the others dance. Greetings, or rude defiances, or trials of wit, or proffers of love to the girls on the shore, or saucy messages, are scattered between them and the spectators along the banks. The boat glides on, until it disappears behind the point of wood. At this moment, perhaps, the bugle, with which all the boats are provided, strikes up its note in the distance over the water. These scenes, and these notes, echoing from the bluffs of the beautiful Ohio, have a charm for the imagination, which although heard a thousand times repeated, at all hours and in all positions, present the image of a tempting and charming youthful existence, that naturally inspires a wish to be a boatman.[12]

Flagg described a flatboat "dropping lazily along with the current" with "its heterogeneous crew of all ages dancing to the violin upon the deck, flinging out their merry salutations among the settlers, who come down to the water's edge to see the pageant pass."[13]

By the time Bingham actually painted *The Jolly Flatboatmen,* the boatmen were disappearing. The rapid spread of steamboats drove the flatboats from all the rivers. Even Mike Fink succumbed.

"He had refused several good offers on the steam boats," an old captain recalled. "He said he could not bear the hissing of steam and he wanted room to throw his pole." Morgan Neville concluded that "the spirit of the Boatmen" died with Mike, but not before they had become, in the words of another firsthand observer, "the representatives of the whole race of pioneers."[14]

It is true, of course, that Mike and the rest had a crude side, which, some have insisted, Bingham omitted from his figures. It was an oversight noted even at the time by a New York reviewer who pointed out that, "His subjects, although taken from common life, are divested of everything like vulgarity." Yet it was surely an intentional omission, for Bingham likely was in full accord with the Art-Union in its effort to establish "an American School of Art" while at the same time creating a "superior unity of national character," and he offered his flatboatmen as authentic representatives of life on the western rivers elevated to art.[15]

For some, however, even this idealized version of life on the western rivers was too common a subject to be held up as an example before the nation. When the Art-Union chose *The Jolly Flatboatmen* to engrave and distribute to its members in 1847, it ran headlong into the age-old conflict between those who felt that art must be noble and uplifting and those who would agree with Ralph Waldo Emerson, who declared to his Harvard University audience in 1837 that "I embrace the common, I explore and sit at the feet of the familiar, the low. Give me insight into today, and you may have the antique and future worlds." The critic for the *Literary World* was clearly not of the Emersonian camp. Not only, in his view, did the painting lack a "standard of taste," because it had no religious or patriotic content, but its "very name . . . gives a death blow to all one's preconceived notions of 'HIGH ART.'" When it was exhibited at the Art-Union a second time in 1847, the *Literary World* columnist reiterated that it was "a vulgar subject, vulgarly treated."[16]

But there were many who understood what Bingham had accomplished. Most of his publicity came, naturally, from Missouri, where he was pronounced "a Western 'meteor of the art'" as

early as 1835. After seeing all Bingham's river paintings to date, a *St. Louis Weekly Reveille* critic declared that, "Bingham . . . is making a brilliant reputation by the delineation of western scenes." A reporter for the *Daily Missouri Republican* ventured that "Mr. BINGHAM has struck out for himself an entire new field of historic painting." Even the reviewer for the *New York Mirror* concluded that, although Bingham's flatboatmen were well scrubbed, he presented them "without their truthfulness being diminished in the slightest degree."[17]

The river series culminates with *The Jolly Flat-*

boatmen in Port (fig. 15), which also could have had its origin in a passage from Timothy Flint: "Almost every boat, while it lies in the harbour has one or more fiddles scraping continually aboard, to which you often see the boatmen dancing." *The Jolly Flatboatmen in Port* retains the core of the original composition, with the dancer as the central figure flanked by the two music makers. The boat is now tied up at the St. Louis landing, indicating the end of the trip and, perhaps, the end of the flatboatmen series. Another flatboat, still out in the river, approaches from downriver, and two more are tied up at the levee

16. *George Caleb Bingham,*
The Wood Boat, *1850,*
oil on canvas, 24¾ × 29⅝ in.
The Saint Louis Art
Museum

17. *George Caleb Bingham,*
Wood-Boatmen on a River
(Western Boatmen Ashore
by Night), *1854,*
oil on canvas, 29 × 36¼ in.
Amon Carter Museum, Fort
Worth

between the assembled group and the steamboat that is docked at the landing. It was probably intended as a reference to the modern craft that pushed the flatboats off the river.[18]

The composition was completed in Düsseldorf and shows evidence of the German influence on Bingham's self-taught style. To begin with, the painting is much more complex than the earlier flatboat pictures, with twenty-one figures instead of seven or eight. The dancer, who evolves through the three paintings, is better painted here, reflecting Bingham's continued study and, perhaps, experience gained in Düsseldorf. The composition is still arranged in the familiar pyramid, but now it is much more complex, with no strong horizontal base. But the sloping sides of the pyramid bring the eye easily to the dancer in the center, as does the more subtle and open approach from the center foreground. As is typical in frontier genre painting, red is a significant part of the design. The dancer wears a bright red vest and waves a red bandanna, and the color is also spotted throughout the picture—the cap of the man standing at the left, the shirt of the man leaning on the pole behind the dancer, and the shirt of the fiddler—to produce a visually cohesive unit. Bingham's European experience is apparent in the painting also in what a contemporary observer called the "faithful and elaborate finish" so characteristic of the Düsseldorf school.[19]

Bingham's second great picture of 1846, *Boatmen on the Missouri* (1846; fig. 14), also reproduces a common sight on the Mississippi—men waiting to sell firewood to a passing steamboat. Bingham was to use this subject again in 1850 with a composition entitled *The Wood Boat* (1850; fig. 16), which he described as depicting "a group such as the traveller daily sees upon the navigable waters of the west." The artist continued to work with the wood-boatmen, experimenting with night settings until he produced one of the most painterly of his compositions, *Wood-Boatmen on a River (Western Boatmen Ashore by Night)* (1854; fig. 17).[20] In it four figures are grouped around a campfire, while a fifth fishes off the back of the docked flatboat. One, at the left, is playing a mouth harp. Another, standing in the center, is leaning on one

of the poles from the flatboat and appears to be laughing or singing along to the music, while the other two are sitting and lying around the campfire in lounging positions typical of Bingham's best work.

As in other paintings of the river series, the four main characters form a pyramid, with the two central figures making a line—with the pole—through the center of the picture. This is, perhaps, Bingham's most successful attempt at using at-mospheric effects to unify the central characters and the landscape in the background, thus overcoming a problem for which he had been criticized in his early efforts.[21] *Wood-Boatmen on a River* is also an experiment in night light, with illumination coming from the campfire and reflecting on the clothing and faces of the figures. The moon backlights the entire scene, showing the fisherman in the background in relief and reflecting off the mists and fog that are so characteristic of the river.

18. *George Caleb Bingham, Raftsmen Playing Cards, 1847, oil on canvas, 28 × 38 in. The Saint Louis Art Museum, Ezra H. Linley Fund*

Raftsmen Playing Cards created a sensation in St. Louis before Bingham shipped it to the Art-Union. Bingham "has taken our western rivers, our boats and boatmen, and the banks of the streams, for his subjects," the *Daily Missouri Republican* reporter wrote. "The field is as interesting as it is novel." The St. Louis reporter testified as to the "perfectly life-like" figures, while a New York reviewer concluded that, "It is truly American."[23]

Bingham's river series, which also included *Watching the Cargo* (fig. 19), was a major accomplishment. He had "studied [the] character [of the boatmen] with the eye and genius of an artist and the mind of a philosopher," the *Daily Missouri Republican* concluded.

He has not sought out those incidents or occasions which might be supposed to give the best opportunity for display, and a flashy highly colored picture; but he has taken the simplest, most frequent and common occurrences on our rivers—such as every boatman will encounter in a season—such as would seem even to the casual and careless observer, of very ordinary moment, but which are precisely those in which the full and undisguised character of the boatman is displayed. . . . He has seized the characteristic points and gathered up their expressive features and transferred them to his canvas with a truthfulness which strikes every observer.[24]

The wood-boat theme was not the only aspect of river life Bingham portrayed after his 1846 successes. *Raftsmen Playing Cards* (1847; fig. 18) is closely related to the flatboatmen pictures in both subject matter and composition. It is no doubt based on his observance of many contemporary "card playing" scenes in real life and on a study of European paintings and engravings such as *The Card Players* (1658; Royal Collection, Buckingham Palace) by Pieter de Hooch, and Charles G. Lewis's engraving (1838) after Sir David Wilkie's painting of the same name.[22]

Bingham's composition again is pyramidal, with the figure seated at the left and the angle of the pole in the back forming one side of the triangle; the standing figure on the right, leaning in toward the center, forms the other. Bingham has moved the observer's position from a nearby boat—as it was in *The Jolly Flatboatmen*—onto the raft itself. The debris in the center foreground leads the eye up to the central figure, the card-player on the right, and the standing figure to his right. Again, the vanishing point of the lines formed by the sides of the raft emphasize the pyramidal shape. It is one of Bingham's finest paintings.

In New York, however, many critics were hostile because of Bingham's subject matter and what they considered his immature style. The reviewer for the *Literary World* denounced both *The Jolly Flatboatmen* and *Raftsmen Playing Cards* as "vulgar subjects," with a pervading "monotonous, dull, dirty pink." Even Bingham's characteristic pyramidal composition, the critic warned, "is only suitable to scenes of the utmost beauty and repose." While a writer in the *New-York Express* damned the paintings for figures that appear "too heavy and dead-like; and all the deeper shadows are nearly of one hue," it is widely recognized today that Bingham captured the colors that are especially evocative of the river: the pale pink of *Fur Traders* and *The Jolly Flatboatmen* and the blues of *The Wood-Boatmen* that blend so wonderfully into the hazy river atmosphere. Despite the negative criticism, the purchasing committee of the American Art-Union realized that, while Bingham could improve certain aspects of his painting, his raw and untutored talent was imbued with an honesty and native integrity that represented a major find in their quest for "truly American" art.[25]

THE ELECTION SERIES

While in the midst of his river paintings, Bingham became intimately involved in the political process that had already begun to attract much of his attention. He was an ardent Whig and had painted banners for several local and state conventions in 1844. In 1846 he announced as a candidate for the state legislature from Saline County, but after a bitter election, which he initially appeared to have won by three votes, the Democratic-controlled state legislature declared his opponent the winner. Although he vowed never to have anything more to do with politics, Bingham ran again in 1848, this time successfully, and became even more deeply involved in Whig politics. He represented the Eighth District of Missouri at the Whig national convention in Baltimore in June 1852 and tried several times to take advantage of his political activities in order to win appointment to a government post in Europe that would allow him to further his art studies.[26] Though he failed to secure such a post, a stunning and original series of paintings sprang directly from his experience on the campaign trail and from his close and thoughtful observations of the electoral process in rural Missouri.

Bingham undertook *The Stump Orator* in 1847, shortly after his political defeat; it was to be his most ambitious composition to date, containing "about sixty" figures. Today, it is known only by a contemporary daguerreotype and descriptions. The painting showed a candidate standing on the stump of a freshly cut tree, presenting his case to the voters.

As with other Bingham paintings, the local reporters were enthusiastic, while the New York critics offered mixed comments. The reporter for the *Daily Missouri Republican* recognized it as characteristic of western political scenes: "For vitality, freshness, grouping, shade and light, and costume, we have never seen anything equal to it."[27] The New York *Literary World* critic declared that "Mr. Bingham's picture . . . makes one's eyes ache to look at it. All the laws of chiar' oscuro are set at defiance, so that the eye is distracted and carried all over the canvas, without a single resting-place. He has evidently no idea of the value of light, and how sparingly it should be used in a picture. In color it is unmistakably bad; its only merit is in the broad exaggerated characters of the heads, which look as if painted from daguerreotypes." Nevertheless, the Art-Union purchased the painting for $350, the most they ever paid for a Bingham.[28]

Before Bingham did a second and more successful version of the campaigning scene, he considered other aspects of the electoral process and painted a picture that, in some ways, may have commemorated his 1846 defeat. *The Squatters* (1850; fig. 20) shows

a family [that] has built its log cabin in the midst of a clearing, and commenced housekeeping. The Squatters as a class, are not fond of the toil of agriculture, but erect their rude cabins upon those remote portions of the National domain, when the abundant game supplies their phisical [sic] wants. When this source of subsistence becomes diminished in consequence of increasing settlements around, they usually sell out their slight improvement, with their "*preemption title*" to the land, and again follow the receding footsteps of the Savage.[29]

During the 1846 election recount, the Whig Bingham bitterly feared that votes cast by squatters, whose affiliations were overwhelmingly Democratic, would end up in the final tally costing him his narrowly won victory. He unsuccessfully argued for a second election, which, he felt, would prove him the clear victor, as the squatters would have pulled up stakes by then.[30]

20. *George Caleb Bingham,*
The Squatters, 1850,
oil on canvas, 25 × 30 in.
Museum of Fine Arts, Boston,
Bequest of Henry L.
Shattuck in memory of the
late Ralph W. Gray

Whatever his feelings about them, Bingham knew the squatters' way of life well. He has imbued the figures with a tension evocative of the transitory nature of their existence. Unlike the flatboatmen, who seem carefree and comfortable with their situation in life, the squatter and the old man stare with a defiant and suspicious look, as if the viewer might be the government land agent come to evict them.[31]

Bingham apparently learned from his critical reviews, for he continued to think about election pictures as he honed his skills on *The Country Pol-*

itician (1849; private collection), *Shooting for the Beef* (1850; fig. 21), *The Wood Boat* (1850; fig. 16), and *The Checker Players* (1850; fig. 23), and in 1852 finished two more pictures in the election series—*Canvassing for a Vote* (1852; fig. 24) and *The County Election* (1851–52; fig. 22)—which earned him universal plaudits. *The County Election* attracted attention from the moment that Bingham began work on it. A *Weekly Missouri Statesman* writer, visiting the artist's Columbia studio to view the painting, reported that

The day of election . . . has engaged the artist constantly for three months, occupies canvass [*sic*] about three by four feet, and is composed of upwards of sixty figures. Prominently on the right, on the main street of a western village, we have the place of voting, the court house, in

the porch of which the clerks and judges are assembled—one of the judges, a thick pussy looking citizen, being engaged in swearing a voter, a well-set Irishman in a red flannel shirt. Near by is a political striker, a distributor of

tickets, *very* politely tendering his services in that regard to an approaching voter. Around and in front is the crowd, composed of many large and prominent figures—some engaged in earnest conversation, some drinking at a cake and liquor stand, some smoking and some hearing a paragraph read from a newspaper. But we cannot give a description of this painting. Several hours would not suffice fully to examine it, so numerous and life-like are the characters. Indeed it is full of reality, a seeming incarnation, prominent in figure, grouped and colored with admirable skill and effect. Persons of highly cultivated taste in the fine arts, and critics in general, will accord to it a remarkable degree of genius and merit.[32]

The *Daily Missouri Republican* and the *Western Journal* in Cincinnati voiced similar praise.[33]

The reviews were merited. Bingham showed considerable improvement in *The County Election,* even according to eastern critics. The courthouse at the right forms the setting for the action, while the rest of the canvas is left open for background, a device that the artist might well have borrowed from William Hogarth's print *Canvassing for Votes* (1757). Bingham arranged two groups of figures, the trio talking at the base of the nearest column and the grouping on the steps, so they would form a "corridor" leading to the two main figures, the voter and the judge administering the oath. His choice of colors sharpens the focus of the composition, for the voter, like the dancer in the flatboatmen series, is dressed in a red coat and the judge in a pale blue one, while those around them are in more muted colors.[34]

The *Philadelphia Register* appreciated the close relation of composition and theme while the *Weekly Missouri Statesman* in Columbia predicted the painting was "destined to become one of the most popular scenes ever produced on this continent."[35] Recognizing the wide appeal of the picture, Bingham's good friend James Rollins appealed to the Art-Union to purchase and engrave the picture:

It is a *National* painting, for it presents just such a scene, as you would meet with on the Arrostock in Maine, or in the City of New York, or on the Rio Grande in Texas, on an election day. He has left nothing *out,* the courtier, the politician, the labourer, the sturdy farmer, the *"bully"* at the poles *[sic],* the beer-seller, the *bruised* pugilist, and even the boys playing "mumble the peg" are all distinctly recognized in the group. . . . As a mere work of art a delineation of character it is superb. But this is not the point of view in which its excellence is to be regarded. The elective franchise is the very corner stone, upon which rests our governmental superstructure and as illustrative of our fine institutions, the power and influence which the ballot box exerts over our happiness as a people, the subject of this painting was most happily chosen, and executed with wonderful skill by its gifted author. . . . From its character and its style of execution, it would arrest the attention of every class of our population it would be admired alike by an exquisite connoisseur in the arts, the most enlightened statesman, and the most ignorant voter, and such a picture *engraved* would be equaly *[sic]* sought after, to decorate the walls of a palace, and those of a log cabin!

Such is my poor opinion of this superior work of art and viewing it, in this light, it would certainly have a great run over mere fancy pieces or even historical works, which cannot be well made to have such a direct bearing upon the most practical as well as the most important duty, belonging to the citizen under our government. . . . [It is] unquestionably the "master piece" of his life.[36]

After its completion, even as Rollins was approaching the Art-Union, Bingham wrote Goupil & Company, the firm then endeavoring to produce prints of two of his other paintings, *In a Quandry. Mississippi Raftsmen Playing Cards* (1851; Virginia Steele Scott Gallery, Huntington Library; engraving, fig. 7) and *The Emigration of Daniel Boone* (1851; Washington University, St. Louis) that "My '*County Election*' has excited more interest than any of my previous productions, and my friends, here, propose to raise a sum which will enable me to publish it, in superior style, upon a large scale."[37]

When the Art-Union declined Rollins's petition, saying that the painting would take too long to engrave, Bingham himself pursued the idea with John Sartain of Philadelphia, one of the best engravers in the country, while he was in the East attending the 1852 Whig national convention. So that Sartain could have the painting to work from, and so he could have one to exhibit during the interim to sell subscriptions to the engraving, Bingham painted a replica (1852; Boatmen's Bank, St. Louis) between mid August and early October 1852 that is yet more successful than the original. In it he manipulated the lighting, shadow, and color, to focus the viewer's attention even more directly on the central characters, and opened up the central approach by removing one of the figures directly between the viewer and the voter. He exhibited it in several Missouri towns before taking it to New Orleans in the spring of 1853, where a reporter for the *Daily Picayune* proclaimed it "AN AMERICAN WORK OF ART." Robert J. Ward of Louisville saw the painting and offered Bing-

23. *George Caleb Bingham,*
The Checker Players
(Playing Chequers), *1850,
oil on canvas, 25 × 30 in.
© Detroit Institute of Arts, Gift
of Dexter M. Ferry, Jr.*

ham twelve hundred dollars for it, the exact amount that Bingham owed Sartain for the engraving that was in progress. Bingham quickly accepted the offer, but bargained to keep the painting through the summer so he could continue to use it to solicit subscriptions for the forthcoming engraving.[38]

Louisville and Lexington newspapers were lavish in their praise of the second version of *The County Election*. Bingham wrote to his friend Rollins that, "The press was profuse in its commendations, and without a dissenting voice . . . pronounced [my picture] superior to anything of the kind which had yet been seen in America." But no sooner had Bingham informed Rollins of his good fortune than a commentator signing himself "PUBLIC WEAL" raised several questions in the *Kentucky Statesman* that continue to provoke comment today. Echoing a charge that the *Literary World* had brought against Bingham, "PUBLIC WEAL" suggested that "another and more elevated view of the subject" was in order. "The painting is supposed to represent correctly our county elections," he wrote, "and in failing to do so, offends against the laws of the land, which would punish the author severely if a private citizen was so characatured [sic] and defamed." Listing the "miserable loafers," a man "too drunk to rise," and a "judge, candidates and voters [who] are a reproach to any precinct or county," the writer concluded the engravings Bingham was offering for sale were no better than "worthless rubbish."[39]

Some recent critics cite Bingham's Whig politics and electoral defeat as sufficient reason for interpreting *The County Election* as a caricature of universal manhood suffrage. And it is undeniable that, deep in the disappointment of defeat, Bingham despaired of the electorate. He wrote Rollins in 1846:

If when you see me again you should not find me that pattern of purity which you have hitherto taken me to be, let the fact that I have been for the last four months full waist deep in Locofocoism plead something in my behalf. An Angel could scarcely pass through what I have experienced without being contaminated. *God help poor human nature.* As soon as I get through with this affair, and its consequences, I intend to strip off my clothes and bury them, scour my body all over with sand and water, put on a clean suit, and keep out of the mire of politics forever.[40]

Several recent commentators have agreed with "PUBLIC WEAL," describing some of the figures in the painting as "self-seeking, bibulous, slick and ingratiating, or crude and ignorant" and pointing out that they mock the Jacksonian motto on the banner that leans against the courthouse pillar in the background: "The Will of the People the Supreme Law." One critic has concluded that almost all the faces in the second version of the painting "reflect some degree of avarice," including a drunk being carried to the polls; another who, having cast his vote, is left holding his head; a political huckster; impassive officials; and rustic farmers who seem victimized by "high-pressure Locofoco campaign techniques." Another notes that the figure standing directly under the voter tossing a coin offers only two possible interpretations, neither positive: that he is tossing the coin to decide who to vote for or that his vote had been bought with the coin.[41]

Whether we see the painting as caricature or celebration does not affect our judgment of its quality. For Bingham's contemporaries, however, caricature was unpatriotic and incompatible with greatness. Despite such dissenting voices as "PUBLIC WEAL," the judgment of Bingham's contemporaries was firmly on the side of greatness. A writer for the *St. Louis Evening Intelligencer,* after viewing the painting before it was complete, predicted that future viewers would wonder "at the artist's presumptuous transfer of such unapproachable greatness to vulgar canvass." When long-time Missouri politician Edward Bates viewed the picture, he confided to his diary that "I was greatly struck with—The last day of the Election . . . . its execution seems as perfectly & as minutely true to nature, as the design is clear & bold." He, too, expressed the hope that Bingham would have it engraved to share with others. Bingham did proceed with plans to have the pic-

24. *George Caleb Bingham,*
Canvassing for a Vote, *1852,*
oil on canvas, 25⅛ × 30¼ in.
The Nelson-Atkins Museum
of Art, Kansas City,
Missouri (Nelson Fund)

ture engraved, putting out feelers to the Art-Union and Goupil, commissioning Sartain to execute the engraving, and finally selling his subscriptions and the rights to the picture to Goupil & Company.[42]

The County Election was not the first business Bingham conducted with the French firm of Goupil & Company; they had previously contracted with him to produce a print of *In a Quandry* and, in 1851, had commissioned a second picture from him, *Canvassing for a Vote,* which Bingham derived from his earlier *Country Politician,* his second recorded political subject. Set in a barroom, *Country Politician,* a "*most* perfect and life-like" scene, includes the "jolly old landlord smoking his pipe," a politician "most earnestly discussing to a very indifferent, listening farmer, the Wilmot Proviso," and "a boy with his coat tail turned up to the stove" while "reading a show bill." The Wilmot Proviso, which would ban slaveholding in the territories acquired in the Mexican War, was a hot political issue of the day, one in which the politician Bingham probably had much interest. The poster at the left also underlines the authentic, contemporary nature of the work. It advertises the Mabie Brothers Circus, which originated in Wisconsin and toured Missouri in nine seasons between 1843 and 1859. Despite such touches of firsthand immediacy, the painting also owes a debt to William Sidney Mount's *The Long Story* (1837; The Corcoran Gallery of Art, Washington, D.C.). Another of Bingham's lifelike interior scenes, *The Checker Players,* or *Playing Chequers* (1850; fig. 23), can readily be traced back to the "gaming" pictures of the late seventeenth century in Italy and Holland by the school of Caravaggio and Dutch masters like Teniers, works with which he was probably familiar.[43] It is thematically related to his earlier *Raftsmen Playing Cards* (fig. 18) as well as the Indian card-playing and checker-playing scenes of Deas (fig. 32), Eastman (fig. 96), and, later, Stanley (figs. 3, 85).

Canvassing for a Vote (fig. 24), done three years after *Country Politician,* moves the trio outside, in front of a hotel. The composition is reminiscent of a Benjamin Harrison campaign print entitled *Log Cabin Politicians* (1840; The Harry T. Peters

"America on Stone" Lithograph Collection, National Museum of American History, Smithsonian Institution) by John Bowen after a now lost painting by William Hall. The structure at the right, in the background, is probably the tavern at Arrow Rock, Bingham's hometown. As in *The County Election,* Bingham perhaps implies certain political asides in the composition. For example, does the proximity of the horse's hind end to the politician reflect Bingham's attitude toward campaigning or the kind of a person who campaigns? Is the sleeping dog in the left-hand corner a comment on the voters' interest in the election, or, perhaps, a suggestion that the politicians would like to have avoided the volatile issues of the campaign, to "let sleeping dogs lie"?[44]

Bingham closed out his election series with two more paintings, a second version of *The Stump Orator* entitled *Stump Speaking* (1854; fig. 25), which was intended as a pendant to *The County Election,* and *Verdict of the People* (1854–55; fig. 26). He painted *Stump Speaking* in Philadelphia while waiting for Sartain to engrave *The County Election.* Because he kept Rollins advised on its progress, there are recorded more of Bingham's own thoughts and comments on this picture than on any other. "As much as you admired the 'County Election,' I think you will be still better pleased with the present work," he wrote on 7 November 1853. "I have found less difficulty in the management of the subject, admitting as it does of a much greater variety of attitude, if not of expression." His self-confidence continued unabated on 23 November: "The fact is I am getting to be quite conceited, whispering sometimes to myself, that in the familiar line which I have chosen, I am the greatest among all the disciples of the brush, which my native land has yet produced."[45]

On 12 December he described the painting in detail:

I have located the assemblage in the vicinity of a mill (Kit Bullards perhaps), the cider barrel being already appropriated in the Election, I have placed [the mill] in lieu thereof, but in the background, a watermelon waggon *[sic]* over which a darkie, of course presides. The waggon and the group in and around, looming up in shadow, and relieved by the clear sky beyond, forms quite a conspicuous feature in the composition, without detracting in the slightest degree from the interest inspired by the principal group in front. In my orator I have endeavored to personify a wiry politician, grown gray in the pursuit of office and the service of party. His influence upon the crowd is quite manifest, but I have placed behind him a shrewd clear headed opponent, who is busy taking notes, and who will, when his turn

comes, make sophisms fly like cobwebs before the housekeepers broom.[46]

These extensive comments, as well as close observation of the painting, permit several conclusions. *Stump Speaking* probably had its origin during Bingham's 1846 campaign. In a speech on the floor of the Missouri House of Representatives, 17 December 1846, he recalled that

Upon the stump I had to contend with the abilities of others besides my competitor. Against me was arrayed, not only a large

25. George Caleb Bingham,
Stump Speaking, *1854,*
oil on canvas, 43 × 58 in.
Collection of the Boatmen's
National Bank of St. Louis

portion of the concentrated wealth of the county in which I reside, but I found, meeting me regularly at my own appointments, the *great* champion of our opponents from the other end of the Senatorial district. Opposed by such a combination; assailed both in front and flank, with an *ex-governor* whenever the occasion offered bearing down on my rear, I still found myself sustained by the consciousness of a good cause.[47]

Some have speculated that the speaker behind the rough-hewn table is Bingham's opponent Darwin Sappington, and that the opponent angrily scrib-

bling on a pad behind him is a self-portrait. Indeed, the high forehead and bushy eyebrows may be recognized in his earlier *Self-Portrait of the Artist* (1834–35; The Saint Louis Art Museum).[48]

The cider barrel, one of the best-known Whig emblems under William Henry Harrison, is no doubt intended as a reference to Whig politics, or at least to the politics of the day, much as Mount's *Cider Making* (1841; The Metropolitan Museum of Art) probably implied a similar reference. The mill is likely an allusion to Henry Clay, the perennial Whig candidate who was popularly called the "mill boy," a reference to his humble, hard-

26. *George Caleb Bingham,*
Verdict of the People,
1854–55,
oil on canvas, 48 × 66 in.
Collection of the Boatmen's
National Bank of St. Louis

working childhood, and recalls Bingham's depiction of Clay as the title character in a political banner, *The Mill Boy* (1844; private collection). The reference to the black man presiding over the wagon is not so much a political reference as it is an indication that Bingham was aware of popular American genre types and had assigned the black man a traditional nineteenth-century role.[49]

The painting would be a major accomplishment for any American artist of the day, particularly for one who, like Bingham, was self-taught. It was a worthy companion to *The County Election,* and Goupil also purchased the copyright to it, Bingham wrote, "upon terms perhaps as favorable as any artist ever obtained from a publisher."[50]

Bingham began *Verdict of the People* (fig. 26) to "*cap the climax*" of his election series shortly after he finished *Stump Speaking.* He informed Rollins on 15 July that "It is much larger, and will combine more striking points than either of its predecessors." He was pleased with the painting, which shows the clerk reading the election results. The overall composition is similar to *The County Election,* except that the courthouse and the mass of figures are now on the left. It is easy to see that Bingham meant the pictures to hang together, for the viewer's attention is directed toward the central figures by a narrow corridor flanked by the man with a wheelbarrow on the left and the fallen and dazed figure on the right. This work, too, derives its authenticity from Bingham's own political experience. The words on the banner waving from the hotel at the right appear to be "Freedom for——AS," which might be read as "Freedom for KANSAS" and relate to one of the most volatile issues of the day, the debate over the Kansas-Nebraska Act and whether or not Kansas was to become a slaveholding territory.[51]

Bingham offered the entire series—*Stump Speaking, The County Election,* and *Verdict of the People*—to the Library Committee of Congress in 1860, but knew in advance that the "depleted state of the treasury" made purchase unlikely. He exhibited them in Washington, Philadelphia, and Cincinnati in the hope of finding a purchaser, before placing them on indefinite loan to the St. Louis Mercantile Library Association in 1862. A contemporary critic concluded that Bingham had "transferred to canvas a *principle* in our government—the exercise of the elective franchise—and submission by the people to the will of the majority."[52]

Perhaps even Bingham himself realized that his creative energy depended upon the dynamism of the pre–Civil War frontier; after 1865 he did not attempt paintings of the scope and grandeur of his earlier efforts. He served as state treasurer from 1862 until 1865 and filled various political offices until he became a professor of art at the University of Missouri in 1877. He completed a few pictures during those years, but was inspired only once to undertake a major effort, *Martial Law,* or *Order No. 11* (1865/1868; Cincinnati Art Museum), a reaction to what he considered the unjust eviction of Missourians from their homes during the Civil War.[53]

Bingham's contribution to what we have called the "exotic genre" lies in his great paintings of life along the western rivers and of the electoral process in the West. He was, in the words of a perceptive New Orleans reporter, "to the Western what Mount is to the Eastern States, as a delineator of national customs and manners. Both are original and both occupy very honorable places in the ranks of American artists."[54] Not only did Bingham help focus on such authentic frontier types as the boatman and the country politician, but he also provided an accurate document of certain elements of frontier society, from squatters and rivermen, to politicians and well-to-do landowners and merchants. His work indeed seems to have been born of his belief that art is "the most efficient hand-maid of history."

Late in his life, Bingham observed that America had produced many great artists—West, Trumbull, Copley, Allston, Church, and others—but that the record of his own day was preserved in Mount's and his own paintings. " 'The Jolly flat Boatmen' and 'County Election' assure us that our social and political characteristics as daily and annually exhibited will not be lost in the lapse of time for want of an Art record rendering them full justice."[55]

NOTES

1. The standard biographies of Bingham are Fern Helen Rusk, *George Caleb Bingham: The Missouri Artist* (Jefferson City: Hugh Stephens Company, 1917); John Francis McDermott, *George Caleb Bingham: River Portraitist* (Norman: University of Oklahoma Press, 1959); E. Maurice Bloch, *George Caleb Bingham: The Evolution of an Artist,* 2 vols. (Berkeley and Los Angeles: University of California Press, 1967); Albert Christ-Janer, *George Caleb Bingham of Missouri; The Story of an Artist* (New York: Dodd, Mead & Company, 1940); and Albert Christ-Janer, *George Caleb Bingham: Frontier Painter of Missouri* (New York: Harry N. Abrams, 1975). For the quote, see Bingham to James S. Rollins, Düsseldorf, 3 June 1857, in C. B. Rollins, ed., "Letters of George Caleb Bingham to James S. Rollins, Pt. 3: September 7, 1856–May 8, 1859," *Missouri Historical Review* 32, no. 3 (April 1938): 353. See also McDermott, *Bingham,* pp. 123–24. The other pictures were *The County Election, Stump Speaking,* and *Verdict of the People.*

2. Bloch, *Bingham,* 1:46, 71. Volume 2 is a catalogue raisonné, and all references in this study are to vol. 1. See also *Daily Missouri Republican* (St. Louis), 16 May 1839, p. 2.

3. Quote in *Daily Missouri Republican,* 4 June 1845, p. 2; see also McDermott, *Bingham,* p. 50.

4. See Bloch, *Bingham,* pp. 79–84, for a discussion of *Fur Traders.* There has been much conjecture and no agreement on what kind of animal this is. It has been called a cat or a wolf, although a later version of this painting, now in the collection of the Detroit Institute of Arts, clearly shows a bear cub. Barbara Novak, *American Painting of the Nineteenth Century: Realism, Idealism, and the American Experience* (New York: Praeger Publishers, 1969), pp. 156–57, is less certain of Bingham's adherence to drawing manuals. One historian has described Bingham's paintings as being similar to a bas-relief, bathed in an even light. See Theodore E. Stebbins, Jr., Carol Troyen, and Trevor J. Fairbrother, *A New World: Masterpieces of American Painting, 1760–1910* (Boston: Museum of Fine Arts, 1983), p. 264. For Bingham's drawings, see E. Maurice Bloch, *The Drawings of George Caleb Bingham, with a Catalogue Raisonné* (Columbia: University of Missouri Press, 1975).

5. Henry Adams argues convincingly in "A New Interpretation of Bingham's *Fur Traders Descending the Missouri,*" *Art Bulletin* 65 (December 1983): 675–80, that the pictures are pendants, that is, companion pieces.

6. John Francis McDermott, "George Caleb Bingham and the American Art-Union," *New-York Historical Society Quarterly* 42 (January 1958): 60–69; "What Has the American Art-Union Accomplished?" *Bulletin of the American Art-Union* 2 (October 1849): 12. For the quotes, see A. Warner to Frederick E. Cohen, New York, 12 August 1848, in Bloch, *Bingham,* p. 81; and Mary Bartlett Cowdry, *American Academy of Fine Arts and American Art-Union Exhibition Record, 1816–1852,* 2 vols. (New York: The New-York Historical Society, 1953), 1:100, 114–15.

7. Bloch, *Bingham,* p. 85; quotes in W[ashington] Irving, *Astoria, or Anecdotes of an Enterprise Beyond the Rocky Mountains . . . ,* 2 vols. (Philadelphia: Carey, Lea, & Blanchard, 1836), 1:141; *Daily Missouri Republican,* 21 April 1847, p. 2; Timothy Flint, *The History and Geography of the Mississippi Valley. To Which is Appended a Condensed Physical Geography of the Atlantic United States, and the Whole American Continent,* 3rd ed. (Cincinnati: E. H. Flint; Boston: Carter, Hendee, and Company, 1833), p. 155; and *St. Louis Weekly Reveille,* 23 March 1846, p. 798. See also John Francis McDermott, "Jolly Flatboatmen: Bingham and His Imitators," *Antiques* 73 (March 1958): 267. The Banvard article is in *Howitt's Journal of Literature and Popular Progress* 2 (4 September 1847): 145. Peter C. Marzio, "The Not-So-Simple Observation of Daily Life in America," in *Of Time and Place: American Figurative Art from the Corcoran Gallery* (Washington, D.C.: Smithsonian Institution Traveling Exhibition Service and the Corcoran Gallery of Art, 1981), p. 183, suggests that the boatmen were new types, but they were already well known in popular literature. See Flint, *History and Geography of the Mississippi Valley,* p. 158, for example.

8. Quote in [Edmund Flagg], *The Far West: or, A Tour Beyond the Mountains. Embracing Outlines of Western Life and Scenery; Sketches of the Prairies, Rivers, Ancient Mounds, Early Settlements of the French, Etc., Etc.* (New York: Harper & Brothers, Publishers, 1838), 1:30.

9. Walter Blair and Franklin J. Meine, *Half Horse, Half Alligator: The Growth of the Mike Fink Legend* (Chicago: University of Chicago Press, 1956), p. 3.

10. Morgan Neville, "The Last of the Boatmen," in Blair and Meine, *Mike Fink,* pp. 47–48.

11. Blair and Meine, p. 56.

12. Flint, *History and Geography of the Mississippi Valley,* p. 157.

13. [Flagg], *The Far West,* 1:31. Another possible source is William Baldwin's painting entitled *The Merry Raftsmen* (1844; The Saint Louis Art Museum). See Perry T. Rathbone, *Westward the Way: The Character and Development of the Louisiana Territory as Seen by Artists and Writers of the Nineteenth Century* (St. Louis: City Art Museum of St. Louis, 1954), p. 186.

14. Neville, "The Last of the Boatmen," p. 260; James H. Perkins, "The Pioneers of Kentucky," *North American Review* 62 (January 1846): 87, quoted in Blair and Meine, *Mike Fink,* p. 24.

15. Quotes in the *New York Mirror* as copied in the *St. Louis Weekly Reveille,* 24 August 1846, p. 977; and Lillian B. Miller, "Paintings, Sculpture, and the National Character, 1815–1860," *Journal of American History* 53 (March 1967): 699. John W. McCoubrey, *American Tradition in Painting* (New York: George Braziller, 1963), p. 34, does not see Mike Fink in Bingham's pictures.

16. Ralph Waldo Emerson, "The American Scholar," in *The Selected Writings of Ralph Waldo Emerson,* edited by Brooks Atkinson (New York: Modern Library, 1940), p. 61. Additional quotes in the *Literary World* 1 (3 April 1847): 209; and 1 (23 October 1847): 277.

17. Quotes in the *Missouri Intelligencer* (Columbia), 14 March 1835, p. 3; *St. Louis Weekly Reveille,* 23 March 1846, p. 798; *Daily Missouri Republican,* 21 April 1847, p. 2; and *New York Mirror,* quoted in the *St. Louis Weekly Reveille,* 24 August 1846, p. 977.

18. Timothy Flint, *Recollections of the Last Ten Years in the Valley of the Mississippi,* edited with an introduction by George R. Brooks (1826; reprinted, Carbondale and Edwardsville: Southern Illinois University Press, 1968); from H. Stewart Leonard, "Catalogue of the Exhibition," in *Mississippi Panorama* (St. Louis: City Art Museum of St. Louis, 1949), p. 62. See also McDermott, *Bingham,* p. 124.

19. The original *The Jolly Flatboatmen in Port* has eight characters. The second version, now in the Terra Museum of American Art, in Evanston, Illinois, begun about 1848 but not completed until 1878, contains seven. Bloch, *Bingham,* pp. 95–96, 204, includes the quote from George Henry Hall, writing to the American Art-Union from Paris, 28 October 1850. Bloch concludes that the Düsseldorf experience was not good for Bingham and that the quality of his work steadily deteriorated after his return, to the point that, in 1867, he merited only a sentence in Henry T. Tuckerman's *Book of the Artists: American Artist Life* (New York: G. P. Putnam & Son, 1867; reprint ed., New York: James F. Carr, 1966), p. 494, the standard work on artists of the nineteenth century.

20. Quote in Bloch, *Bingham,* p. 104 (Bingham to Art-Union, New York, 19 November 1850). See also Novak, *American Painting,* p. 162, for an assessment of *Wood-Boatmen on a River.*

21. Bloch, *Bingham,* p. 107. See, for example, the *Literary World* 38 (23 October 1847): 277; and the *New York Evening Post,* 27 May 1848, p. 1. Bloch, p. 109, says, "In the two night pictures the artist seems to have finally conquered the problem of the unity of form and atmospheric space which had evidently been a conscious concern from his early years as a figure painter."

22. Information on de Hooch and Wilkie are contained in H. Nichols B. Clark, "A Fresh Look at the Art of Francis W. Edmonds: Dutch Sources and American Meanings," *American Art Journal* 14 (Summer 1982): 80, 84; and Catherine Hoover, "The Influence of David Wilkie's Prints on the Genre Paintings of William Sidney Mount," *American Art Journal* 13 (Summer 1981): 22, 27–28.

23. *Daily Missouri Republican,* 21 April 1847, p. 2; *New-York Express* as copied in the *Jefferson City Metropolitan,* 17 August 1848, quoted in Bloch, *Bingham,* p. 98.

24. *Daily Missouri Republican,* 21 April 1847, p. 2.

25. "The Fine Arts," *Literary World* 1 (23 October 1847): 277; *New-York Express* as copied in the *Jefferson City Metropolitan,* 17 August 1848, quoted in Bloch, *Bingham,* p. 98.

26. For Bingham's political activities, see Barbara S. Groseclose, "Painting, Politics, and George Caleb Bingham," *American Art Journal* 10 (November 1978): 6–7. Bingham tried on at least two occasions to get a consular appointment to England, France, Germany, or Italy. See correspondence between Bingham and his supporters and the Department of State in "Letters of Application and Recommendation During the Administrations of James Polk, Zachary Taylor, and Millard Fillmore, 1845–1853," in *Official Records of the United States Department of State* (Washington, D.C.: National Archives Microfilm Publication M873), Roll 7, which was brought to my attention through the courtesy of Colonel Merl M. Moore, Jr., of Falls Church, Virginia.

27. Bloch, *Bingham,* plate 90; quote in *Daily Missouri Republican,* 30 November 1847, p. 2.

28. Bloch, *Bingham,* pp. 130, 134, quoting *Literary World* 3 (3 June 1848): 350–51.

29. Bingham to Art-Union, New York, 19 November 1850, quoted in Bloch, *Bingham,* p. 105; McDermott, *Bingham,* p. 75, cites the quotation as being from the Art-Union catalogue.

30. "These illegitimate Loco focos, whose votes we wish to brush out of our way, have so scattered since the election, over our big praries *[sic],* that it takes a long time, with a good deal of pulling and hauling to get them up to mark. Some of them have gone clear off to parts unknown." Bingham to Rollins, Marshall, 2 November 1846, in C. B. Rollins, ed., "Letters of George Caleb Bingham to James S. Rollins, Pt. 1: May 6, 1837–July 5, 1853," *Missouri Historical Review* 32, no. 1 (October 1937): 15. Perhaps Bingham offered to hold a second election, rather than permit the Democratic-controlled legislature to decide the winner, because he felt that a sufficient number of the "illegitimate" votes would not be around to vote for the Democrats again. Gail E. Husch, "George Caleb Bingham's *County Election:* For or Against the Common Man?" (Paper read at the Middle Atlantic Symposium in the History of Art, National Gallery of Art, Washington, D.C., 5 April 1986), has speculated that Bingham's trust in the wisdom of the voter prompted him to make the offer.

31. *Daily Missouri Republican,* 11 October 1850, p. 2; Bloch, *Bingham,* p. 105. For additional comments on *The Squatters,* see John Demos, "George Caleb Bingham: The Artist as Social Historian," *American Quarterly* 17, no. 2, pt. 1 (1965): 222.

32. *Weekly Missouri Statesman* (Columbia), 31 October 1851, p. 2.

33. *Daily Missouri Republican,* 12 November 1851, p. 2; *Western Journal* 7 (November 1851): 145, quoted in Bloch, *Bingham,* p. 144.

34. Bloch, *Bingham,* pp. 148–49, 152.

35. *Philadelphia Register,* 7 September 1854, copied in the *Booneville Weekly Observer,* 30 September 1854, p. 1, as quoted in Bloch, *Bingham,* p. 147. The opinion is based on seeing the John Sartain engraving rather than the painting itself.

36. Rollins to A. Warner, Columbia, 11 January 1852, AAU Correspondence in the New-York Historical Society.

37. Bingham to Messrs. Goupil & Co., St. Louis, 31 January 1852, photostat in the files of Knoedler and Company, New York, quoted in Ross E. Taggart, " 'Canvassing for a Vote' and Some Unpublished Portraits by Bingham," *Art Quarterly* 18 (Autumn 1955): 240.

38. *Weekly Missouri Sentinel* (Columbia), 28 October 1852, p. 2, commented on the picture, along with *The Emigration of Daniel Boone,* when they were on exhibit in the Grand Jury room of the courthouse in Columbia. See also the *New Orleans Daily Picayune,* 18 March 1853, supplement, p. 1; and Bloch, *Bingham,* p. 143.

39. Highly favorable reviews appeared in the *Daily Louisville Times,* 14 May 1853, p. 3, quoted in Bloch, *Bingham,* p. 139; the *Louisville Daily Journal,* 16 May 1853, p. 2; and the *Louisville Daily Courier,* 18 May 1853, p. 2. Bingham to Rollins, Lexington, 22 May 1853, in Rollins, ed., "Letters, Pt. 1," p. 31. "PUBLIC

WEAL" quoted from the *Kentucky Statesman* (Lexington), 31 May 1853, p. 2.

40. Bingham to Rollins, Marshall, 2 November 1846, in Rollins, ed., "Letters, Pt. 1," p. 15.

41. Robert F. Westervelt, "The Whig Painter of Missouri," *American Art Journal* 2 (Spring 1970): 48; Groseclose, "Painting, Politics, and George Caleb Bingham," p. 8.

42. *St. Louis Evening Intelligencer,* copied in the *Weekly Missouri Statesman,* 9 January 1852, quoted in McDermott, *Bingham,* p. 92. See also pp. 93, 94. Additional quotes in Bingham to Rollins, Philadelphia, 29 May 1854, in C. B. Rollins, ed., "Letters of George Caleb Bingham to James S. Rollins, Pt. 2: October 3, 1853–August 10, 1856," *Missouri Historical Review* 32, no. 2 (January 1938): 183. James Thomas Flexner, *That Wilder Image* (Boston: Little, Brown & Company, 1962), pp. 146–47, noted that "All the elements needed for devastating satire are portrayed—windbags and office holding humbugs, wily or smug; voters idiotic or disreputable, usually drunken; liquor flowing at the polls—yet all is recorded with such admiration as a doting father lavishes on a spirited urchin come home filthy and with his pocket full of frogs."

43. Bingham to Rollins, New York, 30 March 1851, in Rollins, ed., "Letters, Pt. 1," p. 21; *Daily Missouri Republican,* 17 April 1849, p. 2; and E. Maurice Bloch, "A Bingham Discovery," *American Art Review* 1 (September–October 1973): 24. See also Bloch, *Bingham,* p. 116. Although he does not mention Bingham, H. Nichols B. Clark demonstrates the influence that Dutch genre painting had on American artists during the decades before the Civil War in "A Taste for the Netherlands: The Impact of Seventeenth-Century Dutch and Flemish Genre Painting on American Art, 1800–1860," *American Art Journal* 14 (Spring 1982): 23–38, esp. 36–38.

44. Taggart, " 'Canvassing for a Vote,' " p. 230; Barbara S. Groseclose, "Politics and American Genre Painting of the Nineteenth Century," *Antiques* 120 (November 1981): 1212.

45. Bingham to Rollins, Philadelphia, 7 and 23 November 1853, in Rollins, ed., "Letters, Pt. 2," pp. 166–67, 169–70.

46. Bingham to Rollins, Philadelphia, 12 December 1853, in Rollins, ed., "Letters, Pt. 2," pp. 171–72.

47. McDermott, *Bingham,* p. 64, quoting the *Weekly Missouri Statesman,* 22 January 1847.

48. Others have suggested that the speaker might have been the former U.S. Senator from Missouri, James S. Green. Bingham might have had a number of individuals in mind when working on the painting, but it seems doubtful that he intended the figures to represent specific individuals, or that any of the numerous identifications that have been proposed over the years are accurate. Rollins, ed., "Letters, Pt. 2," p. 172, n. 13; McDermott, *Bingham,* pp. 92–93, n. 3.

49. Bloch, *Bingham,* pp. 77–78; Groseclose, "Politics and American Genre Painting of the Nineteenth Century," pp. 8–9. See Marzio for comment on how painters had to create new types. For information on Mount's *Cider Making,* see Alfred Frankenstein, *William Sidney Mount* (New York: Harry N. Abrams, 1975), p. 202; Joseph B. Hudson, Jr., "Banks, Politics, Hard Cider, and Paint: The Political Origins of William Sidney Mount's Cider Making," *Metropolitan Museum Journal* 10 (1975): 107–18.

50. Bingham to Rollins, New York, 17 May 1854, in Rollins, ed., "Letters, Pt. 2," p. 182.

51. Bingham to Rollins, Philadelphia, 16 April and 15 July 1854, in Rollins, ed., "Letters, Pt. 2," pp. 178, 186; Groseclose, "Painting, Politics, and George Caleb Bingham," p. 14.

52. Bingham to Rollins, Washington City, 9 January 1860, in C. B. Rollins, ed., "Letters of George Caleb Bingham to James S. Rollins, Pt. 4: June 6, 1859–June 29, 1861," *Missouri Historical Review* 32, no. 4 (July 1938): 494; *Missouri Statesman,* 16 May 1856, quoted in Bloch, *Bingham,* p. 165.

53. Bloch, *Bingham,* p. 216.

54. *New Orleans Daily Picayune,* 18 March 1853, supplement, p. 1.

55. Bingham to Rollins, Kansas City, 19 June 1871, in C. B. Rollins, ed., "Letters of George Caleb Bingham to James S. Rollins, Pt. 5," *Missouri Historical Review* 33, no. 1 (October 1938): 72.

CHARLES DEAS

CAROL CLARK

During his brief productive life, Charles Deas was recognized both as a promising artist of genre and literary scenes and as one properly devoted to a national subject matter drawn from the Far West. His life was a unified artistic endeavor consisting of equal parts of nature, literature, and imagination, with additional inspiration drawn from striking images by a variety of late eighteenth- and early nineteenth-century artists.

Most information about Deas comes from a long biographical sketch by Henry Tuckerman first published anonymously in *Godey's Lady's Book* in 1846. Tuckerman praised Deas for his depiction of what is "truly remarkable in our scenery," a subject that "has not been more ardently explored by [other] native artists and authors" even though "it is in our border life alone that we can find the materials for national development as far as literature and art are concerned." Curiously, Tuckerman saw the exploitation of native subjects less as a means of exciting the admiration of an American audience than as a way of gaining "instant attention in Europe."[1]

Contemporary reviews of exhibited works reveal a great deal about pictures we know and about others that have disappeared; although Deas was prolific during his twelve-year career, few paintings have survived. Moreover, we have only a very few letters from his hand, and none that discloses much about his attitudes toward his life or

his art. He was included in the travel writings of two of his contemporaries, J. Henry Carleton and Charles Lanman, and some of his works were engraved or lithographed and reached a larger audience. But after his death in 1867 he was accorded no more than brief mention in any histories of art or even in histories of his adopted town of St. Louis. It was not until the 1940s that scholars began to devote some attention to Deas.[2] Using what information is available and combining it with some cautious conjecture, this essay discusses Deas in the context of romantic narrative painting in America, particularly that of the Far West.

Before the artist's birth on 22 December 1818, his family had moved from South Carolina to Philadelphia, where he grew up and was educated in the classics and art. By the autumn of 1835 Deas had moved with his widowed mother to upstate New York; within the year, following an unsuccessful attempt to obtain an appointment to West Point, he set out upon an artistic career.[3] After the critical success of his literary genre pictures, *The Turkey Shoot* (ca. 1836; Virginia Museum, Richmond) and *The Devil and Tom Walker* (1838; Collection of Richard P. W. Williams), at the annual exhibitions, Deas was elected an associate of the National Academy of Design in 1839. One of the requirements of admission was the submission of an original artwork, and the following year Deas offered his *Self-Portrait* (1840; fig. 27).

Deas
Prairie Fire
(detail, see fig. 45)

C. Deas 1840.

The self-portrait reveals a restless man; and we may gather from his having executed at least fourteen pictures in two years that he was energetic—even impatient—as well. He sought new experiences outside of the cities and the domesticated countrysides he had known. Unable to attend West Point or pursue a military career as an officer, he longed for adventure nonetheless, and soon set off in search of it.

Tuckerman gives another clue to a more immediate motive for his western journey. George Catlin's Indian gallery opened in New York on 25 September 1837 with an exhibition of hundreds of Indian portraits and scenes of their dances and hunts, as well as landscapes of the Upper Missouri region, all painted during Catlin's seven-year stay in the Far West. These remained on view for three months. If Deas missed this popular show and the many lectures Catlin delivered to accompany it—unlikely, since the exhibition took place in Clinton Hall, site of the academy classes Deas might have attended in this period—he would have had other chances to see Catlin's work, since that artist reopened his gallery in January 1838 and again in June 1839. And, as Tuckerman observed, "To visit the scenes whence Catlin drew the unique specimens of art, to study the picturesque forms,

costumes, attitudes and grouping of Nature's own children; to share the grateful repast of the hunter and taste the wild excitement of frontier life, in the very heart of the noblest scenery of the land, was a prospect calculated to stir the blood of one with a true sense of the beautiful and a natural relish for woodcraft and sporting."[4]

We know nothing for certain of Deas's aspirations or motives. Perhaps he viewed himself as better equipped and more talented than Catlin. In 1848 he proposed to create his own Indian gallery, but we have no clue that before 1840, the year of the self-portrait, he had Catlin's sense of mission to record, systematically, even compulsively, a vanishing race.

Deas may have shared Catlin's desire to abandon "civilized" society, at least in part, and to wander in the wilderness. Yet Catlin seemed always torn between East and West, ambitious for success within the society he shunned, while Deas compromised more happily for some eight years of artistic activity; he lived in a frontier town, participated in its artistic life, and exhibited his pictures there as well as back east in New York and in Philadelphia.

What became for Deas a changed way of life, an extended opportunity to experience, day-to-day, the conjunction of two potentially antagonistic cultures, may indeed have begun as an intended summer in the wilderness, a visit to his brother's headquarters in Wisconsin Territory. There was another family connection with the West as well, through his maternal uncle, who, as governor of Arkansas Territory, had successfully dealt with the Indians there. And there were the artist's apparent literary interests, which could have turned him to western travel. James Fenimore Cooper's *The Prairie* was published in 1827, and Washington Irving's *A Tour on the Prairies,* recounting an 1832 trip to the West, was issued in 1835. Deas's inspiration for paintings from these authors (*The Turkey Shoot*—taken from *The Prairie*—and *The Devil and Tom Walker*—from Irving's *Tales of a Traveller*) demonstrates that he was aware of their narratives of the West.

Contemporary western artists other than Catlin also may have influenced Deas's interests. The late

1830s saw western travel by several artists, such as the Baltimore painter Alfred Jacob Miller, whose 1837 journey to the fur trade rendezvous may have come to Deas's attention. Seth Eastman, drawing instructor at West Point at the time of Deas's application, had been with the army at forts Crawford and Snelling between 1831 and 1833, and would return to Fort Snelling in September 1841, just after Deas's stay there. George Caleb Bingham, an artist from Missouri, exhibited *Western Boatmen Ashore* at the Apollo Gallery in 1838, the year before Deas made his debut at that very gallery. At this time, too, Bingham may have visited New York and, fresh from study in Philadelphia, may well have met the rising young genre painter.[5] Whatever the specifics that motivated Deas, western scenes and narratives were popular in the late 1830s. Finally, the West may have appealed to Deas as an escape from civilization's pressures, both external and internal—we know that the artist was committed to an asylum in 1848.

Although we have no sense of Deas's attitude toward the Indians before his trip, he did choose to travel among them and, before 1846, recounted to Tuckerman his fascination with their appearance and their ways. In addition to the extant paintings, we have an important document[6] that can be assumed to reflect his mature views on the Indian. Written late in 1848, it is a proposal for an Indian gallery. Deas tried, through an influential relative in South Carolina, to raise five thousand dollars over a five-year period to support himself while he painted from the sketches made during his life in the Far West. He planned to exhibit the paintings in his gallery and divide the profits among the gallery's subscribers and himself. This is the only hint we have of such a project, and we may assume that Deas either did not entice enough subscribers or failed to complete enough pictures to form a gallery. As the document was written after reports of Deas's illness had reached the journals, it is likely that he was not well enough to undertake the task of painting or marketing an Indian gallery.

The language describing the gallery's purpose is very like Catlin's and enlightens us about Deas's attitude toward the Indian after almost eight years of living in the West, traveling to see the people, and painting their images: "[the artist] has it much at heart to save from oblivion a Race, now fast disappearing from the face of the Earth."[7] Deas shared a view of the doomed Indian with Catlin and John Mix Stanley, two other artists who created and toured Indian galleries. The qualified critical if not financial success of those tours may have encouraged Deas; at the time, Catlin's tour of the United States and Europe had ended and Stanley's was in the middle of its five-year run. Deas may have known as well of Charles Bird King's portraits of Indians who were on delegations to the capital; these were in the government's collection in Washington, D.C. Catlin's inability to find support or a permanent home for his collection must not have discouraged the younger artist.

From Deas's proposal we also learn the value he placed on the "several years passed among" the Indians and of his "uncommon opportunities of seeing the different tribes that inhabit the Forests of our vast Western Country,"[8] which gave authority to the paintings he proposed. These "several years" began in the spring of 1840. With Tuckerman as our guide, we can follow Deas over more than a year of travel in Wisconsin Territory.

Only two of Deas's paintings dated to this year survive, but we know from Tuckerman that, at the artist's various stops during his travels, he had opportunity to sketch and to paint. His first look at Indians occurred on the way to Fort Crawford as he traveled the lake route to Mackinaw and saw "genuine sons of the wilderness . . . camped on the beach."[9] He reached his destination through the interior of Wisconsin to Green Bay and via Fort Winnebago and Fox Lake. Fort Crawford at Prairie du Chien on the Mississippi River was his home for most of the next year, and it was from there that he ventured out to see different terrain and other Indian tribes.

Deas seized the opportunity to paint Indians and traders at this important post. Tuckerman reports that, through the auspices of his brother, and the fort's commanding officer, and "gentlemen connected with the Fur companies, he was enabled to collect sketches of Indians, frontier scenery and subjects of agreeable reminiscence and picturesque incident, enough to afford material for a painting." During several seasons at the fort, Deas saw many sides of Indian and frontier life. "The groups of half-breeds, Indians, and *voyageurs,* always to be found about the trading-houses and fur depots, realized all that an artist needs in the way of frontier costume and manners." The artist was able to "observe the expression of Indian character" during a number of incidents at the fort, not the least of which was the confrontation between vengeful Sac and Fox Indians and the Winnebago leader Keokuk, which led to "many serio comic scenes."[10]

Deas also made at least six forays from the fort, especially to see the Winnebago, who that year were being removed from their most recent home in Iowa and settled farther west—a dislocation that may well have excited Deas's sympathy.

At Fort Winnebago he "paint[ed] the likenesses of the prominent members of the tribe," and at Painted Rock he saw Winnebago "to advantage in their every-day life." Tuckerman wrote: "the most extraordinary incidents presented themselves; and in the stillness of the moonlit nights, the echoes of the Indian lover's flute blent with the battle-chant or the maiden's shrill song." In Tuckerman's retelling, the experience was uncommonly romantic, yet not without a consciousness of the reality of the Indian's plight: "sickness in all its stages was there, from the first listlessness of ague to the raging madness of high fever. All were attacked, from the mother with her first-born to the aged crone, from the venerable sachem to the young warrior."[11]

The following summer of 1841, Deas traveled up the Mississippi to Fort Snelling to paint the Sioux, who gathered in tents around the fort. With the persuasive charm he would use again and again in the West, he overcame the Indians' natural reluctance to have their image "taken," and, according to Tuckerman, painted portraits of several of them. He also witnessed the excitement of Sioux games and feasts and "saw some admirable specimens of the human form" and "all the display of which the Indians were capable."[12] Regrettably,

Deas did not have the opportunity to meet Seth Eastman, who returned to Fort Snelling after Deas's departure.

During the visit to Fort Snelling Deas may have painted the large—three and a half by four feet—undoubtedly commissioned *Lion* (Minnesota Chapter of the Daughters of the American Revolution), a portrait of one of territorial governor Henry H. Sibley's wolfhounds. Another painting, more in keeping with his experiences at the forts and with the Indians, probably dates from this trip, or just after, as well. *Fort Snelling* (ca. 1841; fig. 28)[13] is a small, delicately painted landscape of the meeting of Anglo and Indian cultures. Out of a foreground autumnal forest comes an Indian carrying a rifle; he hails figures in a canoe below. The fort, strategically situated on a bluff above the junction of the Minnesota and Mississippi rivers, dominates the scene in the middle ground—as it did the lives of all who dwelled in its shadow. Deas's painting clearly depicts as an idyllic setting the wilderness into which the fort had been introduced just twenty years earlier. Neither the rifle—a symbol of the pioneering frontiersman here appropriated for the Indian's use in hunting and warfare—nor the fort upsets nature's balance. Deas presents the fort as a peaceful presence, and the Indian's gesture of greeting makes the mood of the picture welcoming rather than threatening.

Just a few years before, Deas had longed to become an arms expert and, perhaps, to reside as an officer at an outpost like Fort Snelling, as Seth Eastman had done.[14] Eastman's own painted views of the fort, exhibited at the National Academy of Design in 1838, may have, in fact, inspired Deas's similar effort. Now, after more than a year in the West as a visitor and as an observer of Indian life and frontier culture, he portrayed the fort from the vantage of the Indian and with a sensitivity to the lush landscape around the installation that is apparent in this painting and is further suggested by his choice of the Falls of St. Anthony as one subject for another work, now lost.

Of the many sketches and portraits Tuckerman reported that Deas painted in the West during his year at Fort Crawford and vicinity, only *Lion* and *Fort Snelling,* neither dated, still exist. Yet we know from Tuckerman that Deas painted portraits of the "fine-looking Sioux in the vicinity" of the fort, and from a local newspaper notice that he exhibited "Portraits of several Indians, taken from life" and "Several Portraits" at the autumn Mechanics' Fair in St. Louis, where he had taken up residence by November 1841.[15]

St. Louis, a former Indian trading post and rendezvous for trappers, was a hub of life on the western frontier and one of the gateways to the West. A city active with trade, commerce, and manufacturing, St. Louis was, according to George Ruxton, British traveler and chronicler of the mountain man, home to a varied population of early settlers, merchants and an upper class "who form a little aristocracy even here," a "large floating population of foreigners of all nations," and a "large . . . population still connected with the Indian and fur trade, who preserve all their characteristics unacted upon by the influence of advancing civilization." Ruxton found "the most singular" of St. Louis's "casual population [to be] the mountaineers, who, after several seasons spent in trapping, and with good store of dollars, arrive from the scene of their adventures, wild as savages, determined to enjoy themselves for a time, in all the gaiety and dissipation of the western city."[16] It is difficult to imagine a richer source of imagery for an artist interested in characterization.

From Deas's early participation in the Mechanics' Fairs we also learn something of his political life in St. Louis. Founded in 1839 for the "promotion and encouragement of Manufactures and the Mechanical and usefull Arts," with a membership consisting of "Manufacturers, Mechanics, Artizans, and persons friendly to the Mechanic Arts,"[17] the Mechanics' Institute included stonecutters, carpenters, and a few artists. The group was dominated by merchants, especially of the Whig party, and while Deas may have seen the annual fairs as opportunities to exhibit his paintings and so gain patrons or commissions, his election as a resident member in November 1842 suggests he may also have shared some of the merchants' political views, which supported a federal presence in the territories but opposed continental expansion.

28. *Charles Deas,* Fort Snelling, *ca. 1841, oil on canvas, 12 × 14¼ in. Peabody Museum, Harvard University*

Perhaps through the Mechanics' Institute and its fairs, Deas met John Casper Wild, a Swiss-born, French-trained lithographer who emigrated to the United States and lived in Philadelphia and Cincinnati before coming to St. Louis about 1840.[18] For the frontispiece of Lewis F. Thomas's *Inda, a Legend of the Lakes* (1842), the first volume of poetry published west of the Mississippi, Wild lithographed a portrait of the author from "a splendid painting by C. Deas," no doubt one of the many commissions the artist obtained in St. Louis. Thomas credited Deas with great knowledge of Indian habits and adornment and praised his work: "I may mention, *en passant,* to the curious in Aboriginal matters, that Mr. D. has a large and elegant collection of Indian portraits and graphic sketches, illustrative of their manners and customs, all drawn from nature, and with remarkable skill and fidelity."[19]

The previous year, 1841, *The Valley of the Mississippi Illustrated in a Series of Views* was published, with Thomas as editor and Wild as "painter and lithographer." Although the cover and title-page illustrations are not specially credited, these two views are different from the other illustrations in the book and were most likely taken from works by Deas.[20] The cover (fig. 29) in particular is composed in the manner Deas favored: a principal group or dominant figure to the left looks down and across at small figures at the right; this is the mirror image of Deas's customary *painting* composition and would be expected in a print taken from a painting. What is not characteristic of Deas is the warlike Indian preparing to shoot an arrow at unsuspecting frontiersmen who are felling trees for their log house. If the picture is Deas's, it would be the only example extant in his work of a stereotyped savage confronting the civilizing influence of the settler; the subject may have been given him rather than one he selected.

Several of Deas's extant paintings from his first year or two in St. Louis reflect his interest in the Winnebagos. A pair of small watercolors, *Friends* (1843; fig. 30) and *Winnebagos* (1843; fig. 31), show the daily life of members of the tribe. In *Friends* a small child hails a party on the horizon, and in *Winnebagos* another hailing figure, much like the one in *Fort Snelling,* attracts the attention of a member of a hunting party. The horseman and another figure, who examines a gun, wear brightly colored striped trade-cloth shirts, patterns Deas had favored in *The Turkey Shoot* and *The Devil and Tom Walker* and in which he now took delight as Indian costume.

A yellow-and-silver-striped shirt appears on a player in *Winnebagos Playing Checkers* (1842; fig. 32), one of Deas's most important pictures of this period. Titled, signed, and dated on the reverse of the canvas, this work shows the characterization, narrative potential, and attention to detail that had marked Deas's genre paintings in New York. In the interior of a Winnebago bark wigwam, two braves, highly decorated in ceremonial paint, play a game of checkers. Only one Indian wears a trade-cloth shirt; the others are bare-chested and draped with blankets, one bright red and the other very dark purplish blue, as the shirted player is partially covered in a blanket of forest green. All three are within the ochre walls of their lodge. These color choices demonstrate Deas's awareness of the four-color painting tradition of the Italian Renaissance.

29. John Casper Wild (ca. 1804–46) or Charles Deas, The Valley of the Mississippi Illustrated *(cover illustration), 1841, lithograph, 11½ × 8⅞ in. (sheet). Missouri Historical Society, St. Louis*

30. *Charles Deas,*
Friends, *1843,*
watercolor on paper,
7-½ × 9 in.
John F. Eulich
Collection, Dallas

31. *Charles Deas,*
Winnebagos, *1843,*
watercolor on paper,
7 × 9¼ in.
Mr. and Mrs. Gerald P.
Peters Collection, Santa Fe

Gambling was a favorite frontier pastime, and the game of checkers, introduced by whites, afforded Deas an opportunity to observe and to paint levels of concentration and interaction among the Winnebagos. The observer, smoking a pipe, seems to have commented on the anticipated move of the player seated nearest to him and who, although the game is close, has fewer pieces left on the board. He is decorated with earring and arm cuff, and several rings glitter from his fingers, which barely touch the checker piece, the object of his intense concentration. Startled perhaps by the pronouncement of the old Indian, the opponent suddenly has lifted his hand from the board and has turned his painted face away from us.

Deas scattered objects on the floor and on the walls of the lodge with the attention of a still-life painter. Especially prominent are a gourd rattle and a quiver, possible prizes for the winner of this game, perhaps being played between ceremonial practices at an event like the Council of Winnebago that Deas saw at Fort Crawford or the gatherings he visited at Painted Rock during the summer of 1840. Deas's keen sense of observation and obvious delight in the drama as well as the details of the game, with its painted players and sage kibitzer, engage us in the tension and the humor of the moment.

Winnebagos Playing Checkers is only one of a large group of paintings Deas exhibited at the Mechanics' Fair in 1842, which included "a number of portraits of Indian chiefs, landscape paintings . . . [a] scene of the Illinois troops crossing Cedar Creek, the Interior of a Winnebago Winter Lodge, and the Game of Checkers or Drafts, and the Sesseton Sioux playing at Ball." If the quality of all was as high as suggested by *Winnebagos Playing Checkers,* it must have been an impressive display. The critic for the *Daily Missouri Republican* commended the group as "very fine paintings, as well as accurate in delineation."[21]

The following year, in *Sioux Playing Ball* (1843; fig. 33), Deas painted lacrosse, a more violent game. Lacrosse was played in summer and winter alike and was especially popular with artists as a

32. *Charles Deas,*
Winnebagos Playing
Checkers, *1842,*
oil on canvas,
12⁷⁄₁₆ × 14³⁄₄ in.
Thyssen-Bornemisza
Collection, Lugano,
Switzerland

grand and savage spectacle. Here Deas chose the summer game, played by highly painted, almost naked Sioux. He focuses on the confrontation of two intent players, almost mirror images in their poses and in the efforts of their opponents to bring them down. Deas exhibited a ball game at the Mechanics' Fair in 1842, which may have been the posed and theatrical *Sioux Playing Ball*. This painting interested the critic of the *Broadway Journal* in 1845, although he thought it inferior to *Long Jakes* (fig. 34) and *The Indian Guide* (1846; now lost).[22]

After two years in St. Louis, Deas, as far as we know, ventured onto the plains once more, this time on Major Clifton Wharton's mid-August to mid-September 1844 expedition from Fort Leavenworth to the Pawnee villages on the Platte River. The purpose of the expedition was to confirm friendly relations with the Pawnee and to moderate their disputes with neighboring tribes. Deas's presence is noted in Major Wharton's official journal of the expedition: "Mr. Charles Deas of St. Louis, an intelligent Artist, has become a partner in our expected toils and pleasure." But it is from the unofficial journal of Lieutenant J. Henry Carleton, assistant commissary for the Dragoons, that we learn of Deas's intention to "make many fine additions to his already extensive and truly beautiful gallery of paintings."[23] Deas must have found a kindred spirit in the young lieutenant, who loved the scenic beauty of the prairies the expedition crossed, was fascinated by the animal life observed, had deep interest in the Indians and their lives, and, as something of a writer, desired to express the experiences he shared with the artist.

Carleton describes Deas's exotic appearance in "a broad white hat—a loose dress, and sundry traps and truck hanging about his saddle, like a fur-hunter." Deas's appearance and jaunty attitude prompted the soldiers to call him "Rocky Mountains"; he especially impressed Carleton as a free spirit: "He had a Rocky Mountain way of getting along; for, being under no military restraint, he could go where he pleased, and come back when

33. *Charles Deas,* Sioux Playing Ball, *1843, oil on canvas, 29 × 37 in. The Thomas Gilcrease Institute of American History and Art, Tulsa, Oklahoma*

he had a mind to."[24] Perhaps Deas, the former military academy applicant and aspirant to officer, now took ostentatious pleasure in his independence; or perhaps he needed to separate himself clearly in dress and manner from the life he once contemplated.

Carleton recorded Deas's manner of putting his sitters at ease through humor, cajolery, and an elaborate display of manners as he chattered in French while he painted. "Mr. Deas seemed to possess the whole secret of winning the good graces of the Indians . . . he always gave his salutations in French and with a tone and gestures so irresistibly comic that, generally, the whole lodge would burst into a roar of laughter, though not the shadow of a smile could be seen on his face."[25]

There are no sketches extant of the camp or portraits of Indians from this trip, with the possible exception of an untitled sketch of a military expedition crossing a river (Gerald Peters Gallery, Santa Fe), composed in Deas's typical manner and in which he tried to convey the vast stretches of prairie the party had crossed. For one summer Deas traveled with a military party among the Indians and gathered experiences and painted images to sustain the more settled life to which he returned in St. Louis.

Tuckerman reported that—at least by 1846, when he presumably visited Deas—the artist flourished in his professional life in St. Louis: "from his own testimony, . . . he has there found all that a painter can desire in the patronage of friends and general sympathy and appreciation."[26] He had exhibited at the Mechanics' Fairs and joined their institute, and he was listed for the first time in the St. Louis city directory for 1845 as a "portrait painter," and then again in 1847 as an "artist," with a residence at 97 Chesnut Street. Other than the J. C. Wild engraving after his portrait of Lewis Thomas, only *Portrait of Luke E. Lawless* (ca. 1847; Missouri Historical Society, St. Louis) survives as testimony to Deas's career as a St. Louis portrait painter. And only a few patrons of landscapes and subject pictures are known. John Rosencrants lent *View on the Upper Mississippi, one mile below Fort Snelling* to the Pennsylvania Acad-

emy in 1843, and James E. Yeatman, later treasurer of the Western Academy of Art in St. Louis, included in his collection works by Deas and Bingham, as well as "Old Master" and "after Old Master" paintings. Mrs. Treat and a "Catherwood" owned at least one painting each by 1864.[27] We know almost nothing of local support for Deas while he lived in St. Louis between 1841 and 1847.

His primary activity within the art market between 1844 and 1848 was by exhibition, sale, and "distribution" of his pictures at the American Art-Union in New York. Active in the Apollo Association from its founding in 1839 and with its successor, the American Art-Union, after 1844, Deas benefited from the association's efforts to encourage American artists and their treatment of national subject matter. In ten exhibitions between 1839 and 1850 Deas was represented by about fifteen pictures, eleven of which were purchased by the Art-Union and then distributed by lottery to members at the end of each year. Deas was also a member and actively involved in the appointment of Charles D. Drake as the St. Louis agent for the Art-Union in 1846.[28]

The artist's first great success at the Art-Union came in 1844, with the exhibition of his first western picture there, *Long Jakes (Long Jakes, The Rocky Mountain Man)* (fig. 34). Deas's red-shirted and bearded trapper, astride a gallant stallion, turns in his saddle to inspect something that has caught his attention and alarmed his horse. He is in control, secure in his isolation from the comforts of society, and outfitted not unlike Deas himself as Lieutenant Carleton had described him. According to the critic for the *Broadway Journal, Long Jakes,* also called "Jacques," caused a "sensation among the audience" at the December distribution. The popularity of *Long Jakes* lay in its appealing vision of the western hero as a wild man with a core of urbane chivalry. Long Jakes is "from the outer verge of our civilization" and appears "wild and romantic," yet "there are traits of former gentleness and refinement in his countenance, and he sits upon his horse as though he were fully conscious of his picturesque appearance."[29] Engraved by W. G. Jackman for an 1846 issue of *New York Illustrated Magazine,* Deas's

34. *Charles Deas,*
Long Jakes (Long Jakes,
The Rocky Mountain
Man), *1844,*
oil on canvas, 30 × 25 in.
Vose Galleries of Boston, Inc.

C. Deas. St. Louis May 25 1845

painting inspired an emotional essay by Henry William Herbert, which celebrated "the glorious, the free, the untrammeled sense of individual will and independent power" *Long Jakes* symbolized. Herbert chronicles the mountain man's heroic capture of his wild stallion, a creature noble as his master, and praises the hero's independence in a democratic age "when individuality and personal characteristics and personal influence are yielding everywhere to the pre-eminence of masses." Jakes's attire is perfect, according to Herbert, "everything here is real, useful, yet how showy, and how more than romantic."[30] The American public and critics of 1845 embraced the potential of *Long Jakes* for narrative embellishment and as a political symbol of independence, and they elevated Deas to a new position of prominence in New York and in St. Louis.

"The Rocky Mountain man," as *Long Jakes* was subtitled in the Art-Union catalogue, came not only from "the outer verge of our civilization," but also from an earlier moment in American his-

tory. By 1844 the price of beaver pelts had declined and settlers had begun to invade the territory; the brief heyday of the mountain man had passed. But his apotheosis survived. The publication of Washington Irving's *Astoria* in 1836 and *The Adventures of Captain Bonneville* the next year further fixed the mountain man as a popular literary character. Deas may have read these accounts. He also may have noted John C. Frémont's return to St. Louis in the summer of 1844 after more than a year of far-reaching exploration in the West. Certainly by 1845, when Frémont's report was published, the trapper was even more firmly set in the national imagination.[31]

Long Jakes was reproduced by Jackman in 1846, as we have noted, and was lithographed by Leopold Grozelier about 1855. Copied by many of his contemporaries and especially admired by folk artists, the image, probably in its 1855 printed form, was carried as far as Texas and inspired William M. G. Samuel's *Man on Horseback* (Collection of the Daughters of the Republic of Texas at the Alamo, San Antonio). William Tylee Ranney's *The Trapper's Last Shot* (1850; figs. 55, 56) exists in two versions and may have been inspired by *Long Jakes,* since Ranney could well have seen the painting in St. Louis. Deas himself may have painted several versions of the mountain man or trapper.[32]

Deas's entry in the 1845 Art-Union exhibition, *The Indian Guide,* "whose prototype was a venerable Shawnee who accompanied Major Wharton,"[33] elicited another response from the *Broadway Journal*'s critic, who singled out Deas as "excepting [William Sidney] Mount . . . the most purely American in his feelings of any painter that we have produced." His pictures had "an air of genuineness that impressed you with the feeling of truth." The review goes on to define the special appeal of the mountain man poised between a savage state and civilization:

Pictures of pure savage life, like those by Mr. Catlin, cannot excite our sympathies as strongly as do the representations of beings who belong to our own race. The Indian stands at an impossible remove from civilization, but the

36. *Charles Deas,*
A Group of Sioux, 1845,
oil on canvas, 14⅛ × 16½ in.
Amon Carter Museum,
Fort Worth

half-breed forms a connecting link between the
white and red races; we feel a sympathy for
the Indian guide that we never could for
the painted savage, for we see that he has a
tincture of our own blood, and his trappings
show that he has taken one step toward
refinement and civilized life.[34]

The Indian Guide is now lost, but descriptions
of it suggest similarity in conception and some
details to *The Hunter* (1845; fig. 35), a pen-and-
ink drawing, signed and inscribed "St. Louis May
23, 1845."

Although Deas chose the life of the halfbreed
and the pioneer for several of his works in the
next few years, he did not abandon the Indian as
a subject. Indeed, in 1845, he painted *A Group of
Sioux* (fig. 36), a small, intricately composed picture, serene in some elements but tense as a whole,
which seems to have escaped exhibition in New
York or St. Louis as well as mention in the press.

Deas painted at least one oil sketch, *Figure Group*
(ca. 1845; fig. 37), that is related closely enough
to *A Group of Sioux* to suggest that it is a study
for the major picture.

That Deas understood Sioux culture is evident
in such details as the depiction of the typical Sioux
hairstyle, bullet pouch, and trade items, notably
blankets and striped cloth shirts; the gun on the
ground is also authentic. Yet anomalies appear as
well. The helmet is not typically Sioux, and pipe
smoking would occur more usually in camp, not
on the trail. From these and other details it becomes apparent that Deas has painted a narrative
of a group of Indians fleeing intertribal warfare.[35]
At the upper right a brave signals with a blanket
as a message in smoke appears on the horizon to
the far left, behind a mounted Indian who races
across the plains. This has aroused the group's attention, and their horses, one rearing behind, stir
in anticipation of departure. The brave in white
buffalo robe, seen in profile, stares intently into
the distance as he prepares to mount. A fearful
child holds a horse, which, to judge by its white
man's bridle and woman's saddle, may have been
stolen. In contrast to this tense air of impending
danger, a pipe-smoking elder turns toward a
squaw who looks up at him, and a beautifully at-
tired brave in blue-and-red-striped trade-cloth
shirt and buffalo robe kneels to secure his moccasin near the "still life" to his right. The trappings
of war are present: a gun, hatchet, lance, and
quiver; and the braves' faces are highly painted.
Mysterious and enigmatic but clearly narrative in
its intention, *A Group of Sioux* is a somewhat fanciful interpretation based on Deas's experiences
among Plains Indians.

In the extreme foreground of this picture, Deas
grouped no fewer than eight figures and four
horses in a spiral composition. Through the suggested tension of expressions and of poses of men
and horses alike and the anticipation of action, the
group almost explodes from its center. Deas's
composition and grouping of horses in *A Group
of Sioux* is strikingly similar to Thomas Sully's
The Passage of the Delaware (1819; fig. 38). Since
Deas frequented Sully's studio in his youth, he
may have known this immense canvas, a part of

the collection of the Boston Museum and Gallery of Fine Arts by 1841 and published in their catalogue in 1844.[36] The two works share a circular group of horsemen at the right of the composition, with one horse's head rearing at the back, and attention drawn to distant action at the left. Deas transferred George Washington's revolutionary heroism to anonymous Plains Indians in the Far West.

To judge by Deas's extant paintings and from the titles and descriptions of lost works, 1845 was a productive year that witnessed the reappearance of the artist's popular mountain man, now in deadly combat with an Indian: *The Death Struggle* (ca. 1845; fig. 39). Washington Irving, through Bonneville's voice, recounts the "courage, fortitude, and perseverance of the pioneers of the fur trade, who . . . first broke their way through a wilderness . . . [of the] most dreary and desolate mountains, and barren and trackless wastes, uninhabited by man, or occasionally infested by predatory and cruel savages." Indians "beset every defile, laid ambuscades in their path, or attacked them in their night encampments."[37] The implied tension and anticipated action of *A Group of Sioux*

has here broken loose as a mounted trapper and his Indian adversary plunge off a cliff to certain death.

On exhibition in the late summer of 1845 as the "last arrival at the Rooms of the Art-Union," *The Death Struggle* was acquired by George W. Austen, the distinguished collector and treasurer of the Art-Union.[38] It attracted the immediate and devoted attention of critics for the *Anglo American* and the *Broadway Journal*. With language suited to the dramatic horror of the painting, each spun out a narrative for *The Death Struggle*. According to the *Broadway Journal,* "A Trapper has been found trespassing upon the Indian hunting ground" and in the ensuing fight for the beaver, still in its trap, both Indian and mountain man are wounded; their horses, legs entangled in vines and "maddened by the wounds which had been dealt out alike to man and beast, break from the control of their riders, and rush headlong towards a frightful precipice." The critic continues: "On, on, speed the horses; wilder and wilder they grow in their flight—the height is gained—without let or pause over they go! Man and beast food for the Buzzards! But no! their downward progress is arrested by a boldly

38. *Thomas Sully (1783–1872),* The Passage of the Delaware, *1819, oil on canvas, 146½ × 207 in. Museum of Fine Arts, Boston, Gift of the Owners of the Old Boston Museum*

39. *Charles Deas,*
The Death Struggle,
ca. 1845,
oil on canvas, 30 × 25 in.
The Shelburne Museum,
Shelburne, Vermont

66

jutting rock."[39] So arrested, even momentarily, the bearded trapper's eyes flash in horror, and his hand, holding the knife, clutches at a dead branch above. With the other hand he still holds the beaver, which viciously bites the Indian's arm. This horrific scene is observed from above by the Indian's companion, who strains for a better look. The color red appears throughout the picture, from the trapper's crimson shirt to the Indians' painted faces and the blood on men and animals alike—even snorted from the nostrils of the Indian's mount. The sky, suitably dark and stormy, heightens the drama.

Deas knew many paintings of horses, especially excited and rearing horses. He may have been aware in particular of Benjamin West's monumental *Death on a Pale Horse* (1817; The Pennsylvania Academy of the Fine Arts), which the Pennsylvania Academy acquired in 1836, just after the Deas family moved to New York State. A copy of West's painting toured to St. Louis in March 1844 and was discussed at length in a local paper in June of the next year. In addition, baroque and nineteenth-century compositions of mounted horses must have come to his attention at exhibitions in Philadelphia and New York as well as through publications. Dawn Glanz proposed a very likely source for *Long Jakes* in such nineteenth-century military portraits as Jacques-Louis David's *Napoléon at St. Bernard* (1800; Musée Na-

tional du Chateau de Versailles), popular in America and frequently exhibited in the original and in copies in Philadelphia during the late 1820s and early 1830s. Images of the Roman hero, Marcus Curtius, including Benjamin Robert Haydon's *Curtius Leaping into the Gulf* (1836–42; Royal Albert Museum, Exeter), have been suggested as parallels to *The Death Struggle,* and daring leaps off cliffs were popular images in contemporary comic almanacs, as were fights between frontier heroes and savage Indians, in *Crockett's Almanac,* for example. Further evidence of Deas's interest in the theme of the plunge off a bluff is his *Winona,* now lost, which he exhibited with *The Death Struggle* at the Art-Union in 1845. According to a contemporary description of Deas's painting of this popular story, the young Indian woman, in despair over her impending marriage to someone other than the brave she loves, is shown "in the act of throwing herself from the rock."[40]

The *Broadway Journal* critic praised Deas for his originality and "bold, daring energy in the design," yet chastised him for "too much carelessness in his execution" of *The Death Struggle.* And in noting the "rapid improvement in the artist's conception and execution," this critic singled out the horses for praise: "in no part is the improvement more visible than in the drawing and coloring of the horses."[41] There is a curious relationship between these horses and the composition

40. *William Morris Hunt
(1824–79),*
The Horses of Anahita,
*n.d., plaster,
h. 19¼ × l. 29 × d. 11½ in.
Vose Galleries of Boston, Inc.*

of one of Deas's contemporaries. About two years after Deas completed and exhibited *The Death Struggle,* William Morris Hunt prepared the first designs for what would become in 1878 a mural, *The Flight of Night,* in the Albany State House. Inspired by a Persian poem he discovered as a student in Paris, Hunt drew a pencil sketch of Anahita, goddess of night, fleeing the dawn. She travels in a chariot of clouds pulled by three furious horses of the night, "exemplars of turbulence and superstition." The two horses to the right are virtually identical to Deas's black and white mounts in *The Death Struggle.* Engraved for an 1846 issue of the *New York Illustrated Magazine,* and accompanied by the fanciful Henry William Herbert tale that it inspired, Deas's image may have been known to Hunt first, or each may have drawn on yet another, possibly French, source. Soon after his first sketch, Hunt made a plaster relief, *The Horses of Anahita* (fig. 40), which demonstrates his stylistic debt to Antoine-Louis Barye, the romantic *animalier* sculptor with whom he studied in Paris, and who may have influenced Deas as well. The Deas painting very likely was also inspired by nineteenth-century romantic sculpture, including works by Richard Wesmacott and Pierre-Jean David d'Angers.[42]

After 1845 and Deas's success in New York, the St. Louis newspapers began to recognize his prominence. He was commended for his annual contributions to the Mechanics' Fair each year he lived in St. Louis, and the new *Weekly Reveille* credited "repeated and brilliant proofs of his high standing as an artist." Yet another artist began to attract attention in Deas's adopted city. By 1844 George Caleb Bingham returned to St. Louis after a three-year stay in Washington, D.C., and sent four paintings for exhibition at the 1845 Art-Union. Among them were *The Concealed Enemy* (fig. 12) and what is now titled *Fur Traders Descending the Missouri* (fig. 11). Bingham called this river picture *French Trader and Half-Breed Son,* thereby drawing attention to the *voyageurs* on the Missouri, a subject painted by Deas the same year (fig. 41) and that may have served as inspiration for Bingham.[43]

The lives of traders of French descent, who often intermarried with Indians, sharply contrasted with those of American trappers or mountain men, whose independence Deas had celebrated in *Long Jakes.* Often shown in family groups, the *voyageurs,* as they were known, usually acquired furs through trade with Indians rather than by trapping the beaver themselves. They traveled along the Missouri in dugouts to transport the furs from trading posts in the wilderness to markets like St. Louis and to carry merchandise back to the post.

By the time Deas and Bingham painted the *voyageurs,* they had all but disappeared from the more highly commercialized and, at the time, declining fur trade. The *voyageurs* were regarded as romantic characters by Charles Lanman, who typified those he encountered in the summer of 1846:

By birth he is half French, and half Indian, but in habits, manners, and education, a full-blooded Indian. . . . His dress is something less than half civilized, and his knowledge of the world equal to that of his savage brethren;— amiable, even to a fault, but intemperate and without a religion. . . . He belongs to a race which is entirely distinct from all others on the globe. It is a singular fact that when most troubled, or when enduring the severest hardships, they will joke, laugh, and sing their uncouth songs—the majority of which are extemporaneous, appropriate to the occasion, and generally of a rude and licentious character.[44]

Bingham suspended his fur traders on the placid river at dawn; laden with furs and live and dead game (a duck and a bear cub), they are poised between savage and civilized life in a completely masculine world. The Indian wife who is only implied in *Fur Traders Descending the Missouri* completes the family picture, with other children and a baby, in Deas's *The Voyageurs.* Although similarly composed, the two works present different moods of the Far West. Bingham's trappers regard us with mild interest or amusement, while Deas's *voyageurs* are much more intent on negotiating treacherous waters and preparing for the impending storm.

41. *Charles Deas,*
The Voyageurs, *1845,*
oil on canvas, 24 × 29½ in.
Rokeby Collection, on loan to
The Metropolitan Museum of
Art, New York

Deas's bearded patriarch, in typical beaver hat, controls the dugout from its stern as his eldest son, who has just caught the fish seen behind him, poles the boat forward with his spear. Another child paddles with her father, and a young boy leans over to drink river water from a ladle while his mother holds the youngest child on the covered cargo to which a coffeepot is strapped. A small dog peers over the side of the dugout and into the water. The figures, animal, and objects in the dugout are all reflected in the river below. On its stern the dugout is inscribed "St. Pierre,"

42. *Charles Deas,*
The Trapper and His
Family, *ca. 1845,*
watercolor on paper,
13⅛ × 19½ in.
M. and M. Karolik
Collection of American
Drawings and Paintings,
1815–1865, Museum of Fine
Arts, Boston

which suggests its owner's French origin as well as the possibility that the family may have come from the St. Peters River post in the vicinity of Fort Snelling, which Deas had visited.

Deas intensified the isolation of the French trapper's family by posing them against a forbidding sky, an ominous bank of craggy rocks, and a blasted tree trunk with only a few autumn leaves clinging to it. The oldest son is the only member of the family to acknowledge the presence of an observer in the wilderness.

At about this time Deas painted a watercolor of *The Trapper and his Family* (ca. 1845; fig. 42), which, almost identical to *The Voyageurs,* must be seen as a study or close variant. In 1846, the

year following his first *voyageurs* work, he painted the subject once again (fig. 43) and exhibited the painting at the National Academy of Design in 1847. Before the canvas left St. Louis, however, the critic for the *Weekly Reveille* admired it as "wild and picturesque as nature itself in the solitary regions of the west." He encouraged his readers to sympathize with the plight of the *voyageurs* in their difficult running of the rapids and ever-present danger of Indian encounters. In St. Louis the picture was "true to life," but by the time it reached New York the critic for the *Literary World* found it deficient. Although the color was "not without mellowness," and the faces of "good character . . . the bodies of the figures are too short . . . he has not given them sufficient room."[45]

Any vestiges of the comforts of family life in the 1845 *Voyageurs* have disappeared in the 1846 picture, which shows the rugged traders directly confronting the trials of wilderness life. The craggy trees now close in on the oarsmen, and branches reach over as though to threaten them.

In many ways, Deas's embodiment of the spirit of confrontation suggests an awareness of Cole's series *The Voyage of Life,* which had been seen in two versions in New York in preceding years. Deas may have been made even more aware of Cole's allegorical efforts by Charles Lanman's visit to his studio in the summer of 1846. Lanman's article on Cole's series had appeared in 1843 and 1845.[46] Closest to Cole's depiction of "manhood," Deas's grizzly boatmen steer their allegorical passage through life on the actual waters of the Far West.

A *voyageur* appears once again in Deas's work, as one of the 1847 double portraits in *River Man—Indian Brave* (fig. 44), where the *voyageur's* sage and tired countenance contrasts with that of the wild-eyed Indian with whom he traded and fought. *Portrait of Luke E. Lawless,* of about the same year, undoubtedly commissioned, presents yet another side of frontier life in the formal, austere bearing of the judge, symbolizing the presence of civilizing forces in the wilderness of river man and Indians.

Of the pictures Lanman found in Deas's studio in the summer of 1846, two affirm the artist's concern for the history and present of the American West. As the St. Louis papers carried reports of the Mexican War, Deas painted the daring escape of Texas hero Captain Samuel H. Walker from death at the hands of a Mexican *ranchero*. *The Last Shot* (now lost) appeared at the Art-Union in 1847 and, unlike *The Voyageurs,* exhibited at the National Academy of Design that year, or *The Oregon Pioneers* (now lost), shown at the Art-Union the year before, both of which met with some criticism, this picture was judged to possess "all the force, boldness and freedom of drawing and color characteristic of this artist's works." The picture must have been fierce indeed, as the critic for the *Literary World* warned the potential owner that "the horror of the picture would curdle all the milk of human kindness in his breast," would "haunt him like a night-mare," and would "destroy . . . his peace of mind forever." One critic also noted that Deas was "a candidate to fill the vacant panel in the Capitol at Washington" with a depiction of the eighteenth-century frontiersman George Rogers Clark outwitting Shawnee adversaries, a painting that survives only in Lanman's description of it. Although Senator Thomas Hart Benton advocated Deas for the commission, it was never carried out.[47]

Deas exhibited his last major painting, *Prairie Fire* (1847; fig. 45), at the 1847 Mechanics' Fair.[48] Two months later, he left St. Louis forever. *Prairie Fire* was admired in St. Louis by "a Correspond-

44. *Charles Deas,*
River Man—Indian Brave,
1847,
oil on board, 10 × 14 in.
The Thomas Gilcrease
Institute of American History
and Art, Tulsa, Oklahoma

ent" for the *Literary World* (the article's style and content suggest that it was Henry Tuckerman), who saw a painting of a prairie fire in Deas's St. Louis studio and thought it "the best to our mind which we have had from the easel of Deas":

The figures represent an old hunter on his horse, whose face, and grey beard, and hair, tell the tale of many a hardy adventure through which he has passed. Riding by his side and seated on a noble animal is another figure, the most prominent of the picture, clasping in his arms a young girl, to whom he is betrothed, and supposed to be the daughter of the old hunter. She rests apparently exhausted in the arms of her lover, her hair dishevelled and streaming in the wind. Behind them furiously rages the burning prairie; and one can almost imagine that he hears the crackling of the dry grass beneath the resistless flames. They have just reached a small stream, and are supposed to have gained a place of safety.[49]

This flight recalls the many frenzied horses Deas painted throughout his short career, especially Tom Walker's steed. Two horses and three figures are compressed in the composition to the point of confusion. At the center of the painting is an unconscious woman, whose shoulders and breasts are sensuously exposed as her rescuer clasps her over his horse. The woman's head is thrown back, and her hair streams in abandon, bringing to mind Henry Fuseli's *The Nightmare* (ca. 1782; The Detroit Institute of Arts). A copy after Fuseli's *Nightmare* was exhibited at the Pennsylvania Academy in 1849, too late for Deas to have seen it, but the currency of the image as well as the popularity of prints after the painting make better than conjectural Deas's familiarity with it. In addition, Fuseli's writings were quoted in discussion of Deas's paintings the following year, which indicates contemporary critical awareness of the relationship.[50]

But other sources even closer to Deas present themselves. Prairie fires, a fearsome and spectacular autumn phenomenon, did not escape the notice of travelers to the Far West or of novelists who wrote about the area. Lewis F. Thomas, whose portrait Deas had painted and for whose books he had provided the sources of illustrations, edited *The Valley of the Mississippi Illustrated in a Series of Views* in 1841 and devoted a chapter to the prairies, which were "gloriously beautiful or awfully terrible." In this chapter he graphically described the annual burning of the prairies, caused either by accident or deliberately by hunters to flush out game.

If the wind chances to be high, tufts of the burning material dart like flaming meteors through the air, and, far as the eye can reach, a pall of black smoke stretches to the horizon and overhangs the scene, while all below is lighted up, and blazing with furious intensity, and ever and anon, flaming whisps of grass flash up, revolving and circling in the glowing atmosphere, and lending to the imagination, a semblance of convict-spirits tossing in a lake of fire.[51]

The image of prairies on fire perfectly suited a romantic artist of the Far West.

Thomas's description stresses the natural drama, and J. C. Wild's illustration, which accompanies the text, is a landscape with two deer racing before billowing clouds of flame. Deas's flight has human protagonists, and his image of an old hunter leading a young man and unconscious woman out of danger could have been an illustration of chapters 23 and 24 of James Fenimore Cooper's *The Prairie,* the same work that had inspired Deas's first successful picture. Deas followed enough of the tale of the sage hunter, his companion Middleton, and Middleton's exotic Louisianian bride to demonstrate his familiarity with Cooper's novel.

Finally, a yet more immediate source for this drama of pursuit: the demons raging within the mind of the artist. He was judged insane and committed to an asylum in the summer of 1848. The career of this artist of "early genius and bright promise"[52] ended before he was thirty years old.

Among the works Deas exhibited in 1847 was a western landscape roundly criticized for its inharmonious color, as was another of his contributions, *The Mountain Pass* (now lost). We have

45. *Charles Deas,*
Prairie Fire, *1847,*
oil on canvas,
28⅞ × 36¹⁄₁₆ in.
The Brooklyn Museum,
Gift of Mr. and Mrs.
Alastair Bradley Martin

noted the poor reception given *The Voyageurs.* Deas left St. Louis in the summer of 1847 and, after a stay in Newport, Rhode Island, settled in New York. *The Lord* (or *The Savior*), one of two paintings he showed at the 1848 National Academy of Design exhibition, elicited a sad comment on the artist's lamented "derangement," which might "shield [the picture] from the shafts of criticism." Another critic hoped for "more works like 'Long Jaques' [and] 'The Death Struggle.' "[53]

By the summer of 1848, news of the artist's hospitalization had reached the papers in St. Louis and, quoting an article from the *New York Express,* the *Daily Missouri Republican* attributed the cause of his illness "to a settled melancholy and an unnecessary anxiety about the new science of *magnetism.*" Interest in "animal magnetism"—mesmerism or hypnosis—was reported widely in the St. Louis papers while Deas lived there, as were such incidents as the "cataleptic state" one poor victim entered after an improper "magnetism." Akin to the exorcism of demons, yet with purported scientific basis, magnetism fascinated Deas's fellow painter, William Sidney Mount, who wrote that "In mesmerism there is a sympathy so perfect between the magnetizer and the subject that what he sees, the subject sees." Magnetism faded during the 1840s, but not before Deas had come into contact with it.[54]

Deas called his last picture to appear at the National Academy of Design, in 1849, *A Vision* (now lost). The critic for the *Knickerbocker* described it: "human sufferers" consumed by "winding serpents" with "fangs so wild, so horrible." The critic was astonished by the "beauty and delicacy of the handling, and the correctness of drawing" in so awful a subject, and concluded, "A 'vision'

is it? Yes, and a horrid one! Despair and Death are together, and Frenzy glares from the blood red sockets of the victims, and haunting weird thoughts arise, as we reflect over this singular effort of talent."[55]

To his biographical sketch of Deas, first published in 1846, Tuckerman added, in his 1867 *Book of the Artists,* a paragraph about Deas's derangement and his visionary pictures. "Yet his talent even when manifest in the vagaries of a diseased mind, was often effective; one of his wild pictures, representing a black sea, over which a figure hung, suspended by a ring, while from the waves a monster was springing, was so horrible, that a sensitive artist fainted at the sight."[56]

After the artist's death from apoplexy at New York's Bloomingdale Asylum for the Insane, on 23 March 1867, Daniel Huntington, president of the National Academy of Design, mourned Deas as an associate member who had "early distinguished himself by characteristic pictures of wild border life" and whose latest pictures "reflected the strange dreams of a distempered brain."[57]

Daniel Huntington regarded Deas as of "naturally nervous and sensitive temperament"; an acquaintance in St. Louis later remarked that Deas had been "of a somewhat melancholy disposition, or temperament. Perhaps the malady that finally overwhelmed him was of slow growth. Probably, also, he had a hard struggle to maintain himself, as painters were but poorly remunerated in St. Louis when he lived here; and this may have had a depressing affect [sic] upon his spirit."[58] Temperamentally predisposed and overwhelmed by his circumstances, Deas painted evidence of his spirit throughout his career in scenes of perceived danger, alarm, and flight.

NOTES

1. [Henry T. Tuckerman], "Our Artists.—No. V," *Godey's Lady's Book* (1846), pp. 250–53. This essay was published again in Tuckerman, *Artist-Life: or Sketches of American Painters* (New York: D. Appleton & Company, 1847), pp. 202–14, and with an additional paragraph in Tuckerman, *Book of the Artists* (New York: G. P. Putnam & Son, 1867), pp. 424–29. Unless otherwise noted, quotations refer to the first appearance in *Godey's.*

2. John I. H. Baur included Deas in the company of Fitz Hugh Lane, John Quidor, and the still little-known

Charles Caleb Ward in "Unknown American Painters of the 19th Century," *College Art Journal* 6, no. 3 (Summer 1947): 277–82. During the 1940s, Robert Taft compiled information and a checklist of paintings. This material remains unpublished but can be consulted in the Robert Taft Papers, Kansas State Historical Society. I am indebted to James H. Nottage for bringing this information on Deas to my attention. Richard Mc-Lanathan published a substantial biographical summary in *M. and M. Karolik Collection of American Paintings, 1815–1865* (Boston: Museum of Fine Arts, 1949). The only article devoted to Deas between Tuckerman's "Our Artists" and this study was John Francis Mc-Dermott, "Charles Deas: Painter of the Frontier," *Art Quarterly* 13, no. 4 (Autumn 1950): 293–311, although important contextual analysis of certain of Deas's themes was provided in Dawn Glanz, "The Iconography of Westward Expansion in American Art, 1820–1870" (Ph.D. diss., University of North Carolina, Chapel Hill, 1978); published with some changes as *How the West Was Drawn: American Art and the Settling of the Frontier* (Ann Arbor, Mich.: UMI Research Press, 1982). Since then, more biographical information has come to light, including the date and place of Deas's death, more data on his training, on his family situation and whereabouts during the late 1830s and 1840s, and on his contribution to the proposals for galleries of Indian portraits. Most importantly, we now know of many more paintings by his hand. In 1950, McDermott knew six works by the artist and now thirty are identified.

3. West Point records reveal no reason for Deas's failure to obtain an appointment; we may speculate that he was already exhibiting signs of a "nervous temperament," which rendered him unfit for military service.

4. Tuckerman, "Our Artists," p. 251. For a summary of Catlin's exhibition tour, see William H. Truettner, *The Natural Man Observed: A Study of Catlin's Indian Gallery* (Washington, D.C.: Smithsonian Institution Press, 1979), pp. 36–39.

5. I appreciate Sarah Boehme's help in determining Eastman's whereabouts during this period. The information on Bingham is from E. Maurice Bloch, *George Caleb Bingham: The Evolution of an Artist* (Berkeley and Los Angeles: University of California Press, 1967), 1:48.

6. I am indebted to William Truettner for bringing this document, "Plan for an Indian Gallery," now in a private collection in South Carolina, to my attention.

7. "Plan for an Indian Gallery."

8. "Plan for an Indian Gallery."

9. Tuckerman, "Our Artists," p. 251.

10. Quotes from Tuckerman, pp. 251–52.

11. Quotes from Tuckerman, p. 252.

12. Tuckerman, p. 252.

13. This may be the painting, *View on the Upper Mississippi, one mile below Fort Snelling,* which Deas exhibited at the "Exhibition of paintings, statues, and casts at the Pennsylvania Academy of the Fine Arts," 1843, and which was lent by John Rosencrants. It was the first painting he sent back east for exhibition.

14. This information from Edward P. Livingston to Lewis Cass, 6 October 1835; correspondence in Record Group 94, Adjutant General's Office, "Cadet Application Papers," 1805–1866, National Archives.

15. Tuckerman, "Our Artists," p. 252. *Daily Missouri Republican* (St. Louis), 27 November 1841.

16. George Frederick Ruxton, *Life in the Far West,* edited by Leroy R. Hafen (1849; reprint ed., Norman: University of Oklahoma Press, 1951), pp. 52–53.

17. Typescript copy, Mechanics' Institute, Constitution of the Mechanics' Institute of St. Louis, adopted 16 April 1839, Missouri Historical Society.

18. According to the records of the Mechanics' Institute in the Missouri Historical Society, J. C. Wild joined in 1842, the same year Deas became a member.

19. Lewis F. Thomas, *Inda, a Legend of the Lake* (St. Louis: V. Ellis, 1842), p. 18 n.

20. This was asserted by William Clark Breckenridge in gathered writings by James Malcolm Breckenridge, *William Clark Breckenridge, His Life, Lineage and Writings* (St. Louis: n. pub., 1932), n. page.

21. Quotes from the *Daily Missouri Republican,* 7 November 1842.

22. *Broadway Journal,* 21 June 1845, p. 397. The New York critic states that this "party of Indians at play" has been "lately added to the Exhibition of the American Art-Union." No work of this description is listed in an Art-Union catalogue for this year, and it may be the painting exhibited at the National Academy of Design the year before, 1844, as *Group of Indians Playing Ball,* and subsequently shown at the Art-Union.

23. Wharton quote from "The Expedition of Major Clifton Wharton in 1844," *Kansas Historical Collections* 16 (1923–25): 272, cited in McDermott, "Deas," p. 299. Lieutenant Carleton's journal of the 1844 expedition to the Pawnee was published anonymously in serial form in the *Spirit of the Times* (9 November 1844–12 April 1845) and then reprinted as Lieutenant J. Henry Carleton, *The Prairie Logbooks: Dragoon Campaigns to the Pawnee Villages in 1844, and to the Rocky Mountains in 1845,* edited by Louis Pelzer (Chicago: The Caxton Club, 1943), p. 7.

24. Quotes from Carleton, p. 28.

25. Carleton, p. 100.

26. Tuckerman, "Our Artists," p. 253.

27. For example, see *Catalogue of the First Annual Exhibition of the Western Academy of Art* (St. Louis, 1860) and *Catalogue of the Art Gallery of the Mississippi Sanitary Fair* (St. Louis, 1864).

28. Deas to R. F. Fraser, 7 November 1846, American Art-Union papers, New-York Historical Society.

29. *Broadway Journal,* 4 January 1845, p. 13.

30. Henry William Herbert, "*Long Jakes,* The Prairie Man," *New York Illustrated Magazine* 2 (July 1846): 169–74.

31. For a concise and informative essay on the mountain man, see William H. Goetzmann, "Lords at the Creation: The Mountain Men and the World," in *The Mountain Man* (Cody, Wyo.: Buffalo Bill Historical Center, 1978). Information on Frémont's explorations and publications may be found in Goetzmann, *Army Exploration in the American West, 1803–1863* (New Haven: Yale University Press, 1959), pt. 2, ch. 3.

32. Printed at J. H. Bufford, Boston, and published by M. Knoedler, New York, a copy of the Grozelier lithograph is in the collection of the Amon Carter Museum. On the Samuel painting, see Cecelia Steinfeldt, *Texas Folk Art: One Hundred Fifty Years of the Southwestern Tradition* (Austin: Texas Monthly Press, 1981), p. 24, fig. 4. On Deas's possible influence on Ranney, see Francis S. Grubar, "Ranney's *Trapper's Last Shot,*" *American Art Journal* 2, no. 1 (Spring 1970): 98–99. The view that Deas also painted several versions of his mountain man is argued by John F. McDermott, "Charles Deas' Portrait of a Mountain Man: A Mystery in Western Art," *Gateway Heritage* 1, no. 4 (Spring 1981): 2–9, although I disagree fundamentally with his conclusions.

33. Tuckerman, "Our Artists," p. 253.

34. *Broadway Journal,* 11 April 1845, p. 254.

35. For many of these observations and other discussions about Indian culture I am indebted to Herman Viola.

36. *American Paintings in the Museum of Fine Arts, Boston* (Boston: Museum of Fine Arts, 1969), 1: 262–63.

37. Washington Irving, *The Adventures of Captain Bonneville,* edited by Robert A. Rees and Alan Sandy (Boston: Twayne Publishers, 1977), pp. 8, 9.

38. Quote from the *Anglo American,* 6 September 1845, p. 474. Austen exhibited the painting in Boston under the title *Contest for a Beaver,* no. 75 in *Catalogue of the Twenty-First Exhibition of Paintings in the Athenaeum Gallery* (Boston, 1847).

39. *Broadway Journal,* 13 September 1845, pp. 154–55.

40. The exhibition of the copy after West is discussed in the *St. Louis Weekly Reveille,* 16 June 1845, p. 385, and also in John F. McDermott, "Art in St. Louis," McDermott Research Collection, Southern Illinois University at Edwardsville. Glanz, *How the West Was Drawn,* suggests the influence of military portraits (pp. 92–93, nn. 70–71) and comic almanacs (pp. 95–96). Richard Dorment, "American Mythologies in Painting, Pt. 1: The Indian," *Arts Magazine* 46 (October 1971): 48, points out the Curtius parallel. The description of *Winona* quoted here is from the *Anglo American,* 6 September 1845.

41. *Broadway Journal,* 13 September 1845.

42. I am very grateful to Christopher Wilson, who kindly pointed out the Deas-Hunt relationship to me. The description of Hunt's furious horses and observation of his debt to Barye are from Henry Adams, "The Development of William Morris Hunt's *The Flight of Night*," *American Art Journal* 15, no. 2 (Spring 1983): 43–52. Information on Hunt's mural and its sources is from this study as well as from Adams, "William Morris Hunt's *Chef d'Oeuvre Inconnu*," *Proceedings of the New York State Capitol Symposium* (Albany: Temporary State Commission on the Restoration of the Capitol, 1981), pp. 96–105, 187–91. The engraved illustration of Deas's work was accompanied by an article by Henry William Herbert, "Death Struggle," *New York Illustrated Magazine* 2 (July 1846): 289–94. Sculptures by Wesmacott and d'Angers are illustrated in H. W. Janson, *19th-Century Sculpture* (New York: Harry N. Abrams, 1984), pp. 15, 99.

43. Quote on Deas from the *St. Louis Weekly Reveille,* 19 May 1845, p. 356. For a discussion of the relationship between the two Bingham works, see Henry Adams, "A New Interpretation of Bingham's *Fur Traders Descending the Missouri*," *Art Bulletin* 65, no. 4 (December 1983): 675–80. That Deas may have inspired Bingham's work is suggested by Charles D. Collins, "A Source for Bingham's *Fur Traders Descending the Missouri*," *Art Bulletin* 66, no. 4 (December 1984): 678–81.

44. Charles Lanman, *A Summer in the Wilderness* (New York: D. Appleton & Company, 1847), pp. 141, 146. While in St. Louis, Lanman admired Deas's work and described several pictures in his studio; see pp. 15–17.

45. The review from the *St. Louis Weekly Reveille,* 15 February 1847, is quoted in McDermott, "Deas," p. 308. The unfavorable review is from the *Literary World,* 29 May 1847, p. 397.

46. For discussion of the chronology and bibliography of *The Voyage of Life,* see Paul D. Schweizer, *The Voyage of Life by Thomas Cole: Paintings, Drawings and Prints* (Utica, N.Y.: Munson-Williams-Proctor Institute, 1985).

47. Notice of *The Oregon Pioneers* at the Art-Union appeared in the *United States Magazine and Democratic Review,* January 1847, pp. 64–65. The reviews of *The Last Shot* are from the *Anglo American,* 6 February 1847, p. 381, and the *Literary World,* 30 October 1847, p. 303. It was the critic from the former paper who proposed Deas for the Capitol panel depiction of Clark. Benton's advocacy of Deas for this commission was reported in the *Daily Missouri Republican,* 6 July 1848.

48. *Daily Missouri Republican,* 10 April 1847.

49. [Henry T. Tuckerman], *Literary World,* 24 April 1847, p. 200, reprinted in the *St. Louis Weekly Reveille,* 10 May 1847.

50. *New York Evening Post,* 5 June 1848.

51. Lewis F. Thomas, ed., *J. C. Wild, painter and lithographer, The Valley of the Mississippi Illustrated in a Series of Views* (St. Louis: J. C. Wild, 1841), p. 82.

52. *Knickerbocker Magazine,* July 1840, p. 82.

53. In a letter to R. F. Fraser, 18 June 1847, American Art-Union papers, New-York Historical Society, Henry L. Cobb reported that Deas is "at present on a visit to the East." The *Weekly Reveille* revealed that on 25 August 1847 he was "now at Newport, Rhode Island [and] does not plan to return to St. Louis, but will settle in New York." The reviews of *The Lord* appeared in the *Literary World,* 3 June 1848, and the *New York Evening Post,* 5 June 1848.

54. The *Daily Missouri Republican* report of Deas's illness appeared on 6 July 1848. The case of "improper magnetism" had been reported in the *St. Louis Weekly Reveille,* 26 October 1846. Mount's diary entry for 11 March 1854 is quoted in Alfred Frankenstein, *William Sidney Mount* (New York: Harry N. Abrams, 1974), p. 288.

55. *Knickerbocker Magazine,* May 1849, p. 470.

56. Tuckerman, *Book of the Artists,* p. 429.

57. President's Report, Annual Meeting, National Academy of Design, 8 May 1867. My thanks to Mark Pockros for bringing Deas's death certificate to my attention.

58. Report of Mr. Collet, Board Minutes, Missouri Historical Society, 20 June 1882, Missouri Historical Society, St. Louis.

WILLIAM RANNEY

LINDA AYRES

*Ranney
Scouting Party
(detail, see fig. 60)*

*I*n early 1836, reporting that a large army of Mexican soldiers was on the march against them, Texans appealed to "the Friends of Liberty in the United States of America." In what the *New York Herald* termed a "spirited document," the Texans lamented that "the prelude to the great tragedy has just opened," and "as the frightened babe clings to its mother's breast, our thoughts, as naturally turn to our native country for assistance." Governor Henry Smith's plea, also published in early 1836, asked "those disposed to embark in this struggle . . . to do so promptly, as their services will be needed during the ensuing spring, more than at any time hereafter."[1] One who heeded the call for volunteers was William Tylee Ranney, then an art student in New York. Although Ranney probably spent less than a year in Texas, his experiences there provided inspiration for a group of western scenes created in his studio in the East in the late 1840s and 1850s.

The son of a ship's captain, Ranney was born in Middletown, Connecticut, in 1813, but by 1826 was living with his uncle in Fayetteville, North Carolina. There, at age thirteen, he was apprenticed to a tinsmith, with whom he worked for six years. According to Ranney's obituary, it was while he was in North Carolina that "his natural talent displayed itself by a remarkable facility with the pencil. Devotedly fond of Nature, he delighted to sketch her ever varied and beautiful forms." In

1833 or 1834, Ranney moved to New York, where he began to study painting and drawing and worked in an architect's office. After only a few years, however, Ranney headed south again. Whether his "sympathies [were] aroused by the sufferings of his countrymen," or he tired of the "monotonous duties" of the architect's office and "longed for the free and beautiful country, and to tear himself away from the hated city life," Ranney set out to join in the Texan war for independence.[2]

According to his obituary, Ranney enlisted with Captain Henry A. Hubbel in New Orleans shortly after the fall of the Alamo (which occurred in early March) and headed to Texas. He then served in Captain C. A. W. Fowler's First Regiment Volunteers as paymaster until at least 23 November 1836. For every three months of service—he served nearly nine—Ranney was awarded twenty-four dollars and a bounty grant of 320 acres of land in the new republic. In addition, he may have also received a headright certificate of one-third league (1,476 acres) of land. We cannot be sure that Ranney saw any of his Texas land—indeed, he probably did not—but we do know that he was near the town of Columbia (now West Columbia) for most of his service.[3] Located near the Brazos River, not far from the Gulf of Mexico, Columbia was the capital of the republic from September to December 1836. It was there that the first congress convened and Sam Houston was inaugurated president.

Ranney's widow reported that he "remained in Texas for some time, making sketches for many of his future pictures. He was so charmed with everything he saw; scenes that he long dreamt of were now before his eyes; the wild enchanting prairies, the splendid horses, nature in all her splendor; his poetic mind was filled with the beautiful. . . . On his way home he lingered in a village (the name I forget) near where the City of Austin is now situated." Ranney's obituary further states that he returned to New York in the spring of 1837, and it is believed that he continued his artistic training there.[4] He first publicly exhibited his work in 1838—a *Portrait of Mr. Thompson* (now lost) at the National Academy of Design and a genre painting, *A Courting Scene* (unlocated), at the Mechanics' Institute Fair in New York City.

Ranney may have returned south in the late 1830s, to Fayetteville (where his uncle died in 1840) and perhaps to Texas on business concerning various land claims.[5] New York City directories from 1843 to 1847 list him as a portrait painter, although he submitted not only portraits but also genre scenes and historical episodes from the Revolutionary War to the National Academy of Design and the American Art-Union. Oddly, Ranney does not seem to have painted any works relating to the battles of the Texas war for independence to which he was probably an eyewitness.

However, by 1846 Ranney's paintings began to show the strong influence of his experience in the Southwest. The sketches he made in the West, combined with his memory and creative imagination, served as the foundation for paintings created in his studio. *Hunting Wild Horses* (fig. 46) and *The Lasso* (fig. 47) were executed in that year, and in 1848 Ranney exhibited at the American Art-Union *Prairie Burial* (fig. 49) and *Stampede* (probably *Prairie Fire;* fig. 51). Other scenes of daily life in the West followed: this was to be the sort of "exclusively American" subject for which Ranney gained renown.[6]

What caused Ranney to take up the theme of trappers and pioneers ten years after his sojourn in Texas? Aside from Ranney's possible return to the republic in the early 1840s, two events in the mid 1840s put Texas in the news: its entry into the Union in 1845 and the military conflict that action precipitated, the Mexican War, which began in 1846. The Mexican War created an audience for narratives of the West "by bringing to bear on everything related to the winning of the West the yeasty nationalism aroused by the conflict. The momentary effect was to make the fur trapper and mountain man just such a pioneer of empire as the glorifiers of Kentucky had tried to make of Boone in the earlier decades." These events may have inspired Ranney's western scenes (and possibly those from the American Revolution as well). Moreover, the West as a whole was newsworthy in the 1840s, with increased migration there and the country's desire for westward expansion to the Pacific Ocean. The popularity of American subjects—as evidenced by the American Art-Union exhibitions—must also have played a major role in the development of western genre paintings for Ranney. The Art-Union urged artists to paint native subject matter, cherish American simplicity and freshness, and strive for fuller realization, higher finish, and more accurate drawing. Ranney, for whom the Art-Union was a major patron, sought to bring all these characteristics to his art.[7]

Ranney's figures and scenes are realistically rendered in a linear style that bespeaks his training in draftsmanship. His figures are solid and large, arranged in static, almost classical poses. They seem to be frozen in time, and even Ranney's action-filled canvases (*Hunting Wild Horses* and *The Retreat;* figs. 46, 58) reveal little movement. These attributes reflect the influence of the Düsseldorf style in American art at mid century. Tastemakers, including the Art-Union, suggested that American artists study the precise draftsmanship and highly finished paintings of the German artists whose paintings were shown at New York's Art-Union in 1849 and subsequently displayed in that city at the Düsseldorf Gallery.

The "native subject matter" the Art-Union extolled—genre scenes of American life—sold well and was widely exhibited. The success of such painters of rural life as William Sidney Mount and

Francis William Edmonds was probably not lost on Ranney. Yet there are differences between Ranney's genre paintings and those of these contemporaries. Ranney's scenes are less domestic and humorous than Mount's and Edmonds's, for example, and his paintings are larger than those of many genre painters of the nineteenth century, perhaps because the vast landscape of the West provided the setting for so many of his compositions. He may also have painted large canvases to attract attention to his work.[8]

The subject matter of Ranney's work is more closely related to that of Alfred Jacob Miller and Charles Deas, both of whom earned great critical acclaim for their depictions of trappers and other western types in the 1830s and 1840s.[9] George Caleb Bingham's carefully arranged figural compositions—particularly the flatboatmen (figs. 13, 14, 15)—also find parallels in Ranney's painting.

The influential art and literary critic, Henry Tuckerman, urging artists to adopt novel subjects, observed: "Tales of frontier and Indian life . . . the adventures of the hunter and the emigrant . . . awaken instant attention in Europe. If our artists or authors, therefore, wish to earn trophies abroad, let them seize upon themes essentially American."[10] Ranney took this advice to heart, for he not only seized the opportunity to portray the unusual frontier types of the trapper and pioneer but also built his two-story studio in West Hoboken, New Jersey, to accommodate his many artifacts collected in the West:

It was so constructed as to receive animals; guns, pistols, and cutlasses hung on the walls; and these, with curious saddles and primitive riding gear, might lead a visitor to imagine he had entered a pioneer's cabin or border chieftain's hut: such an idea would, however, have been at once dispelled by a glance at the many sketches and studies which proclaimed that of an artist, and not a bushranger, had here found a home. Yet the objects around were characteristic of the occupant's experience and taste. He had caught the spirit of border adventure, and was enamored of the picturesque in scenery and character outside the range of civilization; and to represent and give them historical interest was his artistic ambition.[11]

And it is picturesque western characters, not the great landscapes of the West, that Ranney gave us.[12] His figures are white males, for the most part, although he also portrayed pioneer families, including women and children. Perhaps because there were other American artists (Catlin, Eastman, Miller, Stanley, Wimar; see pages 131–64) concentrating on Indian subjects and Ranney was eager to carve out his own artistic niche, he depicted few Native Americans. Ranney's art is about representative "types" of Americans—the mountain man and pioneer—people he had met while in Texas, "the guides, trappers, and traders of the Rocky Mountains, who flocked to the standard of Houston, and to whose tales and stories of wild adventure, around the campfire, he was indebted for the style which characterized his paintings ever after," a critic wrote at the time of Ranney's death. "To portraying the picturesque costume and wild life of those hardy mountaineers, he at once devoted his pencil, . . . his works on these subjects will live as faithful historical representations when that race of men—who are even now fast disappearing—will have passed away. His subjects were purely, and almost exclusively, American."[13]

Not only were artists creating scenes of western adventure and American "types," but the image of the frontiersman had become increasingly prevalent in the press, the theater, and in literature, both fiction and nonfiction, since the early nineteenth century. The combination of Jacksonian democracy and expansionism propelled the frontiersman and the West into the public consciousness.[14] The historical figure of Daniel Boone—the earliest archetypal western hero-pioneer in America—and Davy Crockett, who died at the Alamo, inspired biographies and fictional accounts that elevated them to frontier heroes. Boone, in fact, was popular in art as well, as seen in works by Bingham (*The Emigration of Daniel Boone,* 1851; Washington University, St. Louis) and in a fine painting by Ranney entitled *Daniel Boone's First*

View of Kentucky (1849; The Thomas Gilcrease Institute of American History and Art, Tulsa).

Literary journals like the *Western Review* published contemporary tales of frontier life as did numerous books in the 1820s and 1830s, which described trappers and mountain men as independent and brave men who lived like Indians in order to survive, romantic heroes whose lives were dramatically different from those of "civilized" Easterners reading of their adventures.[15]

As early as 1858, one writer noted that Ranney occupied in painting "the same position that FENIMORE COOPER did in literature." This is an intriguing comparison since it was James Fenimore Cooper's cycle of Leatherstocking Tales (five

novels published over the period 1823–41) that perhaps more than all other fictional literature shaped the popular image of the frontiersman in the American mind. These widely read tales presented Leatherstocking in his buckskins as the frontier hero living freely in nature. The public concurrently came to know the mountain men through a large body of literature on the fur trade itself—not only periodicals and books, but published narratives and diaries.[16] Washington Irving's *Astoria* (1836) and *Adventures of Captain Bonneville* (1837) were extremely popular examples of the fur-trade narrative, as was David Coyner's *The Lost Trappers*, published in 1847 and purportedly taken from the journals of a trapper named Ezekiel

47. *William Tylee Ranney,*
The Lasso, *1846,*
oil on canvas, 31 × 42 in.
Private collection

Williams and other sources. Coyner thought the time ripe for bringing such an account before the public:

Indeed any book detailing the trials and difficulties of those early adventurers, will be read with avidity. Any publication, throwing any light on that vast wilderness between the States and the Pacific, and calculated to open its secrets, will be read with interest. Events are now transpiring, that throw around the regions of the far west, an interest, which they never possessed before.[17]

David Coyner felt that the dangers, trials, and hardships—"the stirring scenes of wild western

48. *William Tylee Ranney,*
Study for "Hunting Wild
Horses," *n.d.,*
black crayon heightened with
white on paper, 6⅞ × 10 in.
Private collection

adventure"—of frontier life were exactly the excitement that attracted trappers who "despised the dull uniformity and monotony of civilized life." He wrote, "Look at the trapper as he dashes into a wilderness full of danger. . . . He is conscious that his undertaking is very hazardous. He is aware that he is liable to be discovered by the savages every day, and to be cut off." He saw a trapper's life as one of "sleepless vigilance, of constant toil and danger: and yet he prefers it to any other kind of life."[18]

Books such as those by Irving and Coyner presented eastern audiences with details of a trapper's life—his character and costumes, hardships, and typical incidents—and of frontier scenery. In describing the role of the fur trade in national expansion, they made the fur trappers and mountain men national heroes. These mountain men, in their costume, speech, and marriage to an Indian squaw, exuded a savage aspect. Timothy Flint's *The Shoshonee Valley* (1830) pictured the trappers as "strange, fearless, and adamantine men, renouncing society, casting off fear, and all the common impulses and affection of our nature."[19]

In the early 1840s, the public voraciously read accounts of John Charles Frémont's western explorations and of the trapper-scouts who accompanied his expedition, as they did other narratives by men who had recently traveled to the frontier. Charles Webber's chronicle of life near the Cross Timber in Texas was published in 1848. In *Old Hicks the Guide,* Webber described his job as a Texas Ranger, accompanying eighty families to their settlement at the source of the Trinity River. He told in vivid detail of trouble with the Indians, lassoing mustangs, prairie fires, and "retreats" or runs for safety, all of which appear as subjects in Ranney's paintings.[20] Also in the 1840s, the famous historian Francis Parkman wrote *The Oregon Trail,* and George Frederick Ruxton, an Englishman, published *Life in the Far West,* written after an 1847 visit to Colorado. Ruxton provided a lively picture of the mountain man, his determination and resolve, and was convinced that the "wild and half-savage trapper" exhibited "the energy, enterprise, and hardihood characteristic of the American people."[21]

While we don't know which of these accounts Ranney read, it seems likely that he was familiar with some or all of them, at least by reputation. In any case, the growing body of western literature fueled an interest in the frontier that Ranney shared and from which he profited.

The earliest dated western scenes by Ranney are *Hunting Wild Horses* (fig. 46) and a smaller oil study for it entitled *The Lasso* (fig. 47), both from 1846. Related to them is a preliminary drawing (fig. 48) for the right horse in the large painting, possibly made on the spot during Ranney's days in Texas where wild horses abounded.[22] The action-packed *Hunting Wild Horses* depicts a group of mustangs pursued by a frontiersman through tall prairie grass. In the foreground four panicked horses run in pairs toward each other, portending a collision. They circle a fifth horse—a large white animal—that has been lassoed by the rider and fallen to the ground, his pink tongue hanging out in exhaustion, indicating a long, hard fight. Horses represented the spirit of the West, and the capture of the white mustang has been taken to symbolize the taming of the West by the white man. Dawn Glanz has observed that in early nineteenth-century America, the wild horse represented a life of freedom and was a romantic vision to many writers, including Washington Irving, who described the "prince of the prairies" and the capture of a wild mustang in his 1835 *A Tour on the Prairies.*[23] Alfred Jacob Miller, who painted several scenes of wild horses (see fig. 2), described them in poetic terms:

Among the wild animals of the West, none gave so much pleasure, or caused such excitement, as the bands of wild horses that at intervals came under our view. The beauty and symmetry of their forms, their wild and spirited action,—long full sweeping manes and tails—variety of color, and fleetness of motion,—all combined to call forth admiration from the stoical.[24]

Although the capture of wild mustangs had appeared frequently in popular literature, a legend arose in the 1830s about one extraordinary horse, the "White Steed of the Prairies," a story known widely (through novels, plays, poetry, and sermons) by the 1840s. George Wilkins Kendall, while traveling through Texas in the early 1840s, heard that the horse had been sighted near the Cross Timber and Red River but had eluded his captors, including a Mexican rider who attempted to lasso him in the manner shown in Ranney's painting. The horse was always alone (as it is in *The Lasso,* Ranney's initial conception of the subject). However, by the time Kendall's book was published in 1844, he had learned that after a hard chase, the horse had been captured in Texas, but had died from the fatigue of trying to escape.[25] A long poem about the legend appeared in the *United States Magazine and Democratic Review* in 1843, and Herman Melville even wrote about the animal's "spiritual whiteness" in *Moby Dick.* Glanz believes that Ranney probably knew about the legend and that the capture he depicted can be interpreted both as an end to the horse's wild freedom and the beginning of his servitude and degradation, or, for the captor, as the mastery of the free and creative spirit, an appropriate theme for Ranney as he reached artistic maturity.[26] Indeed, Ranney depicts the triumph of the Westerner over his environment and the artist's own mastery of his chosen medium.

In *Hunting Wild Horses* we see stylistic characteristics that will appear again and again in Ranney's paintings. A large portion of the canvas is devoted to the sky, against which the artist silhouettes the figures and animated animals—in this case, the man's distinguished profile and the horses' rearing heads and frightened, bulging eyes. Usually one white horse is grouped with several dark ones (bay, chestnut, sorrel). Freely painted foreground foliage, including some areas of impasto, contrasts with the more tightly rendered figures and animals. Ranney shows a keen sensitivity to color, with one color—a bright red (seen here in the rider's scarf and sash)—recurring often in his work. The clear, sunlit sky and the blue mountains on the horizon epitomize the western prairie landscape, and Ranney includes clothing and riding gear that is authentic to the period and region depicted.

Prairie Burial (1848; fig. 49) was Ranney's next major western painting. It is a slightly sentimental scene depicting a frequent experience on the frontier during the large western migration of the 1840s. As dark clouds approach, a family mourns the loss of a child (judging from the small size of the grave), perhaps from pneumonia, cholera, yellow fever, smallpox, or dysentery, all prevalent diseases on the frontier.[27] The grave marking to the right suggests an earlier death for the pioneer family, depicted as living in isolation and in hard circumstances—note the small home and the child's torn clothing—on land that seems barren. The stoic pioneers quietly mourn and persevere.

Many lines in the painting point downward to the ground and the grave: the shovel, a child's outstretched leg, a dog's head, the grazing horse's head. All of the family members bow their heads, except for the elderly man who gazes heavenward, perhaps asking for divine guidance or protection against further family losses. One person—the man to the far right—may in fact be a member of Ranney's own family, his brother Richard, who sometimes served as a model.[28] A pink glow—either a sunrise or sunset—covers part of the sky and is reflected on the horse-drawn cart, but it is the characteristic red (in the man's "scarlet cloth" or trade-cloth shirt, the woman's underskirt, the child's moccasin, and the dog's tongue) that gives the somber scene touches of color. Like other Ranney paintings, the surface is highly finished, save for some areas of impasto (on the horse's yoke, pick axe and shovel, soil, older man's shirt collar and buttons, and younger man's boots).

A smaller preliminary version of *Prairie Burial* (1848; fig. 50) displays the basic elements of the larger painting but has minor variations: the palette is lighter and the sky lacks threatening clouds, the pioneer cabin is more evident, there is no grave marker, and the faces of the figures differ slightly.

Exhibited at the American Art-Union in 1848, *Prairie Burial* drew the following comment from a reviewer in the *Crayon:* "[Ranney's] works have a historical value independent of their artistic merit, when it is considered that civilization is fast sweeping away the original picturesque aspects of pioneer life in the far West."[29] Pioneers were im-

49. *William Tylee Ranney*,
Prairie Burial, *1848,*
oil on canvas, 28½ × 41 in.
Private collection

portant to United States expansion in the nineteenth century and to the popular notion of Manifest Destiny. Although the explorers and trappers might open new territories, it was essential that American families populate the land, creating permanent settlements that would help legitimate American claims to the West. As the *Congressional Globe* reported concerning the Oregon boundary dispute with Britain, "All we had to do was to let our women and children go there [to the Oregon territory] and, without assistance from any one, they would take possession of the country."[30]

Ranney was one of the first artists to portray

pioneer families, who represented the westward-advancing American society; they are seen in other works by the artist from the late 1840s and early 1850s: *Prairie Fire* (1848; fig. 51), *The Pioneers* (ca. 1850–57; fig. 52), and *Advice on the Prairie* (1853; fig. 53). After the mid 1840s, pioneers appeared more frequently in American painting. Dawn Glanz has observed that these paintings are more than genre depictions of American life and the pioneer spirit; they also reflect ideas about America's redemptive mission in the world, a belief in the continuous process of civilization, and the debate over whether the Trans-Mississippi West is an arid desert or a new Garden of the World.[31] Ranney's paintings conveyed to his eastern audiences a variety of images and interpretations of the West—images of the West as a place of certain danger but also of endless possibilities.

and a torch to prevent the charging horses—their terror indicated in their eyes—from trampling them and the woman and infant huddled near the wagon. The pinkish-red glow of the rapidly spreading fire is reflected throughout Ranney's

Prairie Fire, conveying a sense of sublime terror, is most likely the painting exhibited under the title *Stampede* along with *Prairie Burial* at the American Art-Union in 1848. The paintings form a pair in their coloration and style and in the theme of frontier hardships. Prairie fires had various causes, including lightning and also Indians, who set fires to scare the white settlers and to render them helpless—causing the loss of irreplaceable equipment and the stampede of horses, the subject of *Prairie Fire.*

Prairie Fire is a dramatic scene, made more so by the nocturnal setting. Men wave hats, cloth,

painting—on the mane of the horse at far left, the canvas of the wagon and tent, saddle, blanket, rope, and on the flesh of the settlers. Yet the figures and horses are frozen in mid action in a kind of classical tableau. In contrast to *Prairie Burial,* in which the woman's face is hidden, the focus of *Prairie Fire* is on the kneeling mother and child. Rena Coen believes that artists, aware of the physical and emotional hardships endured by pioneer women (who, to artists and writers, personified the advance of civilization into the wilderness), depicted women more academically than they portrayed men. They drew largely upon

50. *William Tylee Ranney,* Prairie Burial, *1848, oil on canvas, 14 × 20 in. The Anschutz Collection, Denver*

51. *William Tylee Ranney,*
Prairie Fire, *1848,*
oil on canvas, 38 × 60 in.
Private collection

Christian iconography, classical sculpture, and, particularly, prints after European paintings. In its crowded composition of men and horses surrounding the woman, *Prairie Fire* harks back to a neoclassical French work, Jacques-Louis David's *Sabine Women* (1799; Louvre, Paris), which conveyed the story of heroic women who, forced to leave their homes, accepted their life in a new land and raised their families there. However, the clearest reference to European art (specifically to classical antiquity) in this painting is the central male figure holding the torch; his pose strongly resembles that of the classical statue of a warrior, *Borghese Gladiator* (Louvre, Paris).[32]

Several artists, such as Charles Deas (see fig.

45), Charles Wimar, Alfred Jacob Miller, and George Catlin, depicted prairie fires. Blazes were frequent occurrences on the frontier and appeared often, too, in nineteenth-century popular literature. Ranney's scene presents in paint the "awful darkness," thick smoke, and red glow James Fenimore Cooper described in *The Prairie* (1827). Like Ranney, Charles Webber in *Old Hicks the Guide* also conveyed the terror of being trapped by such a fire.[33]

The West was not only a place of danger but one of opportunity. To many, it was a new Garden of Eden. As pioneer Eliza Farnham reported in her widely read book, "Its magnitude, its fertility, the kindliness of the climate, and the variety and excellence of its productions are unrivaled in our own country, if not on the globe." And Mary Austin Holley's *Texas,* published in 1833, lauded the beauty, climate, prosperity, security, and freedom of that region.[34] *The Pioneers* (fig. 52), begun by Ranney in 1850 and left unfinished at the time of his death, depicts two covered wagons (one in the far background) drawn by oxen and carrying families westward on the flat, open prairie. It is a quiet scene, depicting a family who perhaps left their home in the East following the economic panic of 1837 to search for cheaper land and a better life on the frontier. Crossing the plains was a slow, tedious process (averaging ten to twenty miles per day by wagon); indeed, there were grave risks and difficulties that many travelers were inexperienced to handle.[35] Ranney gives us a more idealized view in this work, which, significantly, bears the same title as Cooper's first Leatherstocking novel. The smiling figures are silhouetted against the "Big Sky" of the plains and the dark interior of the protective wagon. As in *Prairie Burial* and *Prairie Fire,* Ranney (one of the few frontier artists to do so) depicts women settlers, thereby emphasizing their contributions to the civilizing of the West. The scene is reminiscent of the biblical episode, the rest on the flight into Egypt, often depicted in European art, with Ranney's Madonna-like figure sitting sidesaddle on a white horse rather than on a donkey.

A similar feeling is conveyed in Ranney's *Advice on the Prairie* (1853; fig. 53) and its oil study, *The Old Scout's Tale* (fig. 54). The group of figures, arranged in a circle, is dominated by the woman who stands and holds a doll-like infant in her arms. A frontier Eve, she has given birth to a new generation in whose hands will rest the future and who will help her carry civilization to the West. Rena Coen has noted that writers and artists saw women and children as symbols of the "transition from the wild, crude man's world to a domestic and settled one receptive to education, the arts, and an ordered society."[36] Ranney's understanding of the changes taking place in contemporary frontier life is also indicated by his inclusion of a trapper at the caravan's campsite. With the waves of families immigrating into the West came the demise of the trappers and mountain men who had earlier dominated the frontier. But trappers, with their extensive knowledge of topography, Indians, and wildlife, proved to be of great assistance to settlers, often serving as guides or scouts for the wagon trains. In *Advice on the Prairie,* the two come together: trapper and homesteader, wilderness and civilization. The clean-shaven man in his blue velvet jacket is in marked contrast to the bearded trapper in buckskins.

Travelers, eager for the information the trappers provided, were amazed by what the mountain men told them. George Ruxton described a

52. *William Tylee Ranney,* The Pioneers, *ca. 1850–57, oil on canvas, 24 × 36 in. Private collection*

campfire scene similar to *Advice on the Prairie* from his travels in the West, recalling

the rough conversation of the . . . mountaineers, whose . . . narration of their everyday life is a tale of thrilling accidents and hairbreadth 'scapes, which . . . appear a startling romance to those who are not acquainted with the nature of the lives led by these men.[37]

In Ranney's painting, the homesteaders listen intently to the trapper's story. The scene parallels an incident reported by one traveler, whose caravan encountered a party of trappers that included the famous folk hero, Jim Bridger. After dinner, Bridger, known for his tall tales, recounted the trappers' adventures. The settlers' interest was keen, for "what they had met we would likely encounter; the chances that had befallen them would likely happen to us; and we looked upon their life as a picture of our own."[38]

America is rich in the tradition of oral storytelling, an art form that particularly flourished in the West and Southwest. Tall tales were considered typical of the frontiersman, and Ranney's painting also reflects this aspect of western life and recalls the artist's own experience of listening to the trappers' stories around the campfire (see page 81). It may also reveal Ranney's admiration for the work of William Sidney Mount, since the seated trapper with gesturing arms, seen in three-quarter right profile, and the seated listener holding a pipe, seen in left profile, are types strongly reminiscent of those portrayed in Mount's *The Long Story* (1837; The Corcoran Gallery of Art, Washington, D.C.).[39]

Rather than focusing on the difficulties of frontier life, as in *Prairie Burial* and *Prairie Fire, Advice on the Prairie* presents us with a peaceful scene set in a clearing in the tall prairie grass as the setting sun illuminates the sky. The family appears well clothed and fed, warm and comfortable in their outdoor environment. There is a sense of contentment but also one of anticipation for what lies ahead. This is one of Ranney's finest efforts, not only as a scene of contemporary pioneer life, but also for its tight compositional groupings and mastery of color, detail, and texture. The juxtaposition of pinks and blues and pinks and greens as well as the inevitable "Ranney red"—in the fire, trapper's shirt and moccasin top, boy's undershirt, and woman's shawl trim—unites the whole. The artist's careful attention to detail can be seen in the trapper's costume and gear and the braiding on the rope, and his deftness in rendering a variety of textures is evident in the metal equipment, buckskin, wooden keg, rope, animal fur, and the many types of cloth that appear in the scene.

Despite his attention to pioneer families, women, and children, it was the masculine world of the frontier, the world of the trapper and mountain man that Ranney most often portrayed in his western scenes. Paintings such as *The Trapper's Last Shot* (two versions, figs. 55, 56), *Halt on the Prairie* (fig. 57), *A Trapper Crossing the Mountains* (two versions, one in fig. 63), *The Retreat* (fig. 58), *The Trappers* (fig. 64), and *The Pipe of Friendship* (fig. 65) were all executed between 1850 and 1857, the year of his death, and are the works for which Ranney is best remembered. While the pioneers and their "prairie schooners" crossing the oceanlike plains were the symbols of westward progress, it was the trappers who were the first navigators, charting their courses and making their emigration possible. Trappers, or mountain men, served as the link between the old civilization in the East and the new and future one in the West. The fur trade, an important element in the United States economy of the early nineteenth century—especially during the 1830s—generated a great deal of interest in the Trans-Mississippi West, and the unconventional men who trapped beaver held an irresistible appeal for various elements of society. They appealed to the romantic who was intrigued by adventure, to the patriot and moralist (the trapper's courage and resourcefulness were seen as *American* characteristics), and to the pragmatist (because they paved the way for future commerce).[40] The fur trapper, with his fringed buckskin suit and J&S Hawken rifle, was a fundamentally American creation and became known to the public both through literature (see pages 81–84) and art in the early and mid nineteenth century.

It was William Ranney who perhaps best characterized this particular breed of self-reliant American. Numbering fewer than one thousand over the approximately twenty-year period (ca. 1820–40) that the fur trade was most active, the mountain men were not only hard-working capitalists but important agents of America's Manifest Destiny, helping to "extend national boundaries and national consciousness to continental completion." William Goetzmann credits them in large measure for winning the empire of the West for

53. *William Tylee Ranney,* Advice on the Prairie, *1853,* oil on canvas, 40 × 54 in. *Private collection*

54. *William Tylee Ranney,* The Old Scout's Tale, *ca. 1853,* oil on canvas, 13½ × 19½ in. *The Thomas Gilcrease Institute of American History and Art, Tulsa, Oklahoma*

the United States by establishing a de facto sovereignty over it. Trappers explored the mountains and plains of the West, served as pathfinders and trailblazers for the homesteaders heading to Oregon and California, and "advertised" the possibilities of the West through letters and reports sent back east.[41] Ironically, it was the mass migrations to the West they made possible (along with the Panic of 1837, which drove down the price of beaver skins) that led to the decline of the mountain man.

Ranney's portrayal of trappers (probably the southwestern trappers he most likely met while in Texas) suggests several interpretations. The mountain man is a "symbol of wilderness fast disappearing before the crush of civilization," and a nationalistic figure, claiming the West for America.[42] But the trapper is also a representative of his class, a working man pursuing his daily life. However, Ranney does not depict the trappers *trapping* (as Alfred Jacob Miller did). Instead he shows them always on the move, with their horses —so invaluable to their way of life. Although the trappers in Ranney's paintings may stop to rest, there is a feeling of momentary inactivity only. This is but a brief part of a continuing journey as the trappers advance civilization westward, carrying on the work of earlier heroes like Daniel Boone.

Rather than depict large groups of "company" trappers, indentured to the large firms, Ranney gives us the free trapper, who hunted where he wanted, sold his furs to the highest bidder, and used his own horses and equipment. The free trapper was the epitome of American freedom and independence. Ranney's characters are brave—his trappers are large—and self-sufficient; they go about their business despite loneliness, Indian attacks, lack of food, and other difficulties.

Perhaps Ranney's most famous trapper painting was his first effort on the theme, *The Trapper's* *Last Shot* (1850). Also known as *The Last Shot* and *The Last Bullet*, Ranney executed two versions of the painting—one for the Western Art-Union (fig. 55) and the other for the American Art-Union (fig. 56)—images that became known to thousands of Americans through an engraving (fig. 125) by T. Dwight Booth, made for the Western Art-Union

56. *William Tylee Ranney,* The Trapper's Last Shot, *ca. 1850, oil on canvas, 28½ × 36 in. Private collection*

in Cincinnati, and later by a Currier & Ives lithograph (fig. 126). A number of oil copies by unknown artists, after the prints, are also known to exist. The Western Art-Union announced its scene as being "of peculiar interest," and Francis Grubar believes that this painting was the first of the two, since it is signed and dated. It also appears that the Cincinnati organization had already purchased its painting and had announced the Booth engraving as its annual gift print when Ranney completed the larger painting subsequently purchased and exhibited by the American Art-Union in New York.[43]

The American Art-Union catalogue described the work in this way: "A western pioneer riding through a stream, is beset by Indians, at some of whom he is preparing to discharge his rifle." Earlier paintings by Charles Deas may have provided inspiration for *The Trapper's Last Shot*. Deas's *Long Jakes* (fig. 34), exhibited at the American Art-Union in 1844 and engraved in 1846 in *New York Illustrated Magazine* (fig. 122), presents a lone trapper on horseback, twisting to the rear. Later, more dramatic works by Deas—*The Last Shot* (1847) and *The Trapper* (1846 or 1847), both unlocated—may also have influenced Ranney. A contemporary account of Deas's *The Trapper* describes a trapper on horseback "at the moment, apparently, when some noise in his rear has awakened his attention. Resting his right foot in the heavy wooden stirrup, he has drawn the other out, with body turned in the saddle, is holding his rifle steady for any hostile surprise. The horse, with his head turned to one side, is also listening attentively to the alarm. . . . The whole picture conveys at a glance the lonely, perilous, and daring character of the western trapper." Contemporary critics linked Deas and Ranney: "A few of Mr. RANNEY's pictures of single prairie cavaliers, on the watch for Indians and other 'varmint' remind us somewhat of DEAS' treatment of similar subjects. One or two verge on the melo-dramatic."[44] *The Trapper's Last Shot* in turn influenced Arthur Tait's *The Prairie Hunter—One Rubbed Out!* of 1852 (fig. 69).

A still and silent tension pervades *The Trapper's Last Shot*. The only possible sound is from the horse's legs in the water (small pools circle them). The water reflects the horse (more so in the Western Art-Union version) as the dramatic and colorful sky silhouettes the rider. The Western Art-Union work is thinly painted, although the brushwork in the tall thick grass is loosely and richly applied, with impasto near the top.

The Trapper's Last Shot was favorably received. The American Art-Union in New York, in outlining the advantages of membership, called attention to the annual lottery by which artworks, including "Ranney's truthful renderings of character and every day life," were distributed. The *New York Herald* found the painting to be "a picture of strong character, and well managed. The intense eagerness of the horseman is admirably conveyed." And a painting entitled *The Trapper's Halt* (probably this same work), which brought $340 at the Ranney Benefit Sale, was cited for "combining all his best characteristics."[45]

The Trapper's Last Shot is not only one of Ranney's most admirable scenes but also one that, in its ambiguous title, gives the viewer the opportunity to interpret the painting's meaning. Will the trapper's last shot reach its mark and allow him to escape or will the imminent bullet be the last he fires before his death? Will he live to see another sunset? The sense of entrapment and fear is even more apparent in the larger (American Art-Union) version of the painting, in which the horse and rider are brought right up to the front of the picture plane, the space is more constricted with a higher horizon line, the Indians are more clearly defined and closer to the trapper, and the expressions of terror shared by man and horse are more exaggerated. The trapper is himself trapped.

According to Joe Meek, the flamboyant mountain man who claimed to be the subject of the painting, the story had a happy ending. Meek recalled that the incident took place in 1837 when a party of trappers went to the headwaters of the Missouri River and encountered a group of Blackfeet. They battled the Indians for two days, with Meek in the thick of the fight. Meek's gun, "Sally," had one last shot, and it found its mark in the Indian closing in on him. The trapper rode to safety.[46]

We cannot know for certain if Ranney's painting depicts this particular person—who was described as a tall, broad-shouldered, powerful, and handsome man with an olive complexion, "fierce, dark eyes and a classical nose and chin"—and this event (about which the artist might have heard during his stay in the West) or if Ranney knew of similar people and incidents. In any case, Ranney's trappers and mountain men are anachronistic portrayals of a breed whose heyday had passed. By the time Ranney executed *The Trapper's Last Shot,* Joe Meek had retired as a trapper, settled in Oregon, become a farmer, and served in a variety of civic posts. But Ranney presents the archetypal trapper or mountain man as national hero. Always ready to fight, he survived by his wits and prided himself as much on his recklessness as his courage.[47] The Western Art-Union painting more saliently describes the trapper's defiant bravery, al-

though it is the American Art-Union version in which the figure takes on a larger-than-life monumentality.

The *Bulletin of the American Art-Union* for April 1850 announced that Ranney had "finished two characteristic scenes—the *Last Bullet* and *The Halt on the Prairie,*" and the Art-Union exhibition catalogue described the latter work (fig. 57): "Two trappers, each with two horses, one is mounted; the other is standing, and engaged in adjusting his saddle-girth. The scene is the broad prairie, and the time is afternoon."[48]

Like *The Trapper's Last Shot, Halt on the Prairie* received favorable notice when exhibited and was said to be "especially admired, not without reason."[49] The vastness of the frontier—and its powerful effect on the mind—probably impressed Ranney's eastern audiences, just as it must have seemed "otherworldly" to Ranney when he first

57. *William Tylee Ranney,* Halt on the Prairie, *1850, oil on canvas, 36¼ × 53¼ in. Archer M. Huntington Art Gallery, The University of Texas at Austin, Gift of C. R. Smith, 1985*

arrived in the West in 1836. The painted landscape is minimal—comprised of bands of muted color—with the artist's and viewer's attention focused on the trappers and their animals. Ranney has taken great care in rendering the animal skins they are taking to trade, the dog's fur, the horses' manes and tails, and the jacket draped over the left rear horse. The prairie Ranney gives us is a desolate and remote landscape where the trappers survive by their frontier skills and by their reliance on one another. The barren prairie sets the mood of Ranney's quiet but powerful paintings; it intensifies the utter isolation of the trappers.[50] The tightly knit group stands out, like so many sitting ducks, against the huge sky and boundless plains, vulnerable to every conceivable danger.

A painting with a similar title, *Halt on the Plains* (1857; fig. 9) projects a different feeling. Here three scouts, their horses, and dogs stop to rest cattle on their way across the Great Plains. This landscape, with water and vegetation, is more inviting than the one in *Halt on the Prairie* and, with the introduction of the cattle and distant mountains, takes on a tamer character. Painted during the last year of Ranney's life, the painting harks back in spirit to a small (eight-by-fourteen-and-a-half-inch) work entitled *Halt on the Prairie* (ca. 1850; collection of Mr. and Mrs. John Merriam), which depicts a wagon train crossing the prairie, accompanied by cattle and a number of scouts.

The Retreat (1850; fig. 58) contains one of Ranney's rare depictions of Indians (albeit a cameo appearance in the far background of the painting) and is one of his most action-filled pictures. We see the dramatic flight of several trappers who are pursued by a small band of Indians. It has been suggested, due to the pack horse's brand with Ranney's initials, that the canvas depicts an incident in the artist's life. While there is no documentation for this theory, the event shown in *The Retreat* was often related in popular literature on frontier life. The trapper in the left background (in a pose and situation that took on greater meaning in *The Trapper's Last Shot*) holds off the Indians while his partners, arranged in a pyramidal grouping, escape with the pack horses carrying their supplies. The riderless horse in the right background indicates a fallen comrade. With no cover on the "wide expanse of prairie ocean," their only chance is to outrun the Indians.[51] As one nineteenth-century storyteller described a similar situation:

It was riding for dear life, for it was clear that, unless we could gain some position of advantage, . . . our smaller party would, in any event, be annihilated. On we hurried, with the reckless speed which desperate apprehension furnishes, feeling that every step we gained was so much between us and certain destruction. Our horses were greatly fagged by our long travel, but we used both quirt and spur with an energy that fairly maddened them into the most tremendous exertion.[52]

Ranney showed *The Retreat* and *The Scouting Party* (either fig. 60 or fig. 62) at the annual exhibition of the National Academy of Design in 1851. The *Bulletin of the American Art-Union,* in reviewing the show, noted: "2 or 3 of Ranney's pictures have a blunt vigor about them which is appropriate to their subjects, drawn from the life of the prairie."[53] And a writer for the *New-York Daily Tribune* cited *The Retreat* for its "good movement," and continued:

The spirit of the whole and the concentration of the action are very admirable. We could have wished for a more spacious view of the Prairie, which by its vastness and magnificent monotony of the line would have intensified the interest by revealing no rocks, or trees, or devices of escape. But the scene throbs with characteristic life.[54]

Despite the review's criticism of the limited viewpoint, it is precisely the *constriction* of space and the placement of riders and horses near the viewer at the front of the picture plane that gives this painting such a thrilling feeling of immediacy and an empathy and identification with the fleeing trappers, silhouetted against the sunset sky of pink, orange, and blue. The hair of the man at far right is blown back by the speed at which he and his horse are traveling. This type of composition, with trappers galloping across the foreground and with Indians in the distance, was also used by Arthur Tait (fig. 70) and by Alfred Jacob Miller, for instance, in his watercolor entitled *Escape from Blackfeet* (Walters Art Gallery, Baltimore).[55] A small pen and ink study (fig. 59) for *The Retreat,* in an arched-top format, gives us the early compositional elements of the painting, although the middle horseman, Indians, and riderless horse had yet to be added.

Ranney continued the theme of the trapper the following year with two paintings entitled *The Scouting Party* (figs. 60, 62). One (ca. 1851; fig. 60) especially illustrates the "international brotherhood" of trappers, a spiritual and psychological

kinship fostered by their geographical detachment. The two trappers with brimmed felt hats greeting a French Canadian trapper (indicated by his fur cap) are Americans. It appears that the French Canadian (whose deep-set eyes and nose resemble a *Self-Portrait* by Ranney [ca. 1830s; fig. 61]) and one American are sharing a pipe, a symbol of friendship since tobacco was a rare and luxurious commodity, a "true consolation" on the frontier. The cove in which they meet, surrounded by mountainous terrain, provides shelter and a sense of

safety for their gathering. The triangular group of figures gives a stable focus to the composition, and the pink sunset glow lends a quiet, contemplative air. Again, as in *Halt on the Prairie,* Ranney successfully captures textures, from the wood and metal of the rifles to the dry foreground foliage, the buckskin garments, and the coats of the dog and horses.[56]

Although we do not know which of the two paintings called *The Scouting Party* was exhibited at the National Academy of Design in 1851, we do have a description of the painting purchased the following year by the American Art-Union: "A party of trappers with their horses on a high bluff watching the movements of Indians who are betrayed by fires in the prairie below." This is the smaller *Scouting Party* (1851; fig. 62), which was engraved for the Art-Union.[57] The pose of the figure at far left echoes that of *The Trapper's Last Shot* of the previous year, while the horses and rider—seen in the other *Scouting Party* as well—form a pyramidal composition. The bluff on which they stand provides a stage for the protagonists, who are spotlit in an otherwise dark scene. Ranney has executed a magnificent nocturnal sky, the clouds illuminated below by the setting sun, while the dark blue sky is dotted with stars. Danger is nearby, indicated by the smoke in the distant valley, but these trappers have the advantageous position and can avert a potential fight with the Indians.

A Trapper Crossing the Mountains (ca. 1853; two versions, one in fig. 63, the other in the J. B. Speed

61. *William Tylee Ranney,* Self-Portrait, *ca. 1830s, oil, 10¾ × 9½ in. (oval). Private collection*

62. *William Tylee Ranney,* The Scouting Party, *1851, oil on canvas, 22 × 36 in. Thyssen-Bornemisza Collection, Lugano, Switzerland*

63. *William Tylee Ranney,*
A Trapper Crossing the
Mountains, *ca. 1853,*
oil on canvas, 20 × 25 in.
The Anschutz Collection,
Denver

Museum, Louisville) is Ranney's only winter scene from his trapper series. The cold, dreary landscape indicates the isolation the trappers endured, while the forlorn look on the figure's face and the weary manner in which his pack horse hangs his head reinforce this feeling of loneliness. Ranney's trapper may be lost (as was Alfred Jacob Miller's *Lost Greenhorn;* fig. 100), since trappers usually began the season at the river's headwaters in the mountains, reaching the milder climate of the plains before winter.

The figures, horses, and pack horse seen in Ranney's *The Trappers* (1856; fig. 64) are taken from such earlier paintings as the two entitled *The Scouting Party*. Two trappers, one American and one French Canadian, are traveling together (for protection against the ever-present threat of Indian attack and simply for companionship) through a mountainous landscape with dead trees. They are heading westward, toward the sunset, which sheds a pink cast on the greenish water of the lake they cross, and on the rocks and trees, on the pack

64. *William Tylee Ranney,*
The Trappers, *1856,*
oil on canvas, 23½ × 36 in.
Enron Art Foundation/
Joslyn Art Museum,
Omaha, Nebraska

horse's mane, and on the gear on his back. Ranney's characteristic red appears throughout as well, on the saddle blanket, jacket, hat, belt, and shirt. *The Trappers* is a quiet, meditative work painted a year before Ranney's death and calls to mind a scene described by Sir William Drummond Stewart in his account of the mountain man, *Altowan* (1846): "The evening was fading; and the universal calm, the open solitude around, the gigantic range of mountains in front—might have furnished for the poet and the painter, admirable subjects for their finest productions."[58]

The Pipe of Friendship (1857–59; fig. 65), continuing the theme of trappers of different nationalities meeting on the frontier and sharing a pipe of tobacco, is almost identical in composition to *The Scouting Party* (fig. 60). Ranney, however, changed the setting from that seen in the earlier work to the flat plains location of *Halt on the Prairie* (fig. 57). *The Pipe of Friendship* is one of the paintings left unfinished at Ranney's death and that William Sidney Mount is known to have com-

pleted (the work is inscribed "W. Ranney 1857 & WSM Fcb. 1859"). It is through Mount, who considered Ranney "a glorious fellow,"[59] that we have a better idea of Ranney's painting technique:

Commenced touching up an unfinished picture by W. Ranney. He appears to make a careful drawing of his design and then glazes over the figure (or whatever he is painting) with red, blue, yellow, brown, Green, purple etc., and then works into the above while wet, or otherwise as the [time] or case may be.

In some of his skys he changes the tint very often—blue and white, red and white, and yellow and white—and when the atmosphere is hazzy [sic], he also scumbles different tints upon his figures and animals—colors broken—in patches.[60]

William Ranney died of consumption, at age forty-four, on 18 November 1857 at his home in West Hoboken, New Jersey, The *New York Times* hailed him as "in every sense of the word, an

65. *William Tylee Ranney and William Sidney Mount (1807–68),* The Pipe of Friendship, *1857–59, oil on canvas, 23 × 36 in. The Newark Art Museum, Gift of J. Ackerman Coles, 1920*

American artist." *Leslie's Illustrated* stated: "His pictures were stamped with American character, and he chose the most striking features of American scenery for his subjects." The *New York Herald* likewise emphasized the native character of Ranney's work and the "graphic truthfulness" with which he illustrated western life: "Owing none of his gifts to foreign sources of inspiration, Mr. Ranney might with truth be said to be a genius born of the American soil and to be racy of its peculiarities."[61]

Aware of the financial situation of his family—Ranney had been ill since 1853—fellow artists organized the Ranney Fund Exhibition and sale, held in December 1858 in rooms provided by the National Academy of Design. The event included works by Ranney and such luminaries of American art as Asher B. Durand, Frederic Church, John F. Kensett, George Inness, and Jasper Cropsey, who contributed their paintings to the sale. Noting that Ranney was "certainly one of the most patriotic of painters," who concentrated on "scenes and stories of his native land," one newspaper article exhorted all those "who wish to see American artists devote themselves successfully to the illustration of American life" to support the forthcoming sale strongly.[62]

Ranney had been a popular contributor to the annual exhibitions in New York. He was favored by the public, critic Henry Tuckerman felt, not so much on the strength of his artistic skills but because of his paintings' "freshness and force derived from a congenial subject," and their "dramatic truth, natural and local interest, [and] picturesque effect." The *Crayon* deemed "a specimen of Ranney . . . indispensable wherever a collection of American Art exists."[63] Nostalgia and nationalism played a large role in the appreciation of Ranney's work. He had been in the West at an exciting time, a time of great change when the dominance of trapper and mountain man was ending and the migrations of homesteaders beginning. While the West of the Mississippi and the Missouri had been depicted eloquently by George Caleb Bingham, it fell to Ranney to bring to urban, eastern audiences the Far West—the exotic and remote territory that was to become part of America's destiny. Ranney gave them both the mountain man who helped win the West and the pioneer families who followed the trails they blazed. A genre painter, he presented "types" of both groups and blended romantic and somewhat idealized characteristics with realistically rendered details of frontier costumes, equipment, and events. A consummate storyteller, he brought forth two images of the West: a territory of trial and wild hardship and a place of serenity and natural peace.

NOTES

1. *New York Herald,* 4 March 1836, p. 1. Committee of Vigilance and Safety, *Resolutions Adopted by the Committee on January 15 and 20, 1836.* Broadside on microfilm, "Texas as Province and Republic, 1795–1845," Amon Carter Museum Library. Texas (provisional government) Commissioners, *To the Public,* printed in Nashville in 1836. New York City newspapers and the public followed the story of the Texas war with great interest. On 7 January 1836 the American Theatre in the Bowery staged *Venice Preserved,* for the "Benefit for the Relief of THE TEXIANS, Now struggling against Tyranny and Oppression." The handbill for this performance is on the microfilm series listed above.

2. His uncle, William Nott, adopted young Ranney after Captain Ranney was lost at sea in 1829. The facts about Ranney's early life are from Francis Grubar, *William Ranney: Painter of the Early West* (New York: Clarkson N. Potter, 1962). On p. 6, Grubar mentions his apprenticeship to a tinsmith, but Ranney's obituary in *Leslie's Illustrated,* 28 November 1857, p. 407, states that he was apprenticed to a blacksmith. The quote about Ranney's sketching talent and the view that he went south to escape city life are from the same obituary. The statement that he was drawn there by the sufferings of his countrymen was expressed by Margaret Ranney, the artist's widow, in a questionnaire she completed for *Appleton's Cyclopedia of American Bi-*

ography in 1883 (transcript in the possession of Ranney's descendants). Despite her comments, it has been questioned when—and even if—Ranney went to Texas; several authors have suggested that the author fought not in the 1836 war but in the Mexican War of 1846–48. William H. Goetzmann in Goetzmann and Joseph C. Porter, *The West as Romantic Horizon* (Omaha, Neb.: Joslyn Art Museum, 1981), p. 102. However, documents in the Texas State Archives and the state's General Land Office confirm Ranney's presence in Texas in the 1830s and his participation in the war for independence. James Tylee, a native of New York City who moved to Texas in 1834 to join Stephen Austin's colony, died at the Alamo in 1836. Ranney's middle name raises the question whether he might be related to James Tylee and whether the latter's involvement in the Texas war for independence inspired Ranney to join the Texas army. Thus far, I have been unable to ascertain if there was a connection between the two men. Ranney's paternal grandmother was Hannah Tiley or Tilley of Saybrook, Connecticut. See Charles Collard Adams, *Middletown Upper Houses* (Canaan, N.H.: Phoenix Publishing, 1983), p. 191.

3. Although Goetzmann, *Romantic Horizon,* p. 102, and Pauline A. Pinckney, *Painting in Texas* (Austin and London: University of Texas Press, 1967), p. 39, state that Ranney fought in the Battle of San Jacinto, William Ranney's name does not appear in the published list of men who fought at San Jacinto. A C. Raney (sgt.) and an L. Raney (pvt.) are listed, however. See *Documents of Major Gen. Sam. Houston, Commander in Chief of the Texian Army, to His Excellency David G. Burnet, President of the Republic of Texas: Containing a Detailed Account of the Battle of San Jacinto* (New Orleans: John Cox & Co., Printers, 1836). G. H., "Death of William Ranney" (an unidentified clipping from 1857 in *The Ranney Collection,* New-York Historical Society), stated that "on the day following the battle of San Jacinto, the company to which he was attached joined the forces of Houston." A photocopy of the Muster Roll of Captain Fowler's First Regiment Volunteers indicates that Ranney enlisted in that company on 18 May 1836. A photocopy of a receipt for $48 shows that Ranney was still in the military at Columbia, Texas, on 23 November 1836. Both documents are in the Texas State Archives, Austin. I checked the pension rolls and mil-

itary service records for the Mexican War (both on microfilm at the National Archives, Washington, D.C.) and could find no reference that William Ranney returned to Texas in the 1840s to serve in the army. I thank Michael Green at the Texas State Archives and Dr. Michael Hooks at the General Land Office, Austin, for their assistance in providing photocopies of documents relevant to Ranney's stay in Texas in the 1830s.

In 1847, Ranney received a bounty land grant of 320 acres in Bosque County for service from 12 March–12 June 1836. He later received 640 acres (in McLennon and Milam Counties) for service from 18 May–18 November 1836, although one patent for 205 acres was cancelled due to an incorrect field survey. Another grant of 320 acres (in Hamilton County) for service from 2 July–2 October 1836 was also cancelled. See Thomas Lloyd Miller, *Bounty and Donation Land Grants of Texas, 1835–1888* (Austin and London: University of Texas Press, 1967), p. 545. We cannot be certain that it was the artist William Ranney who received the headright certificate of over one thousand acres since the documents concerning the land transactions were signed by a William "Reney." Misspellings do occur in the nineteenth century, but it is doubtful that Ranney would be the same person as "Reney" since the signatures on the documents do not appear to be identical to the artist's. However, no Reney is listed in Miller's *Bounty and Donation Land Grants.*

4. Margaret Ranney, in questionnaire for *Appleton's Cyclopedia.* Although Pinckney, *Painting in Texas,* p. 39, states that Ranney studied at the Institute of Mechanical Arts in Brooklyn, I can find no record of such an institution. I thank Jean Ashton of the New-York Historical Society Library for checking the Brooklyn and Manhattan city directories for the Institute of Mechanical Arts. Perhaps Ranney studied at the Mechanics' Institute (founded in 1830), which was located in Manhattan and in whose 1838 fair he exhibited.

5. See G. H., "Death of William Ranney" and Grubar, *Ranney,* p. 7. Ranney or Reney (see note 3) would have had to appear in person before the land commissioners at Harrisburg (now Harris) County near Houston in 1838 to claim his headright certificate and to sell it in 1839 to James W. Seymour. The original documents concerning these transactions are in the General Land

Office, Austin. Letter, Michael Q. Hooks to Linda Ayres, 6 May 1986.

6. G. H., "Death of William Ranney."

7. Quote from Henry Nash Smith, *Virgin Land: The American West as Symbol and Myth* (1950; reprint ed., Cambridge, Mass.: Harvard University Press, 1970), p. 84. On the Art-Union's influence, see Maybelle Mann, *The American Art-Union* (Otisville, N.Y.: ALM Associates, 1977), p. 22. The American Art-Union purchased twenty-six paintings from Ranney.

8. William Sidney Mount noted in his journal entry for 7 December 1846: "I must paint larger pictures—takes no more time and more effective in an exhibition." He frequently made similar observations, writing on 3 April 1854 that large, highly finished paintings would be noticed in an exhibition. Quoted in Alfred Frankenstein, *William Sidney Mount* (New York: Harry N. Abrams, 1975), pp. 7, 144, 145, 182, 273.

9. Miller was the first painter to see the legendary Rocky Mountain trappers, and he exhibited his western scenes in May 1839 at New York's Apollo Gallery to sensational reviews, praising him for the originality of his subject matter. Ron Tyler, ed., *Alfred Jacob Miller: Artist on the Oregon Trail* (Fort Worth: Amon Carter Museum, 1982), pp. 36–37.

10. Henry T. Tuckerman, *Book of the Artists: American Artist Life* (New York: G. P. Putnam & Son, 1867: reprint ed., New York: James F. Carr, 1966), p. 425. This first appeared as an anonymous article, "Our Artists.—No. V," *Godey's Lady's Book* (1846), pp. 250–53.

11. Tuckerman, *Book of the Artists,* pp. 431–32. Ranney settled in West Hoboken in 1853, having lived in Weehawken in the late 1840s and in New York City for a brief time around 1850. A description of his West Hoboken studio also appeared in the *Crayon* 5, pt. 1 (January 1858): 26. The Ranney house, demolished in 1927, was located at Thirteenth Street and Palisades Avenue in what is now Union City, New Jersey. Ranney also built a stable where he kept the horses that so often appear in his paintings. Hoboken attracted such other artists as Charles Loring Elliot, Robert Weir, and William Mason Brown, who lived there in the nineteenth century.

12. In fact, the scenery he depicts cannot positively be identified as Texas or western landscapes. Although the prairie scenes (in *Hunting Wild Horses, Halt on the Prairie,* and *The Retreat*) resemble the coastal plains near Columbia, Texas, where he served in the army, other works by Ranney may have imaginary landscapes. My thanks to Ron Tyler for this observation.

13. G. H., "Death of William Ranney." Ranney, in his travels after the war, could have met some of the trappers working in Texas. By 1835, a Missouri fur-trading firm had an office in Galveston, not too far from Columbia. American trappers in Texas were exporting between five and ten thousand dollars worth of furs (beaver, otter, badger, bear, buffalo, and deer) annually through Nacogdoches during the years 1830–38. The city was also a headquarters for mountain trappers unable to get to Taos or Santa Fe. Paul Chrisler Phillips, *The Fur Trade* (Norman: University of Oklahoma Press, 1961), 2: 519–20.

14. Jules Zanger, "The Frontiersman in Popular Fiction, 1820–60," in *The Frontier Re-examined,* edited by John Francis McDermott (Urbana, Chicago, and London: University of Illinois Press, 1967), pp. 147–52.

15. Richard Slotkin, *Regeneration through Violence: The Mythology of the American Frontier, 1600–1860* (Middletown, Conn.: Wesleyan University Press, 1973), pp. 403, 413, 417.

16. Quote from "The Ranney Fund," *New York Times,* 10 December 1858. Cooper's first novel in the cycle was *The Pioneers* (1823), followed by *The Last of the Mohicans* (1826), *The Prairie* (1827), *The Pathfinder* (1840), and *The Deerslayer* (1841). By the early 1830s, weekly newspapers printed enough diaries and letters from the trappers to locate all the landmarks of their travels. Bernard DeVoto, *Across the Wide Missouri* (Boston: Houghton Mifflin Company, 1947), p. 4.

17. David H. Coyner, *The Lost Trappers, A Collection of Interesting Scenes and Events in the Rocky Mountains* (Cincinnati: J. A. and U. P. James, 1847); micropublished in *Western America: Frontier History of the Trans-Mississippi West, 1550–1900* (New Haven, Conn.: Research Publications, 1975), pp. xi, xii. Coyner described the trapper's life and such incidents as prairie fires,

writing that the "great fires are sometimes very beautiful and even grand when seen in a dark night" (p. 57).

18. Coyner, pp. xii, xiii.

19. Flint, who was also an early biographer of Daniel Boone, is quoted in Dawn Glanz, *How the West Was Drawn: American Art and the Settling of the Frontier* (Ann Arbor, Mich.: UMI Research Press, 1982), p. 28, which notes how these men became heroes. Smith, *Virgin Land*, p. 81, comments on their savage aspect. Flint is quoted in Smith, p. 82. Smith also cites Charles Sealsfield's [pseud. Karl Anton Post] *Life in the New World; or, Sketches of American Society* (published in German in 1835–37; English edition in New York in 1844), Coyner's *The Lost Trappers* (see above), Emerson Bennett's *The Prairie Flower; or, Adventures in the Far West* (1849), and Lewis H. Garrard's autobiographical narrative *Wah-To-Yah* (1850) as popular works that described the unusual life of the Westerner. See Smith, pp. 82–84.

20. Old Hicks was a guide on a trip in search of gold mines near the Red River in Texas. Webber published many popular frontier stories in such magazines as the *American Whig Review* and the *United States Magazine and Democratic Review* as well. See Charles W. Webber, *Old Hicks the Guide or, Adventures in the Camanche Country in Search of a Gold Mine* (New York: Harper & Brothers, Publishers, 1848), pp. 17, 52, 73, 335.

21. George Frederick Ruxton, *Life in the Far West,* edited by LeRoy R. Hafen (1849; reprint ed., Norman: University of Oklahoma Press, 1951), p. 51.

22. The *Arkansas Gazette* (10 July 1839, p. 3) reported: "The mustang or wild horse is certainly the greatest curiosity . . . that we met with upon the prairies of Texas. They are seen in vast numbers, and are oftentimes of exceeding beauty. . . . We still meet with many in the lower counties, and during the summer hundreds were seen in the neighborhood of Houston." Columbia, where Ranney was stationed, is in the southeast area of the state, as is Houston.

23. Glanz, *How the West Was Drawn,* p. 91.

24. Marvin C. Ross, ed., *The West of Alfred Jacob Miller,* rev. and enl. ed. (Norman: University of Oklahoma

Press, 1968), no. 92. Miller's painting, *Hunting Wild Horses,* emphasizes the colorful Indians on horseback rather than the stampeding horses.

25. George Wilkins Kendall, *Narrative of the Texan Santa Fe Expedition* (New York: Harper and Brothers, publishers, 1844), 1:88–89. Walter Blair states that when James Hall visited Texas in 1845, people were still telling stories about the white steed. See Walter Blair, *Native American Humor* (New York: Harper & Row, Publishers, 1960), p. 72. Hall's book, *The Wilderness and Warpath,* was published in New York in 1846.

26. Glanz, *How the West Was Drawn,* p. 95. The poem, by J. Barber, and Melville's reference to the legend are on pp. 92–93.

27. Sandra L. Myres, *Westering Women and the Frontier Experience, 1800–1915* (Albuquerque: University of New Mexico Press, 1982), pp. 128–29.

28. Elizabeth Moran, the artist's great-granddaughter. Claude Ranney, the artist's grandson, believed that Richard Ranney (1815–59) posed for the kneeling figure in *Duck Shooting* (1850; The Corcoran Gallery of Art, Washington, D.C.). See Grubar, p. 36. The same figure appears in *Prairie Burial*.

29. "Sketchings—Exhibitions," *Crayon* 5 (December 1858): 354–55.

30. Glanz, *How the West Was Drawn,* pp. 59–61, includes the quote from *Congressional Globe,* 29th Congress, 1st Session, 1846, p. 130.

31. Glanz, pp. 56–58.

32. Rena N. Coen, "David's Sabine Women in the Wild West," *Great Plains Quarterly* 2, no. 2 (Spring 1982): 67–76. The famous Hellenistic marble *Borghese Gladiator* (first century B.C.) is illustrated in Francis Haskell and Nicholas Penny, *Taste and the Antique: The Lure of Classical Sculpture, 1500–1900* (New Haven and London: Yale University Press, 1981), fig. 115. Washington Irving developed images of Indians as classical sculpture, describing the Osage as having "fine Roman countenances" and looking like "figures of monumental bronze." See Irving's *A Tour on the Prairies* (1835; reprinted, Norman: University of Oklahoma Press, 1956), pp. 21, 22, 32, 43.

33. Glanz, *How the West Was Drawn*, p. 72, notes Cooper's description. The scene in Webber, *Old Hicks the Guide*, is on pp. 73–75.

34. Eliza W. Farnham, *Life in the Prairie Land* (1846), quoted in Myres, *Westering Women*, p. 14. On Holley, see Annette Kolodny, *The Land before Her: Fantasy and Experience of the American Frontiers, 1630–1860* (Chapel Hill and London: University of North Carolina Press, 1984), p. 129.

35. There were inadequate supplies, and no proper tools for setting up a household (they could take with them only the barest necessities), no time for leisure, no resources for pleasure, long periods of isolation, and often the loss of one or more family members, as seen in *Prairie Burial*. See Kolodny, *The Land before Her*, esp. pp. 94–96, 121–22, 133, 140, 237.

36. Coen, "David's Sabine Women in the Wild West," p. 69.

37. George Frederick Ruxton, quoted in Glanz, *How the West Was Drawn*, p. 54.

38. James Bridger, a guide, mountaineer, and Indian trapper, was born in Richmond, Virginia, but raised in St. Louis. Bridger began his career as a mountain man in 1822, discovered the Great Salt Lake in 1824, and, in 1830, became a partner in the Rocky Mountain Fur Company, followed by the firm of Fitzpatrick, Sublette, and Bridger, and then the American Fur Company. Alfred Jacob Miller met Bridger at the 1830 rendezvous and noted that "no one has travelled here within the last thirty years without seeing or hearing of him." Bridger established Fort Bridger (which became one of the principal trading posts for western emigrants, a military post, and Pony Express station), and, in the 1850s, served as a guide for a number of expeditions. He died on his farm, near Little Santa Fe, Missouri, in 1881. See Cornelius M. Ismert, "James Bridger," in *The Mountain Men and the Fur Trade of the Far West*, edited by LeRoy F. Hafen (Glendale, Calif.: Arthur H. Clark Company, 1968), 1:87–104. The settler's response is an unidentified quote in the Ranney family files. Grubar, *Ranney*, p. 41, reported that Ranney descendants believe that the figures on the right side of the group were friends of the artist.

39. On the western tradition of oral storytelling, see Blair, *Native American Humor*, pp. 70–72. Zanger, "The Frontiersman in Popular Fiction," p. 148, reports that nineteenth-century fiction writers attributed frontiersmen with the gift of telling long, exaggerated stories. Seated storytellers also appear in several canvases by George Caleb Bingham, including *Canvassing for a Vote* (fig. 24).

40. Glanz, *How the West Was Drawn*, p. 27.

41. Quote from DeVoto, *Across the Wide Missouri*, p. 228. William H. Goetzmann, *The Mountain Man* (Cody, Wyo.: Buffalo Bill Historical Center, 1978), pp. 12, 23.

42. Quote from William H. Goetzmann, *Exploration and Empire: The Explorer and the Scientist in the Winning of the West* (New York: Alfred A. Knopf, 1966), p. 106. Glanz, *How the West Was Drawn*, p. 145, has pointed out that the equestrian portrait tradition in America was primarily used for national leaders—military heroes and heads of state. She believes that the use of the equestrian tradition in trapper paintings indicates the national and heroic stature of the American trapper.

43. *Transactions of the Western Art-Union* (Cincinnati, 1850), p. 15. Francis S. Grubar, "Ranney's *The Trapper's Last Shot*," *American Art Journal* 2, no. 1 (Spring 1970): 97. Grubar points out that Ranney also made more than one version of *Boone's First View of Kentucky* and *On the Wing*, among others. When Ranney created multiple versions of a subject, the signed and dated work was usually the original effort.

44. The catalogue description of *The Trapper's Last Shot* is in Mary Bartlett Cowdrey, *American Academy of Fine Arts and American Art-Union Exhibition Record, 1816–1852* (New York: The New-York Historical Society, 1953), p. 295. The account of Deas's *The Trapper* appeared in the *St. Louis Weekly Reveille*. See Glanz, *How the West Was Drawn*, p. 146 and p. 172, n. 71. The link between Ranney and Deas is noted in "Fine Arts, The Ranney Exhibition," unidentified clipping postdating the Ranney Sale of December 1858, in *The Ranney Collection*, New-York Historical Society.

45. The three favorable reviews are from the *Bulletin of the American Art-Union*, 1 November 1850, p. 123; "The Fine Arts," *New York Herald*, 8 September 1850; and an unidentified clipping (possibly from the *Com-*

mercial Advertiser), 22 December 1858, in *The Ranney Collection,* New-York Historical Society.

46. Meek said that the painting was by John Mix Stanley, but Stanley did not go to the frontier until the 1840s. Meek often misremembered dates and events. Frances Fuller Victor, *The River of the West* (Hartford, Conn., and Toledo, Ohio: R. W. Bliss & Co., 1870), pp. 228–31. DeVoto, *Across the Wide Missouri,* p. 304, also recounts the fight. In addition to the Victor biography, there is a good account of Joseph LaFayette Meek by Harvey E. Tobie in Hafen, *The Mountain Man and the Fur Trade,* 1:313–35. Meek, born in Virginia in 1810, joined William Sublette of the Rocky Mountain Fur Company in 1829 and spent eleven years in the Rocky Mountains. He went to California with Joseph Walker, hunted with Kit Carson, and, in 1840, helped to blaze a new wagon trail to Oregon.

47. Victor, *The River of the West,* pp. vii, 50, 105, includes the description of Meek and notes how recklessness combined with courage in the trapper. Glanz, *How the West Was Drawn,* p. 45, makes the connection between such works as Deas's *Long Jakes* and Ranney's *The Trapper's Last Shot* and traditional equestrian portraiture of heroic figures.

48. *Bulletin of the American Art-Union,* 1 April 1850, p. 15. The catalogue description is in Cowdrey, *American Academy of Fine Arts and American Art-Union Exhibition Record, 1816–1852,* p. 295.

49. *New-York Daily Tribune,* 27 November 1850.

50. Glanz, *How the West Was Drawn,* pp. 49–50.

51. The suggestion that *The Retreat* depicts an incident in the artist's life comes from "Forthcoming Auctions," *New York Sun,* 28 May 1938, p. 9. Ruxton, *Life in the Far West,* p. 55, presents the image of prairie as ocean.

52. Webber, *Old Hicks the Guide,* p. 336.

53. *Bulletin of the American Art-Union,* 1 June 1851. I thank Mark Thistlethwaite for calling my attention to this review.

54. "The Fine Arts: Exhibition of the National Academy, VI," *New-York Daily Tribune,* 21 June 1851, p. 6.

55. Glanz, *How the West Was Drawn,* p. 35, mentions the Miller parallel.

56. Glanz, pp. 49–50, comments on the "international brotherhood" of trappers and distinguishes the French Canadian from the Americans. Ruxton, *Life in the Far West,* p. 25, points out the meaning of tobacco on the frontier. According to notes made by Claude Ranney, the artist's grandson, the black stallion seen here was owned by Ranney's friends, the Kerrigan family, in West Hoboken.

57. The painting is described in Cowdrey, *American Academy of Fine Arts and American Art-Union Exhibition Record, 1816–1852,* p. 295. The print, drawn on wood by Miller and engraved by Richardson, appeared in the *Bulletin of the American Art-Union,* 1 September 1851, p. 89.

58. Sir William Drummond Stewart, *Altowan* (1846), edited by J. Watson Webb, quoted in Goetzmann, *The Mountain Man,* p. 38.

59. Charles Lanman, *Haphazard Personalities: Chiefly of Noted Americans* (Boston: Lee and Shepard, 1886), p. 177.

60. Mount's diary entry dated 3 February 1859, quoted in Frankenstein, *Mount,* p. 339. Since *The Pipe of Friendship* was completed by Mount in February 1859 (see inscription on the painting), it is likely that this is the painting to which Mount's comments on technique refer. It is not known how many of Ranney's paintings Mount completed.

61. "American Artists," *New York Times,* 5 December 1857. *Leslie's Illustrated,* p. 407. "American Art—The Late William Ranney," *New York Herald,* 3 December 1857.

62. Unidentified clipping, "A Good Deed Gracefully Done," 1858, in *The Ranney Collection,* New-York Historical Society. Of the 212 works in the sale, 108 were by Ranney. Ninety-five artists donated paintings. The sale raised over seven thousand dollars for Ranney's family. This event led to the formation of the Artist's Fund Society. See Grubar, *Ranney,* pp. 11–12; and "Ranney Collection," *Crayon* 6, no. 2 (February 1859): 58.

63. Tuckerman, *Book of the Artists,* p. 432. "Exhibitions," *Crayon* 5, no. 12 (December 1858): 355.

ARTHUR F. TAIT

WARDER H. CADBURY

*I*n his classic *Across the Wide Missouri,* Bernard DeVoto faulted the accuracy of Arthur Fitzwilliam Tait's western work. Although he described the artist's style as that of a "conscientious realist," DeVoto saw in the eight large Currier & Ives prints of Tait's prairie genre scenes "a curious mixture of truth and fantasy." In *Portrait of the Old West,* Harold McCracken went even further, criticizing these lithographs as "purely pictorial and by no means factual." But, he pointed out, "they became very popular. Many people in the East formed their conception of life on the plains from reproductions of Tait's paintings." Neither scholar mentioned that Tait never set foot on the prairie—indeed, never ventured farther west than Chicago (which he visited on the occasion of the 1896 World's Columbian Exposition)—and thus never saw the lively scenes he painted with such color.[1]

More recently, in his essay "Fact and Fiction in the Documentary Art of the American West," John C. Ewers criticized Tait—along with others—for trying "to visualize the plains grasslands from the security of their New York studios."[2] Ewers continued: since a picture may linger in the memory long after written words are forgotten, an inaccurate painting can do even more harm than a false statement and ought not to be exhibited or published.

And there are further problems with Tait as a

Tait
Buffalo Hunt
(detail, see fig. 75)

western artist. He was a prolific painter whose active career in and out of Manhattan spanned the entire second half of the nineteenth century. He earned a solid reputation as a specialist in birds and animals, not as a worker in genre. An enthusiastic sportsman, he found in the wild deer and bear of the Adirondacks, which he visited annually for thirty years, his artistic province. Currier & Ives published more than two dozen of his paintings of hunting and fishing themes. In later years his canvases featured domestic sheep and chickens in the farmyards of the rural Hudson River Valley just north of the city. Louis Prang produced ten different best-selling chromolithographs of Tait's ducklings and chicks. In contrast, Tait's prairie scenes were few in number, and they all date from the earliest chapter of a long career in this country, when he was fresh off the boat from England and not yet an American citizen. Indeed, out of a lifetime total of more than seventeen hundred paintings, large and small, only twenty-two have a western motif, depicting the trapper's life, and these were done between 1851 and 1862.[3] Some of these paintings were studies or copies of others, leaving a mere thirteen different compositions, of which two are still unlocated. Eight of these eleven known pictures were published by Nathaniel Currier and, later, Currier & Ives as large folio prints.

What inspired Tait to make these few pictures

in the first place? That eight of eleven were reproduced as lithographs points to the quite mundane explanation that he was simply trying to make a living by doing whatever pleased the printmakers. Other facts support this conclusion as well. Once he was successfully established in his career, by the mid 1860s, he ceased to paint genre scenes of any kind, whether of western trappers or Adirondack sportsmen. This suggests that Tait preferred to paint exclusively his lustrous portraits of animals and birds when at last he was financially at liberty to do so. It may indicate Tait's attitude about the work he did for the printmakers that, in his otherwise systematic records, he occasionally forgot to note a painting executed for them.

Since almost all of Tait's western works were special commissions for Currier & Ives, it is possible that the publisher furnished the idea as well as some details for each image. James Ives, a man of many talents who joined the firm in 1852, almost certainly played some role. As a businessman, he enjoyed a shrewd journalistic sense of what was timely and would appeal to the public taste. He was also a connoisseur of art, both highbrow and low. It is reported that in deciding what to publish he was "unusually adept in showing how an idea could be used to best advantage. His criticism of sketches was keen and he was clever at combining features from various sketches into a well-designed composite whole."[4]

Little or nothing is known about Tait's methods of composition. If, after some initial discussions with the publishers, he submitted preliminary sketches for further suggestions and alterations, none have survived. We do know that once a composition was approved and completed by his hand, he was neither inclined to experiment with further changes nor to tolerate them from the printmakers. While still a novice, he sometimes made a second or third canvas of exactly the same image and identical in every detail, except that the copy for the lithographer often had the same dimensions as the intended print and was less highly finished than usual for him.

The theme of nearly all of Tait's prairie compositions is the armed conflict of the white man against the Indian, a motif that appealed to many mid-century Americans, caught up in the spirit of expansion, as the expression of the nation's identity and destiny. Eastern newspapers were full of accounts of the wars in Texas, the wagon trains on the Oregon Trail, and gold seekers en route to California. A few book-length accounts of the adventure-filled lives of the trappers and scouts, overland expeditions, and military explorations caught the public's fancy, and nearly every narrative had its own dramatic tales of Indian skirmishes. Printmakers were quick to profit from a public eager to buy inexpensive pictorial images of these encounters.

Except for *The Pursuit* and *The Last War Whoop,* the Indians portrayed in Tait's scenes are either entirely unseen, lurking somewhere out of the picture, or depicted as small figures in the background. A conscientious realist, Tait could hardly have handled the Indians otherwise. He did not have the knowledge to paint their costume and accoutrements with any authority. Instead, Tait relied on the viewer to use his own imagination to visualize the dangerous enemy and to speculate on the denouement of each drama. With the help of often splendid draftsmanship, Tait's pictures sometimes evoke an anxious tension and palpable vitality that distinguish them from ordinary documentary, history, or narrative paintings. The same combination of a fluid dynamism and a sure handling of line appears in some of his Adirondack hunting and fishing scenes and probably reflects his early acquaintance with British sporting prints.

The dominance of the figure of the trapper in Tait's western paintings tempts the inference that he was trying to justify the conquest of the continent and the endless killing of Native Americans. But such an assumption is probably mistaken, as Tait did not see in his art any didactic purpose or even symbolic meaning. While the conflict between civilization and the wilderness, pioneer versus the Indian, and the notion of Manifest Destiny preoccupied many Americans, including some of the artists discussed in this book, Tait was, after all, a newcomer to the United States.

Not long after Tait's birth in 1819 in Liverpool,

his father's prosperous business in the shipping trade suffered severe losses, and the boy was sent to live on a farm with relatives. Instead of receiving a gentleman's education, he became interested in animals and acquired an affection for hunting and fishing—enthusiasms that lasted all his life and determined the scope of his artistic calling.

Tait's career began in his early teens when he was hired as a clerk in Thomas Agnew's Manchester gallery. There he became familiar with prints and paintings and began to teach himself the fundamentals of drawing. So strong was his impulse to pursue art that he arranged with the janitor of the Royal Institution to open its door to him before dawn so he could sketch the plaster casts of classical statuary before his day's work began.

With marriage at nineteen, Tait gave up clerking at Agnew's and became a "professor of drawing"—as he was listed in the Manchester city directory. At this time he taught himself the painstaking skills of the recently improved technology of lithography. He saw great promise in this inexpensive way to mass-produce pictures. In addition to such commercial uses as package labels and advertisements, lithography could produce modestly priced prints, reproductions, and illustrated books for an increasingly literate and discriminating public. Tait thus learned a new trade that put him in the mainstream of contemporary developments in British graphic arts.

During this period there was a special enthusiasm for medieval antiquities, the "Gothic Revival," and Tait soon found employment freelancing as draftsman and lithographer for a pair of ecclesiastical architects who published a large folio of plates illustrating the design and decorative details of some churches of the Middle Ages. By 1842, Tait had moved back to the busy port city of Liverpool, where he was commissioned to execute a large print of Saint Jude's Church.

As a more ambitious and independent venture in lithography, Tait shifted his focus to the newly built railways, which were just beginning to bring the Industrial Revolution to the English countryside. He spent much time in the field sketching landscapes with bridges, viaducts, tunnels, and stations, and then copied his compositions onto stones for the printer. In 1845 he published a series of twenty lithographs of such topographical views on the Manchester & Leeds Railway.

The commercial failure of a second series of railway prints may have been a factor in Tait's decision to become more independent and to advance his career by shifting to painting in oils. The shift in medium marked a shift in subject matter as well, to canvases depicting domestic animals and sporting scenes in the Highlands of Scotland. His earliest known oil painting, done in 1848, was a handsome portrait of a thoroughbred horse.

Just two years later, in 1850, Tait immigrated to the United States. Although our information is tantalizingly sketchy, the idea of immigrating may first have occurred to him as a consequence of an acquaintance with George Catlin. From 1840 to 1842 Catlin had exhibited his Plains Indians paintings in London, in conjunction with something he called *Tableaux Vivants*. He hired twenty Englishmen to dress in Indian costume and paint their faces, and he taught them to dance and sing and give a most convincing war whoop. It was the first Wild West show, long before Buffalo Bill entertained Queen Victoria. At the same time, Catlin published an account of his years with the Indians, embellished with over three hundred of his own illustrations.

In May 1842, Catlin accepted an invitation to show his Indian gallery at the Mechanics' Institute in Liverpool, where he was well received. In the fall his success prompted him to put his paintings in storage and take his troupe of dancers on a tour of several cities, but by early 1843 he had reopened his gallery in Manchester for several months before leaving for London.

Tait and Catlin may have met at this time; more than a hundred years later Tait's son recalled: "Father joined Mr. Catlin and travelled with him in what father and Mr. Catlin called 'the Circus' during part of the year."[5] That Tait might even have been a member of Catlin's troupe is consistent with his known enjoyment of the theater and his occasional bouts of wanderlust.

Indeed, it was just such an adventure that brought Tait to the United States. His cousin, George Danson, was a scene painter and sometime artist who staged outdoor fireworks displays in conjunction with reenactments of dramatic historical events. Tait had lithographed an advertising poster for a show depicting Mount Vesuvius and the destruction of Pompeii, and, when Danson decided to bring his entertainment to America, Tait accepted his offer to go along. After all, his prospects as a sporting artist in England did not look promising. He could not work from nature in a countryside posted against trespassing and hunting. He lacked the academic training and the entrée to aristocratic patrons competitors such as Sir Edwin Landseer enjoyed.

Soon after Tait arrived in New York in the fall of 1850, it was clear that the fireworks venture was going to fizzle, but the artist had been testing his options by painting a variety of themes—game stalking in Scotland, grouse and partridge shooting, and deer hunting. He even executed a group portrait of George Washington and his generals. That Tait should also have tried western scenes is not a surprise. The excitement of the California gold rush was in the air, and the newspapers were full of notices and narratives of overland expeditions to the Rockies and beyond.

Perhaps he was encouraged to paint such scenes by the proprietors of Williams, Stevens & Williams, a shop for mirrors, cut glass, art prints, and painters' supplies. There were no commercial art galleries in the New York of those days; so this store displayed some of Tait's canvases in its Broadway window to attract customers. But the more significant influence upon Tait was surely William Ranney, who also did business at Williams, Stevens & Williams. Ranney, who had served with the army during the Texas war and brought home with him many artifacts from the West, regularly exhibited his scenes of western life in New York.

With characteristic generosity, Ranney probably offered Tait the use of these artifacts as props to give his paintings authenticity. The community of artists in New York at the time was small and intimate. If Ranney and Tait did not first meet while exhibiting their works in the same shop window, the affairs at the National Academy of Design and the American Art-Union offered further opportunities to get acquainted. Ranney lived in West Hoboken, not far from the Jersey marshlands, and Tait shared with him a passion for sporting; that they both painted duck-shooting scenes confirms a kindredness of spirit. Nearly a decade later, at the time of Ranney's tragic early death, it was Tait who played a major role in organizing an art auction to benefit his friend's widow and children.

But the most direct evidence of Tait's use of Ranney's collection of western gear as props is the appearance of nearly identical objects in the two artists' canvases. It would seem that not long after his arrival in New York, Tait borrowed a buckskin tunic, rifle, powder horn, rakish hat, and beaded Indian pouch and sandals and went to a photographer's studio to have his picture (fig. 66) taken so he could be his own model.

66. *Photographer unknown, A. F. Tait in Western Garb, ca. 1848–52(?), photograph. Adirondack Museum, Blue Mountain Lake, New York*

For his first western painting, the 1851 *On the Warpath* (fig. 67), Tait simply used a grid to transfer the posed photograph of himself onto a large canvas. The picture shows a trapper who has silently dismounted, concealed himself behind a rock outcropping from some Indians passing by off to the right, and shouldered his rifle. To the left is his faithful horse, whose anxious eye seems to recognize the threat of danger.

The tunic and leggings of buckskin, seen in the photograph and painting, were typical of the trapper's costume. The fringes along the outside seams were not only decorative, but served useful purposes; their wicking action helped to shed rainwater more quickly, and they provided a convenient supply of "whangs" or short leather strips for mending moccasins or saddle.[6] As for the rifle, neither the photograph nor the several paintings in which it appears are clear enough to reveal the exact make and model. But such long, lightweight, accurate, and graceful firearms were generally called Kentucky rifles, named for the volunteer sharpshooters from that state who distinguished themselves at the battle of New Or-

leans. Nor is it possible for the ethnologist to identify exactly the beaded pouch on the trapper's belt, which appears in at least two other non-western paintings by Tait. The painting does clearly show how the curved powder horn conveniently fits the contour of the body. Although the costume and accoutrements are authentically western, some critics have noted that the forested background and large deciduous tree trunks look more like the Adirondack woodlands of James Fenimore Cooper's novels than the Trans-Mississippi plains.[7]

In the register in which Tait kept records of nearly all his paintings, this one is titled *Trapper at Bay,* the artist noting that it was sold to Williams, Stevens & Williams. Following the English practice of producing pictures in pairs to make them more salable as decorative art, he painted another canvas of the same size as its companion, which he called *Trapper at Bay—Alarm.* Neither this painting nor even a description of it has been located.

In 1852, a scant year and a half after his arrival in New York, Tait was invited to submit work for the annual spring exhibition of the National Academy of Design. Of the six canvases accepted, only one had a western theme; entitled *Trappers at Fault, Looking for the Trail* (fig. 68) in the exhibition catalogue, it was a later version of a scene exhibited at the Boston Athenaeum with the title *Prairie Scene (Discovering an Indian Trail)*.[8]

As with *On the Warpath,* many of the details of *Trappers at Fault* confirm Tait's use of borrowed props from Ranney's studio. The trapper on the left, for example, is wearing the beaded pucker-toe moccasins so characteristic of the time and place. The artist Alfred Jacob Miller noted in 1837 that the Indian women made such articles with "the utmost neatness, taste and dexterity. Everybody here wears them in preference to either boot or shoe—they are verily the most comfortable covering for the feet that can be fashioned."[9]

The stirrup of the horse of the kneeling trapper is a variant of what was sometimes called a Mexican or block stirrup, made from a flat block of wood three or four inches thick with a slot cut through at the top for the stirrup leather and a large D-shaped hole carved entirely through for the foot. The skin or blanket laid on the seat of the saddle to soften the ride was called an epishemore. The tin canteen hanging from the saddle's pommel may have been military issue from Ranney's tour of duty in Texas.[10] Inaccurate, perhaps, is the fly net on the horse to the right, commonly used in the East for workhorses and draft animals, but not for riding horses.

The variety of headgear duplicates what is found in the works of Ranney and others, and suggests the independence and cocky self-reliance of the trapper's nomadic and dangerous life. When his store-bought felt-rimmed hat was lost or had worn out, he fashioned such exotic replacements as the jaunty creations depicted by the more romantic brush of Alfred Jacob Miller two decades earlier.[11]

It was precisely such colorful costumes in this painting that earned Tait his first—and mixed—reviews in local newspapers during the spring of 1852. The *New York Herald* critic declared that "As a colorist, Mr. Tait has a considerable portion of merit, although his manner is a melange made up from the manners of many. . . . He seems to have been bitten by Mr. Ranney, and to have imbibed all his extravagance, with little of his fidelity and fire." In a somewhat similar vein the *Literary World* called *Trappers at Fault* an example of "a style of painting that is becoming painfully conspicuous in our exhibitions and shop-windows, of which glaring red shirts, buckskin breeches, and a very coarse prairie grass are the essential ingredients; and in which Mr. Ranney had the honor to lead the way; but with him there was some character of individuality, which Mr. Tate [sic] lacks."[12]

The striking presence of the color red in the art of the American West caught the eye of other contemporary critics and deserves some discussion. Even Charles Baudelaire, writing of the work Catlin exhibited in the Salon of 1846, was struck by "Red, the color of blood, the color of life, [which] flowed so abundantly in his gloomy Museum that it was like an intoxication."[13]

Whatever the aesthetic effect, the truth is that red flannel cloth goods were as real a part of the prairie landscape as redskins. Both white men and Indians had a special passion for red flannel, with the consequence that it persistently appears in the literature and the painting of the fur-trade era and later. The red flannel cloth was exported from England specifically for trade with the Indians; it was only natural that western traders and trappers would begin to use it for themselves as well. Soon, the cloth was ubiquitous in the West, and Tait and his contemporaries cannot be faulted for painting the territory as red as it really was.[14]

After only a year in this country, Tait found another way to make his name and work known. His experience with fine art prints at Agnew's gallery, together with his mastery of engraving on stone, prompted him to test the market for lithographs copied from his paintings. He contacted Nathaniel Currier, presenting as a sample of his work a large painting he described in his records as "One rubbed out. (Galloping Trapper on horse)." The picture (fig. 69) was favorably received; Tait next noted that he made a small copy of it, "Purchaser, Mr. Currier for publishing. 14 x 20. Price received $50." In January 1852, the

lithograph was copyrighted and offered to the public as *The Prairie Hunter.* "*One Rubbed Out!*" (fig. 112).

Where did Tait get such a thoroughly American colloquialism for his subtitle? Perhaps he read George Frederick Ruxton's *Life in the Far West,* published in book form in 1849, a work excelled by none in the literature of the fur trade for color, charm, and authenticity. In a poignant paragraph, Ruxton explained the Indians' belief that their own fate and that of the buffalo were inseparable: "the Great Spirit has ordained that both shall be 'rubbed out' from the face of nature at one and the same time . . . and that before many winters' snows have disappeared, the buffalo and the Red man will only be remembered by their bones, which will strew the plains." If, as seems to be the case, Ruxton was the first to translate from the Indian tongue this colorful idiom and introduce it into the English language, its appearance on Tait's print certainly helped it become used more widely.[15]

The picture itself, said Bernard DeVoto, is "admirable. A few details of the horseman's equipment are surprising, but he is a genuine

mountain man, the Indians are right, and the landscape is authentic." DeVoto's suggestion that it derives from an unknown painting by John Mix Stanley,[16] however, is less plausible than a kinship to Ranney's *The Trapper's Last Shot* (figs. 55, 56). If Tait didn't see the painting in Ranney's studio or at the exhibition of the American Art-Union, he would have had easy access to the steel engraving (fig. 125) published by the Western Art-Union in Cincinnati. Obvious are such similarities as the buckskin tunic and leggings with decorative fringes, red saddle blankets, and the placement of the horse and rider at an angle oblique to the pic-

ture plane. But Tait made some interesting changes in the composition that effectively alter the somber tension of Ranney's canvas and even suggest the possibility of a happier ending, a more cheerful mood that would make the print more attractive to paying customers.[17] Tait did not borrow anything like Ranney's forlorn title, and he removed the ominous storm clouds and brightened the sky. He lowered the horizon and thus suggested the opportunities for making a run for it across the prairie's broad expanse. Though he made the threatening Indians more visible in the background than Ranney had, they are at a suf-

ficient distance to give the trapper a chance to make a getaway. More important still, whereas Ranney mired the horse in swampy water over its hocks, Tait has him on firm ground and moving away, off to the right of the viewer, at a good clip.

To a modern audience, however, the figure of the horse in motion seems stiff and primitive. The explanation is that the artist faced a dilemma in depicting the horse at a gallop: the naked eye is not quick enough to determine the position of each leg, and yet the artist must choose to depict a single moment in a complex sequence of movements.

The convention employed here is a time-honored tradition that art historians call the "flying gallop" (or, sometimes, "the rocking-horse gallop").[18] Tait could have learned this widely known artistic device in England from the very popular sporting prints of Henry Alken, for example; in any case, the appearance of the horse did not seem strange or stilted to him or to his patrons more than a century ago.

Nathaniel Currier must have been pleased with his first Tait lithograph; he soon bought a second painting as a companion, published and copyrighted in February 1853 with the title *A Check*.

70. *Arthur F. Tait,*
The Check, *1854,*
oil on canvas, 30 × 44 in.
The Thomas Gilcrease
Institute of American History
and Art, Tulsa, Oklahoma

71. *Arthur F. Tait,*
Trapper Looking Out,
1852,
oil on canvas, 24 × 36 in.
Philbrook Art Center, Tulsa,
Oklahoma

"*Keep your distance!*" As he did on a number of occasions, Tait seems to have painted several versions of this scene, differing only in size, or the position or number of figures in the right background, or the arrows in the blanket roll. The version illustrated here, *The Check* (fig. 70), is a later one, dated 1854. Since Tait added "U.S.A." to his signature on the front, this is presumably the canvas noted in his records as "repainted for London." During the first few years in this country, Tait sent a few other paintings back to his homeland to sell, but with what success is not clear.

The likely source for Tait in this instance was Ranney's *The Retreat* (fig. 58), which he saw in 1851 at the National Academy of Design's spring exhibition. A notice of Ranney's painting in a newspaper at the time praised the picture, but added that "a more spacious view of the Prairie" would have been desirable. Tait took this advice

for his own picture by lowering the horizon again (as he had in *The Prairie Hunter—One Rubbed Out!*) and widening the scene to show more clearly the band of hostile Indians at a distance to the right, while the trapper's companion rounds up the pack horses on the left. To the pommel of the saddle Tait has attached an odd-shaped but characteristic gourd canteen as an authentic touch.[19] From the trapper's belt hangs what is probably his strike-a-light pouch in which flint, steel, and tinder were kept for starting fires. Behind the saddle is secured his "possibles" bag, containing a few personal possessions.

This picture caught the eye of Captain Randolph B. Marcy, a veteran of twenty years of campaigns and explorations from the Missouri to the Rocky Mountains and beyond. In *The Prairie Traveler,* crammed with information and advice for greenhorns planning to make the trek overland to the West, Marcy reprinted *The Check* as a strikingly

72. *Arthur F. Tait, American Frontier Life (Trapper Retreating Over River), 1852, oil on canvas, 24⅜ × 36¼ in. Yale University Art Gallery, Whitney Collections of Sporting Art, given in memory of Harry Payne Whitney, B.A. 1894, and Payne Whitney, B.A. 1898, by Francis P. Garvan, B.A. 1897, M.A. (Hon.) 1922*

apt illustration of a life-saving tactic in dealing with the Indians, which he describes as follows:

A small number of white men, in traveling upon the Plains, should not allow a party of strange Indians to approach them unless able to resist an attack under the most unfavorable circumstances. It is a safe rule, when a man finds himself alone in the prairies, and sees a party of Indians approaching, not to allow them to come near to him, and if they persist in so doing, to signal them to keep away. If they do not obey, and he be mounted upon a fleet horse, he should make for the nearest timber. If the Indians follow and press him too closely, he should halt, turn around, and point his gun at the foremost, which will often have the effect of turning them back, but he should never draw trigger unless he finds that his life depends upon the shot; for, as soon as his shot is delivered, his sole dependence, unless he have time to reload, must be upon the speed of his horse.[20]

Tait's final western genre scenes for 1852 were a pair of large canvases, *Trapper Looking Out* (fig. 71) and *American Frontier Life (Trapper Retreating Over River)* (fig. 72). Both feature the trapper on his horse seeking among the trees and shrubs that rim the beds of creeks and streams safety from an unseen enemy. Both give Tait a further chance to demonstrate his growing skill at depicting the form and textures of animals and, it must be added, reveal his less polished way of handling foliage and landscape. Both feature the same fringed buckskin garb, red saddle blanket, tin canteen, and characteristic hats.

It is interesting to note that in his *American Frontier Life (Trapper Retreating Over River)*, Tait illustrates how cumbersome a defensive weapon the long-barreled, muzzle-loading Kentucky flintlock could be. His companion behind the tree, with gun at the ready, covers his rear, while the trapper, having already fired his gun, must carefully pour powder from his horn into the pan near the hammer, a tricky maneuver while astride a moving horse.

By the mid 1850s, Tait had become increasingly busy and successful in other areas of interest. He did varied scenes for Currier: trout fishing on Long Island, duck shooting in the Jersey meadowlands not far from Ranney in Hoboken, and some dead game panels. More important was his

discovery of the Adirondack forests and lakes in upstate New York, where he could both enjoy himself as a sportsman and paint the deer, grouse, and bear that inhabited the wilderness. These canvases attracted buyers (and promised to be more lucrative than commissions from printmakers), earning him election to the National Academy of Design as associate member in the spring of 1854.

It was February 1856 when Tait's next western scenes were lithographed and published. James Ives, who had recently joined Currier's firm, felt there was a market for more prairie adventures. He escorted Tait and Louis Maurer, a talented li-

thographer he had hired, to the Astor Library, where they could study the rare folios and books of Catlin and Karl Bodmer.[21]

In *The Pursuit* (fig. 73), Tait's debt to Catlin for authenticity is the clearest. In describing a very similar scene of his own, Catlin declared the Comanche Indians to be without equal as horsemen:

Among their feats of riding, there is one that has astonished me more than anything of the kind I have seen or expect to see, in my life: a strategem of war, learned and practiced by every young man in the tribe; by which he is able to drop his body upon the side of his horse at the instant he is passing, effectually screened from his enemies' weapons as he lays in a horizontal position behind the body of his horse, with his heel hanging over the horse's back; by which he has the power of throwing himself up again, and changing to the other side of the horse if necessary.

In this wonderful condition, he will hang whilst his horse is at fullest speed, carrying with him his bow and his shield, and also his long lance of fourteen feet in length, all or either of which he will wield upon his enemy as

74. *Arthur F. Tait,* The Last War Whoop, *1855, oil on canvas, 30 × 44 in. Milwaukee Art Museum Collection, Gift of Edward S. Tallmadge*

he passes, rising and throwing his arrows over the horse's back, or with equal ease and equal success under the horse's neck.[22]

The companion painting to *The Pursuit, The Last War Whoop* (fig. 74) exhibits the same authenticity in the depiction of the Indian's weapons. The bow, for example, may seem too small, but experience had taught the Indians that short bows were more effective on horseback. The shield, or arrow-fender, was also surprisingly useful; made of parfleche—rawhide from the buffalo, smoked and hardened with glue from the hoofs—it could stop or deflect an arrow or even a bullet that did not strike it head on.[23] In both paintings, the weapons of the trapper include for the first time in Tait's work the handgun. If it came from Ranney's studio, it was probably a heavy-duty "horse pistol," since the revolver had not been invented at the time of Ranney's service with the military in Texas. In any case, Tait here documented an interesting stage in the history of the winning of the West. The American long rifle was a fine weapon in the eastern woodlands, where a man had both feet firmly on the ground, adequate cover, and time to reload. It was less effective in the open expanse of the prairies, where all the combatants were mounted. To be sure, it had greater range and accuracy than the Indian's bow and so was useful in persuading the enemy to keep his distance. However, the trapper with a double-barreled rifle would have at most two shots and then would need as much as a minute at a standstill to stop, reload, and take aim—an often fatal interval, which gave the Indian a chance to attack at full gallop and, from his snapping bow, aim and shoot as many as twenty arrows before closing in for the kill with his lance. With a pair of loaded pistols in his belt, however, the trapper could surprise the enemy with weapons especially effective from horseback at close range.

Tait may have gotten the idea for the paintings from an incident narrated in Rufus Sage's exciting adventure, *Scenes in the Rocky Mountains,* first published in 1847 but reprinted the very year Tait did the painting and Maurer copied it onto stone. The story tells of a trapper spurring his horse to its speediest to escape from a band of dreaded Blackfeet:

Four mounted Indians immediately started in pursuit, and gained rapidly upon him till they came within shooting distance, when the lone trapper turned upon them, and with his double-barreled rifle picked off two of their number and again fled.

Confident of securing their intended victim, now that they supposed his fire-arms were uncharged, the remaining two hurried after him, and in a few moments were within range of pistol-shot. The trapper then again halted, and the discharge of a pistol brought the third to the ground.

Drawing a second [pistol] from his belt, the work of slaughter would have been complete, had not the terrified savage, in his turn, fled with the utmost precipitancy.[24]

As he had sometimes done before with print-maker's commissions, Tait made two copies of different sizes for each of this pair of paintings, the smaller designed to match more closely the dimensions of the stone plate.

It is interesting to note that just two years after the print version (fig. 113) of *The Last War-Whoop* (the hyphen occurs in the print's title but not the painting's), Maurer himself composed a nearly identical scene for Currier & Ives entitled *The Last Shot.* In this version of a direct confrontation between the Indian and the white man, however, it is the latter who has fallen. The Indian dismounts and raises his tomahawk for the fatal blow when he is suddenly surprised by a last shot from the trapper's pistol. Such a scene, it has been suggested, reflected a stereotype of the Indian as a savage who, "brave and cunning as he might be, was doomed to extinction because his technology was inferior to that of Anglo-Saxon civilization."[25]

Tait himself did not seem to harbor such views of the justice of Manifest Destiny. In 1858 he was elected to full membership in the National Academy of Design and was the subject of an informative article in the *Cosmopolitan Art Journal* embellished with a woodcut portrait by Samuel Putnam Avery, a helpful friend of Tait's who was at the beginning of a career as a distinguished art dealer. Avery may also have written the article, which reports "the artist's purpose to visit the Far West, where, by domesticating with the Indian, he may become the more fully acquainted with aboriginal and forest life, and thus glean the knowledge necessary for the elaborate and original works to which he proposes to devote his best powers. It is only by such study that any artist can fully succeed."[26] As it turned out, Tait never did realize what may have been his hope ever since youth, when he met Catlin, to go west as Catlin had done. Perhaps he thought it would be foolhardy to leave New York just when his artistic talent was bringing him recognition from peers and the public. His wife, whose health was not the best, may have objected to the idea as well.

With the Civil War came an increased demand for decorative prints, especially of scenes that offered rural tranquillity or escapist adventure to provide relief from the terrible events of the battlefield reported in the daily newspapers. So in 1862, Currier & Ives commissioned Tait to paint several Adirondack sporting scenes of camping, deer hunting, and trout fishing. Two western scenes have a similar sporting motif, perhaps because the former themes of danger and death in a war between Indian and white man were no longer very palatable.

In *Buffalo Hunt* (fig. 75), Tait has painted a vivid scene of what, according to DeVoto

seems to have been the finest of all sports on this continent, perhaps the finest sport hunters have enjoyed anywhere. Every variety of big game, from elephants to grizzlies, has its own devotees, but everyone who ever hunted buffalo on horseback in the West . . . found it the consummation of the sportsman's life. This was not because the buffalo was cunning or crafty, for it was the stupidest of mammals, nor because it was hard to come by, for it existed in far greater masses than any other large animal on earth, nor because it was dangerous in itself. What gave the hunt an emotion equivalent to ecstasy was the excitement, the speed, the thundering noise, the awe-inspiring bulk of the huge animal in motion, the fury of its death, and the implicit danger of the chase. . . . For forty years this was a notable and unique American experience . . .[27]

As one of a pair of prints jointly titled *Life on the Prairie,* Currier & Ives published *The Trapper's Defense, "Fire Fight Fire"* (fig. 76). Tait was paid seventy-five dollars for his painting, twenty-four by thirty-six inches in size. As was customary, when the printmakers had finished copying the original painting onto stone, they disposed of it at an auction sale a week before Christmas 1863. The present location of this canvas is not known to us, but there is a nice preliminary sketch on millboard of the same scene in a private collection.

Those who were witnesses to the real drama of a prairie on fire sometimes were moved to write powerful descriptions of their experience in vivid prose. This, for example, is Rufus Sage's account, published in 1846:

Here was, indeed, an *"ocean of flame!"* far as the eye could reach—dancing with fiery wavelets in the wind, or rolling its burning surges, in mad fury, eager to lick up every vestige of vegetation or semblance of combustible that appeared in its way!—now shooting its glowing missiles far, far ahead, like meteors athwart the sky, or towering aloft from the weeds and tall grass, describing most hideous and fantastic forms, that, moving with the wind, more resembled a cotillion of demons among their native flames than aught terrestrial!—then driving whole sheets of the raging element into the withered herbage in front, like the advance scouts of an invading army, swept onward its desolating course, leaving in its tracks naught save a blackened waste of smoking ruins![28]

In this print Tait repeats many of the authentic details of his earlier lithographs: fringed buckskin leggings and tunic, red flannel shirts, epishemores in place on the saddles, and the gourd canteen. The most specific critique of Tait's accuracy has been John C. Ewers's complaint that, like Felix O. C. Darley, who also never saw the West, he painted "tall, thick, wheat-like grass which bears no resemblance to the ground cover of the short-grass plains on which the nomadic tribes of Plains Indians hunted buffalo." There is some merit to the criticism, though it does not apply equally to all of Tait's western scenes. In his *Buffalo Hunt,* for example, the grass looks about eight inches tall. The type and height of ground cover apparently varied a good deal as one traveled toward the Rockies. In his own description of prairie fires, Catlin distinguished between "the elevated lands and prairie bluffs, where the grass is thin and short [and] the fire slowly creeps with a feeble flame" and "the war, or hell of fires, where the grass is seven or eight feet high. . . . There are many of these meadows on the Missouri, and the Platte,

75. *Arthur F. Tait,*
Buffalo Hunt, *1861,*
oil on canvas,
24½ × 36½ in.
Private collection

and the Arkansas, of many miles in breadth, which are perfectly level, with a waving grass so high that we are obliged to stand erect in our stirrups in order to look over its waving tops."[29]

In the late winter of 1861, Tait made two small sketches, each nine by twelve inches, for Currier & Ives to consider. One of these Tait called *The Rescue;* it was apparently turned down, and nothing more is known about it. The other sketch was accepted for publication, so Tait painted a larger version for the lithographer to copy. He described it in his record book: "The Stratagem.—3 trappers in foreground laying in ambush for Indians in background with camp fire & sham figures & Indians." This painting is also unlocated, but there is the large folio print, copyrighted September 1862, with the title *American Frontier Life. The Hunter's Stratagem* (fig. 77).

It is questionable whether this was intended to be a western scene at all, despite the familiar fringed buckskin shirt and leggings. The deep forest background, the Indians on foot instead of on horses, and even the old trick of stuffing clothes to look like real men in order to deceive the attackers—all this looks more like something from Cooper's Leatherstocking tales, set in the Hudson and Mohawk valleys. Even the shift in title, from trapper to hunter, suggests the same conclusion. On the other hand, it cannot be grouped with Tait's other work of contemporary Adirondack sporting scenes, for the danger from Indians had long vanished from the region he knew so well. Perhaps, then, it is only a historical fiction to suggest an entertaining story at a time when our country was divided and at war.

To make up the customary pair of prints, there

appeared in January 1863 the second *American Frontier Life* lithograph with the title *On the War-Path* (fig. 78). It would appear that Currier & Ives selected this work as a replacement for Tait's still unlocated sketch, *The Rescue,* which for some reason was not chosen for publication. The print derives from the painting *On the Warpath,* of 1851 (fig. 67). In preparing the lithographic stone, some changes were made in the pose of the trapper-hunter that, it will be recalled, was a copy of a studio photograph of Tait himself garbed in borrowed buckskins. The trapper in the print has his hat off and, more appropriately, is crouched down somewhat, the better to conceal himself from the Indians. Presumably this alteration in Tait's original composition was made with his permission, for such tampering is something he would not ordinarily tolerate. In fact, a year or so later, after

they had changed another picture, this time clearly without his consent, Tait summarily ended his association with Currier & Ives.[30]

This period also marks the conclusion of Tait's work as a painter of western genre scenes. Since he continued to paint as a successful artist for another forty years until his death in 1905, it is natural to wonder why he ceased to portray western motifs. Perhaps, as what DeVoto called a "conscientious realist," he abandoned the subject after he had exhausted his knowledge of it. Without having traveled to see the prairies with his own eyes, he may have decided that to paint more western scenes would turn him into a mere copyist or illustrator. And, by the time the turmoil of Civil War and Reconstruction had subsided, Tait's career was too deeply committed to other fields of art for him simply to drop everything and go

77. *After Arthur F. Tait, American Frontier Life. The Hunter's Stratagem, 1862, lithograph, 20⁹⁄₁₆ × 27¼ in. Published by Currier & Ives. The Old Print Shop, Inc., New York (Kenneth M. Newman)*

west. Furthermore, like James Ives, Tait had a shrewd eye for changing public tastes and may have suspected that the market for western art was no longer so promising.

Tait found his métier as a painter of animals closer to home in the lakes and forests of the Adirondack Mountains in upstate New York and then, as he became less active as an outdoorsman, the pleasant country farms just north of Manhattan. He began by painting the horse, which appears in all his western canvases, but he became more comfortable depicting the deer and grouse, chickens and sheep.

In the history of the iconography of America's westward expansion during the mid nineteenth century, Tait's popularity was mainly a consequence of convincing realism, appealing color, and dramatic style. A largely unsophisticated public found it more difficult to appreciate the sometimes more subtle manner of his competitors, from the exotic images of the trapper by Alfred Jacob Miller to the romanticism of Charles Deas and the more democratic but often moody work of William Ranney. One reviewer, in 1854, early in Tait's career, pronounced the work of this "young Englishman" to be "thoroughly American, and in his province he paints better altogether than any of his competitors in this region."[31] Even Buffalo Bill Cody—at least according to Tait family tradition—once asked the artist how he had learned to paint the prairies with such fidelity. That these apparently realistic images were broadcast via the medium of Currier & Ives makes Tait all the more important. The popular and inexpensive lithographs reached a far wider audience than the pic-

78. *After Arthur F. Tait,* American Frontier Life. On the War-Path, *1863, lithograph (hand colored), 20³/₁₆ × 27¹/₄ in. Published by Currier & Ives. The Harry T. Peters Collection, Museum of the City of New York*

tures of his competitors, and thus he became the artist most responsible for the image of the trapper and plainsman held by the American public in the 1850s and 1860s.[32]

It is remarkable that, more than a century later, his compositions are, if anything, even more widely familiar. While the original large folio lithographs are now expensive collector's items, they have been for the past fifty years often reproduced, among other places, on a popular advertising calendar of the Travelers Insurance Company in editions of more than a million copies annually. Most of his original western canvases now hang in public museums.

Apart from the intrinsic merit of his paintings, Tait's significance today is his role in delineating what has evolved into one of the most durable icons of the West. From the trapper to the trader, scout, guide, buffalo hunter, cavalry trooper, and cowboy, it is the figure of an ordinary, weatherbeaten, often solitary man on horseback doing his job in an extraordinary country.

NOTES

1. Bernard DeVoto, *Across the Wide Missouri* (Boston: Houghton Mifflin Company, 1947), p. 397. Harold McCracken, *Portrait of the Old West* (New York: McGraw-Hill Book Company, 1952), p. 128.

2. John C. Ewers, "Fact and Fiction in the Documentary Art of the American West" in *The Frontier Reexamined,* edited by John Francis McDermott (Urbana: University of Illinois Press, 1967), pp. 79–85.

3. Warder H. Cadbury and Henry F. Marsh, *Arthur Fitzwilliam Tait, Artist in the Adirondacks. An Account of his Career . . .* [and] *A Checklist of His Works* (Newark, Del.: University of Delaware Press, 1986). With over 450 illustrations, this volume is based in part upon Tait's manuscript register of paintings, which, together with some other biographical materials, is at the Adirondack Museum, Blue Mountain Lake, N.Y. Unless otherwise noted, the book mentioned above is the source for the material contained in this essay.

4. Harry T. Peters, *Currier & Ives, Printmakers to the American People* (Garden City, N.Y.: Doubleday, Doran & Company, 1942), p. 8.

5. These recollections are part of the Tait Biography Project, housed in the library of the Adirondack Museum.

6. This is told of Bill Williams, an eccentric old mountain man, in George Frederick Ruxton, *Life in the Far West,* edited by Leroy R. Hafen (1849; Norman: University of Oklahoma Press, 1951), pp. 124–25. Buckskin, however, was not the most desirable of materials for clothing. Too hot in warm weather, it was miserably cold and clammy when wet, and took forever to dry out. Where possible, the thermal properties of a wool shirt made it the preferred garment. See Colin Taylor, "The Plains Indians' Leggings," *The English Westerner's Brand Book* 3 (January 1961): 2–8.

7. H. J. Swinney in *Currier & Ives, Chronicles of America,* edited by John Lowell Pratt (Maplewood, N.J.: Hammond Incorporated, 1968), p. 94.

8. Tait painted two versions of this canvas, and it was probably the earlier version (checklist no. 51.16), dated 1851, which went to Boston. In the second version here Tait has added a second horseman in the right background. Both paintings are thirty-six by fifty inches in size.

9. The moccasins are discussed in James A. Hanson and Kathryn J. Wilson, *The Mountain Man's Sketch Book* (Chadron, Neb.: The Fur Press, 1976), 1:36. Miller is quoted from Marvin C. Ross, *The West of Alfred Jacob Miller,* rev. and enl. ed. (Norman: University of Oklahoma Press, 1968), plate 174.

10. The Mexican Stirrup is described in Charles E. Hanson, Jr., "The Spanish Cross Stirrup," *Museum of the Fur Trade Quarterly* 15 (Spring 1979): 5. On the epishemore and the canteen, see Hanson and Wilson, *The Mountain Man's Sketch Book,* 2: 31, 42. Compare, for example, the canteen in Ranney's *Squire Boone Crossing the Mountains with Stores for his Brother Daniel, Encamped in the Wilds of Kentucky* (1852), p. 316.

11. The trapper's headgear is discussed in Hanson and Wilson, 1:6. For an example of Miller's versions, see Ross, *The West of Alfred Jacob Miller,* plate 29.

12. Reviews quoted from the *New York Herald*, 17 February 1852, p. 2; and *Literary World*, 1 May 1852, p. 316.

13. Jonathan Mayne, *The Mirror of Art, Critical Studies by Charles Baudelaire* (Garden City, N.Y.: Doubleday & Company, 1956), p. 73. The description of Charles Deas's *Long Jakes* that appeared in the *Broadway Journal*, 4 January 1845, p. 13, also took note of that trapper's "blazing red shirt." See pp. 60–62 for a detailed discussion of the Deas work.

14. For additional information on the history of red flannel cloth, see Florence M. Montgomery, *Textiles in America, 1650–1870* (New York: W. W. Norton & Co., 1984), pp. 352–53.

15. Ruxton, *Life in the Far West*, p. 106. That Ruxton introduced the term into English is suggested by John Russell Bartlett, *Dictionary of Americanisms. A Glossary of Words and Phrases Usually Regarded as Peculiar to the United States*, 2d ed. (Boston: Little, Brown & Company, 1859), p. 373. See also Peter Watts, *A Dictionary of the Old West, 1850–1900* (New York: Alfred A. Knopf, 1977), p. 277.

16. DeVoto quote from *Across the Wide Missouri*, p. 397. Stanley's North American Indian Gallery opened on Broadway on 28 November 1850 and closed in late February of 1851. For an admission ticket of twenty-five cents, Tait certainly could have seen them, but it would have been some months before he painted his own canvases. The later catalogue description of the two paintings of Joe Meek's escape from a band of Blackfoot Indians are the specific canvases that, DeVoto argues, "exactly describe" this pair of Tait's (p. 451). In fact, the descriptions don't exactly match. Furthermore, these works by Stanley are dated 1851 and may well have been painted after February of that year when the collection went to Washington. It is difficult, therefore, to entirely agree that "these are the Stanley pictures which I suspect Tait studied most carefully."

17. Charles Deas's now lost painting of *The Last Shot* of 1847 was apparently even more gloomy than Ranney's. See the review excerpts quoted on p. 71.

18. For a thorough discussion, see Irma B. Jaffe, "The Flying Gallop: East and West," *Art Bulletin* 65 (June 1983): 183–200. In 1887 Eadweard Muybridge published the final folio of his pioneering high-speed photographs in his *Animal Locomotion*, proving that the flying gallop was not true to nature. As a consequence, its use by artists was generally abandoned.

19. The review of Ranney's work appeared in the *New-York Daily Tribune*, 21 June 1851, p. 6. Tait's gourd canteen is noted in Hanson and Wilson, *The Mountain Man's Sketch Book*, 2:31.

20. Randolph B. Marcy, *The Prairie Traveler* (New York: Harper & Brothers, Publishers, 1859), p. 208.

21. Peters, *Currier & Ives*, p. 21.

22. George Catlin, *Illustrations of the Manners, Customs, and Condition of the North American Indians . . .* (London: H. G. Bohn, 1866), pp. 65–66 and plate 167.

23. Here and in the following paragraphs I am indebted to chapter 3 in Walter Prescott Webb, *The Great Plains* (New York: Grossett & Dunlap, 1931).

24. Rufus B. Sage, *Scenes in the Rocky Mountains*, edited with letters and papers by LeRoy R. Hafen (Glendale, Calif.: Arthur H. Clark Company, 1956), 2:182.

25. Dawn Glanz, *How the West Was Drawn: American Art and the Settling of the Frontier* (Ann Arbor, Mich.: UMI Research Press, 1982), p. 52.

26. *Cosmopolitan Art Journal* 2 (March and June 1858): 103–4.

27. DeVoto, *Across the Wide Missouri*, p. 36.

28. Sage, *Scenes in the Rocky Mountains*, pp. 161–62.

29. Quotes from John C. Ewers, "Not Quite Redmen: The Plains Indian Illustrations of Felix O. C. Darley," *American Art Journal* 3 (Fall 1971): 93; and George Catlin, *Letters and Notes on the Manners, Customs, and Condition of the North American Indians* (London: by the author, 1841), 2: 16–17, 20–21, and plate 128.

30. See Bartlett Cowdrey, "Arthur Fitzwilliam Tait, Master of the American Sporting Scene," *American Collector* 13 (January 1945), cover and p. 1. It was in 1865 that Currier & Ives published a later version of Tait's picture of quail, *The Cares of a Family*, with alterations from the original design that irritated Tait.

31. *New York Evening Mirror*, 21 April 1854, p. 2.

32. Glanz, *How the West Was Drawn*, p. 30.

THE AMERICAN INDIAN GENRE PAINTINGS OF CATLIN, STANLEY, WIMAR, EASTMAN, AND MILLER

HERMAN J. VIOLA, WITH H. B. CROTHERS AND MAUREEN HANNAN

Miller
Trapper's Bride
(detail, see fig. 101)

The American Indian has been a popular artistic theme since the discovery of the New World. The first artists, often without much information upon which to base their drawings, sought to satisfy the curiosity of Europeans about the appearance and customs of the native peoples who inhabited the remote and newly discovered wilderness across the sea. By the turn of the nineteenth century, much curiosity about the Native Americans remained, even on this side of the Atlantic. In addition to curiosity, however, concern arose that the Indians would disappear because of diseases and assimilation before their customs and way of life could be fully recorded. Thus, in the second quarter of the nineteenth century several documentary artists risked health and fortune by traveling into the western wilderness to record the appearance and lifeways of the Native Americans while the opportunity to do so still existed. Five of them—George Catlin, John Mix Stanley, Charles Wimar, Seth Eastman, and Alfred Jacob Miller—are the subjects of this essay.

First into the field and the one to whom all other artists of the American Indian are compared was Catlin (fig. 79), who established an impressive gallery of Indian portraits, genre scenes, and artifacts. He may not have been the most gifted of these artists, but he was certainly the most dedicated and the most influential. He was the first white man to paint the Plains Indians in their homeland, paintings that gave the American public its first and most enduring images of the West. Were it not for his example to other artists, the pictorial record of the tribes that lived west of the Mississippi would today be meager indeed.

A native of Wilkes-Barre, Pennsylvania, born 26 July 1796, Catlin was the son of a country lawyer who expected him to follow in his footsteps. Catlin did study law and was admitted to practice, but art was his ruling passion.[1] By 1821, he had moved to Philadelphia and was exhibiting his work at the Pennsylvania Academy of the Fine Arts. He developed some skill in painting miniatures in watercolor and received a few commissions for oil portraits, his most notable being of Governor DeWitt Clinton of New York.

The origin of Catlin's interest in painting Indians is unknown. He claimed that seeing a delegation of western Indians striding the streets of Philadelphia in 1824 inspired his decision to record their way of life. The real reason, however, may be revealed in a comment by the prominent art critic of the day, William Dunlap, who considered Catlin "utterly incompetent" and derided his portrait of Clinton as "the worst . . . which the city of New York possesses." Dunlap thought Catlin's decision to devote his talents to painting Indians a wise one, for he would have "no com-

by the Detroit artist James Otto Lewis, whom he commissioned to make portraits of Indian leaders at treaty conferences in Michigan Territory.[3]

Although Catlin's initial motivation for painting Indians may be obscure, his career as a recorder of their way of life is well documented. His earliest known Indian subject is an unfinished portrait of the Seneca leader Red Jacket, dated "Buffalo 1826." Two years later, while in Washington, D.C., he painted portraits of several members of a delegation of Winnebago Indians visiting the president of the United States. (The fact that King also did portraits of this delegation suggests that Catlin may well have been inspired by the War Department gallery; the inclusion of Indian genre scenes and the concept of a traveling exhibition were evidently Catlin's own contributions.) The aspiring artist did not actually launch his ambitious plans until 1830, however, when he left for St. Louis, then the hub of the American fur trade and the jumping-off point for adventurers like himself. By then he was thirty-four years old and married to Clara Gregory, who was to give him four children before her premature death in 1845.

For the next six years, Catlin roamed the West—from Lake Michigan to the High Plains and from North Dakota to the Gulf of Mexico—in a relentless search for Indian portraits and scenes. His mentor in this effort was the veteran explorer William Clark, then Superintendent of Indian Affairs in St. Louis and the ideal person to introduce an artist to the Indian tribes of the Far West. Although Catlin's exact itinerary during this six-year period is difficult to determine, he covered a remarkable amount of territory, sometimes alone, more often with fur traders or dragoons; but, extensive as his wanderings were, there is no evidence to justify his claim that he had traveled the Oregon Trail and visited the Rocky Mountains.

One thing is certain. Catlin was an incredibly fast worker. He had two styles. One is termed his studio-portrait style; the other, which forms the bulk of his oeuvre, is his field-sketching style. He could capture a human likeness, landscape, or action scene with a few deft strokes of the brush. The general character is there but details are lacking. It was this pictorial shorthand that enabled

petitor" and "nothing to ruffle his mind in the shape of criticism." Perhaps recalling this overharsh assessment, Catlin later urged viewers to judge his Indian paintings as a record of a vanishing people and not as works of art.[2]

Catlin did not originate the idea of an Indian gallery. Thomas L. McKenney, the first commissioner of Indian Affairs, had begun such a gallery in the nation's capital as early as 1822. By the time McKenney left office eight years later, his War Department gallery featured more than one hundred portraits and a collection of Indian "curiosities." Most of the portraits were by the popular Washington artist Charles Bird King, whose subjects were members of the many Indian delegations that visited the city each year. McKenney had also supplemented his collection with portraits

Catlin to compile his remarkable collection. Indeed, he seldom took the time to make a finished painting. When he did, it could be very good, as in his outstanding portrait of the Seminole leader Osceola, who was dying in prison when Catlin documented his appearance for posterity.[4]

Catlin began exhibiting his paintings in various midwestern communities as early as 1833, but it was not until he had completed his western ramblings four years later that his gallery took real shape. He opened it at Clinton Hall in New York City in late 1837 to rave reviews and packed audiences and then went on to similar triumphs in Boston, Philadelphia, and Washington.

Heady with success, Catlin decided to try his luck in Europe. In 1839, he left for England, where for five years he exhibited his gallery to appreciative audiences in London's Egyptian Hall. His catalogue lists 507 numbered paintings, 310 of them portraits, as well as an impressive collection of costumes, utensils, and weapons. The focal point of his gallery was a full-size Crow tipi with a cover made from twenty-five buffalo skins. A born showman, Catlin preceded Buffalo Bill as impressario of a Wild West show by half a century. He took to wearing Indian costume himself and even hired white actors to perform as Indians on stage. He later replaced the actors (perhaps including Arthur F. Tait; see p. 111) with various troupes of Indians who happened to be touring Europe at the time, paying them to perform to improve attendance.

When interest in his gallery began to wane, Catlin took it to Paris. The move was ill fated. There his patient and long-suffering wife fell ill and died, leaving him responsible for their four children as well as the gallery. Her death was followed a year later by that of his only son, of typhoid. Catlin, however, seems to have been oblivious to the suffering his family had to endure on behalf of his gallery. Since it seldom met expenses, he was constantly besieged by creditors. Although his prospects took a turn for the better in France, he got caught up in the revolution of 1848 and was lucky to escape the country with his gallery.

By now hopelessly in debt and trying to care for his three daughters, Catlin sought to sell his gallery. It was not a new idea. As early as 1838, he had offered it to the federal government for $150,000. He could raise little support for the purchase even when he lowered the price to $60,000. Efforts to sell it in Europe were equally fruitless, and by 1852 his financial situation had become desperate. His children went to live with his wife's family in the United States, and Catlin went briefly to debtor's prison. When it appeared that his life's work was about to fall before the auctioneer's gavel, an angel appeared in the guise of a wealthy American named Joseph Harrison, who paid most of Catlin's debts—to the tune of $40,000—but took the bulk of the gallery to America as security.

Catlin never recovered financially. He did make another set of paintings based on sketches he had retained, and he added new paintings made during later travels in South America and the Far West, but by the 1860s his gallery was no longer a novelty, and he fell into obscurity. Destitute and convinced his life had been a failure, he died in Jersey City, New Jersey, on 23 December 1872.

Meanwhile, efforts were under way to salvage his original gallery, which since Harrison's purchase had languished in a Pennsylvania warehouse, surviving two fires. Thanks to the interest of officials at the Smithsonian Institution, Harrison's widow gave the badly deteriorated collection to the federal government in 1878. It is now in the custody of the National Museum of American Art at the Smithsonian.

Although genre paintings were of secondary importance to Catlin, he appreciated the need for lively scenes of everyday life to relieve the monotony of a large series of portraits, and he included some two hundred in his gallery. For the most part, these are a disappointment to ethnologists because Catlin worked so hurriedly. The pace he kept simply did not allow much opportunity for close observation. Moreover, because his purpose was to develop a Wild West show, he tended to paint exciting hunting scenes and spectacular ceremonies rather than Indians performing mundane tasks. His genre scenes generally show Indians in large groups in dramatic settings. As

historian John Francis McDermott so aptly points out, "one turns to Catlin for a sense of the wildness of the West, not for the daily round of everyday life."[5]

Scholars agree that Catlin's finest scenes of Indian life are the Mandan Okipa ceremonies, which he witnessed in 1832. This series of paintings, which includes the striking *Bull Dance, Mandan O-Kee-Pa Ceremony* (fig. 80), is executed with unusual care and attention to detail. Perhaps he realized the unique opportunity that the Mandans had given him as an outside observer and consciously attempted to paint as accurate a depiction as possible. Whatever his motivation, scholars

owe him an enormous debt because smallpox virtually exterminated the Mandans within a few years of his visit. Ironically, invaluable as these paintings are today, they subjected Catlin to severe criticism at the time because the public found his portrayal of Mandan self-torture difficult to believe.[6]

Such criticism was not isolated. From ineptitude or perhaps myopia, Catlin distorted perspective and exaggerated the size of objects. From haste, he necessarily took shortcuts, omitted details, limited his palette, and otherwise simplified his work, thereby leaving himself open to the criticism that his paintings were misrepresentative and even untruthful. Naturalist John J. Audubon, upon seeing the Mandan earth lodges in 1843, noted in his journal: "The Mandan huts are very far from looking poetical, although Mr. Catlin has tried to render them so by placing them in regular rows, and all the same size and form, which is by no means the case. But different travellers have different eyes." The artist Alfred Jacob Miller was more caustic. "There is in truth . . . a great deal of humbug about Mr. George Catlin," he wrote. "Luckily for him there are but few persons who have travelled the same ground."[7]

Eventually, however, historian Bernard DeVoto, stressing Catlin's contribution to ethnology, began the process of rescuing the artist from the oblivion to which contemporary critics had consigned him: "It is true that he was an enthusiast and even a monomaniac . . . [and] made many mistakes, and even that he falsified or invented some details. Nevertheless, he is in the main reliable and . . . American ethnology may be said to begin with Catlin."[8]

Ball Play of the Choctaw—Ball Up (fig. 81), one of a series of excellent paintings on this topic that he sketched near Fort Gibson in 1834, is a fine example of Catlin's work. Catlin loved the excitement of Indian games and claimed he would go twenty miles out of his way to attend one. "In this game," he wrote, "every player was dressed alike, that is *divested* of all dress, except the girdle and the tail, . . . and in these desperate struggles for the ball, when it is *up* (where hundreds are running together and leaping, actually over each other's heads, and darting in between their adversaries' legs, tripping and throwing, and foiling each other in every possible manner, and every voice raised to the highest key, in shrill yelps and barks)! there are rapid successions of feats, and of

81. *George Catlin,*
Ball Play of the
Choctaw—Ball Up,
1834–35,
oil on canvas mounted on aluminum, 19½ × 27½ in. National Museum of American Art, Smithsonian Institution, Washington, D.C., Gift of Mrs. Joseph Harrison, Jr.

incidents, that astonish and amuse far beyond the conception of any one who has not had the singular good luck to witness them."[9] The detail in is remarkable, for in many of his group scenes most of the figures are mere stickmen.

Hunting scenes were another favorite with Catlin, who was at his best when depicting buffaloes. As DeVoto affirmed, "from Catlin on every artist who painted the West . . . did at least one 'buffalo chase' in exactly Catlin's terms."[10] *Buffalo Chase, Mouth of the Yellowstone* (fig. 82) was sketched on the Upper Missouri in 1832.

Catlin described the scene "as animals dying on the ground passed over." According to William Truettner, who has examined the artist's work in great detail, Catlin composed this painting from several buffalo and landscape studies. The other scene, *Buffalo Chase in Winter, Indians on Snowshoes* (fig. 5), reflects the artistic license Catlin sometimes took. He never saw Plains Indians hunting in snow, and the hunters here are wearing their summer war clothes![11]

Mention should also be made of Catlin's writings, for his genre scenes really depend on them to be fully understood. He took copious notes on the religious practices of the Indians, their ceremonies, laws, codes of morality, and games. In fact, he recorded virtually every intimate and traditional aspect of their lives his informants were willing to share. His most popular publications, besides the catalogues that described the paintings and artifacts in his gallery, are *Letters and Notes on the Manners, Customs, and Condition of the North American Indians,* published in London in 1841; and *Catlin's North American Indian Portfolio* (fig. 108), consisting of twenty-five lithographs, which appeared three years later. In addition to supplementing the author's always precarious income, the publications were intended to complement his gallery. They also demonstrate his passionate commitment to interpreting the life and customs of the American Indian to the rest of the world.

Catlin is a controversial figure in the history of American art, his position rather analogous to Audubon's. He was not the most talented painter of his time, not even of Indian life. He sometimes took liberties with the truth—like his claim to have visited the Rocky Mountains—and he had a strong streak of the huckster in him. Nevertheless, Catlin deserves the plaudits that only recently have been accorded him by DeVoto and others. In art, as well as anthropology, his niche should be secure.

The documentary artist closest to Catlin in scope and importance is John Mix Stanley (fig. 83). In fact, their careers have amazing parallels. Both saw Indian paintings as a way to fame and fortune. Both tried to sell their galleries to the Smithsonian Institution. Neither closed the sale, but Catlin's gallery, which survived two fires while in storage, is at the Smithsonian today, whereas Stanley's gallery, placed there for safekeeping, was destroyed in the Smithsonian fire of 1865. Were it not for that fire, Catlin's reputation might well be overshadowed by that of Stanley, often acclaimed the better artist by contemporaries. Seth Eastman, for one, considered Stanley's paintings "far superior" and declared that they gave the viewer "a better idea of the Indian than any works in Mr. Catlin's collection."[12] This is high praise coming from a fellow artist who, of those here under discussion, was the only one to know Indians from extended firsthand experience.

John Mix Stanley was born to a tavernkeeper on 17 January 1814, in Canandaigua, New York, once the heartland of the Iroquois Confederation.[13] Legend has it that Indians, including Red Jacket, whom Stanley later featured in his large oil painting *The Trial of Red Jacket* (1868; Buffalo and Erie County Historical Society), patronized his father's tavern. These visits supposedly left a lasting impression upon the young boy who, at age fourteen, was apprenticed to a wagonmaker in nearby Naples. Six years later, Stanley moved to Detroit, where he became a house and sign painter and befriended James Bowman, an itinerant portrait painter, who admired his work and offered him free instruction. Stanley and Bowman eventually moved to Chicago, where they may have opened a short-lived studio and gallery. If they did, the venture quickly failed and they went their separate ways. Stanley wandered about the Old Northwest, visiting Galena, Fort Snelling, and Green Bay before returning to the East. He lived briefly in New York, Philadelphia, and Baltimore, apparently supporting himself as a portrait painter while working to improve his artistic skills.

By 1841, according to his notices in the local newspaper seeking commissions, Stanley had reached Troy, New York. This move marked the turning point in his life because here he decided to concentrate his energies on creating a gallery of Indian portraits and formed a partnership with another young man, Caleb Sumner Dickerman. An aspiring artist himself, Dickerman worked as a clerk in his father's marble yard. Although little is known of the actual arrangement, Dickerman

appears to have been the business agent and Stanley the artist.

While in Troy, Stanley also learned the use of the Daguerrean camera. Perhaps he thought the camera would have a detrimental impact on the careers of aspiring portrait painters and wanted to develop a backup skill, or perhaps he saw it as a useful tool in his work. Whatever the explanation, Stanley is known to have carried a camera with him in his search for portraits, making him one of the earliest photographers of the Indian.

Stanley probably decided to paint Indian portraits in hopes that they would be more exciting and profitable than the paintings he had been doing. Certainly, on the surface, it would appear that Indian galleries were a means to financial success. Not only had Catlin's gallery, now in Europe, enjoyed a handsome patronage during its brief eastern United States tour, but also Thomas L. McKenney seemed to be reaping a fortune by selling lithographic copies of the portraits in the War Department gallery. McKenney and his partner, James Hall, for several years had been

advertising their monumental project, titled *History of the Indian Tribes of North America,* which consisted of biographies and portraits of 120 Indian leaders taken from the War Department collection. Published on a subscription basis, the project had been before the public for almost a decade by the time the lithographs were completed in 1842. Still another gallery was being offered for sale by James Otto Lewis, the painter of some sixty portraits in the War Department gallery. When Lewis learned of McKenney's publication plans, he immediately brought out his own collection under the title *The Aboriginal Port-Folio* (fig. 84), which actually appeared before the more ambitious and polished *History of the Indian Tribes.*[14] What Stanley and Dickerman could not have known, of course, was that, appearances notwithstanding, none of these ambitious projects was actually profitable.

Despite such formidable competition, the partners must have thought the market could stand yet another Indian gallery. The fact that their portraits would not duplicate many of those in either the King or Catlin galleries was a point in their favor. The partners intended to focus their efforts on the Far West, the region between the Rocky Mountains and the Pacific Ocean just then being opened to settlement.

Dickerman wrote the secretary of war for a "general letter of introduction" to the officers commanding the military posts on the western frontier giving the partners permission "to take the portraits of the most prominent chiefs of the various tribes" and to obtain "a collection of Indian curiosities similar to the one collected by George Catlin." The approval came not from the secretary of war but the commissioner of Indian Affairs, who assured them that "it has been the practice of the Department to allow citizens of the United States to enter the Indian Country, when their purposes are lawful, and that [they] may receive the aid and protection of the officers of the government written permits have been given to them for that purpose."[15]

Armed with the necessary approval, the partners proceeded immediately with their plan. December 1842 found them at Fort Gibson, a military outpost in the northeast corner of present-day Oklahoma. Stanley was to paint there and in areas as far south as Texas for the next three years. During this time, he attended three intertribal councils, which gave him ample opportunity to obtain portraits. The most significant council was at Tahlequah, the Cherokee capital, which was attended by ten thousand Indians from more than a dozen tribes.

By the middle of 1845, Stanley and Dickerman were in Cincinnati preparing their gallery for exhibition. According to the catalogue, it included eighty-three paintings and an assortment of Indian artifacts. Most of the paintings were portraits, but there were about a dozen landscapes and scenes of village life: The critics were enthusiastic but attendance left much to be desired. From Cincinnati, the partners took their gallery to Louisville, where they again suffered a poor patronage although newspaper editors described Stanley as "a young artist of great merit. His pictures are larger

84. *James Otto Lewis (1799–1858),* The Aboriginal Port Folio *(cover), 1835–36, lithograph, 18¼ × 11½ in. Collection of Herman J. Viola*

than those of Catlin and, we should judge, not inferior in execution. The whole form an excellent and life-like representation of Indian life and manners."[16]

Despite their indifferent success, the partners were not unduly discouraged. Stanley closed the gallery in March 1846 and returned to the West to obtain more portraits. In Kansas he did portraits of Keokuk and other Sac and Fox leaders before continuing on to Santa Fe, where the outbreak of war with Mexico interrupted his plans. Stanley decided to join the Stephen Watts Kearney expedition to San Diego, serving as a draftsman with the topographical engineers. From San Diego, he went to San Francisco and then Oregon, where he had a narrow brush with death when he stumbled into an Indian uprising at Marcus Whitman's mission station at Waiilatpu. Only because the hostiles mistook him for an employee of the Hudson's Bay Company was his life spared. During these wanderings Stanley evidently lived much as he had in Indian Territory, painting portraits of whites for his livelihood and of Indians for his gallery.

Stanley went next to Hawaii, where he was to spend eighteen months. Although he did portraits of the royal family, he seems to have done relatively little painting, and his stay there remains a mysterious interlude.

Leaving Hawaii in November 1849, Stanley returned to Troy and once again joined up with Dickerman, who had spent the preceding four years there waiting for him and taking care of the gallery. The partnership evidently remained intact, despite Stanley's prolonged absence, because in the fall of 1850 they again took the gallery—now enlarged to 134 paintings—on the road. As before, they moved from city to city, hoping for the best but faring poorly at the door. "If I had known the extent of the task I had assumed, the adversity, the privations and the fatigues to which I was to be exposed, and the frequent despondencies that were to come over me," Stanley later confessed, "I would no longer have prosecuted the work upon which I had embarked."[17]

From Troy, the partners went to Albany, New Haven, Hartford, New York, and Washington,

D.C., which became the gallery's final destination. Somehow Stanley persuaded Joseph Henry, the first secretary of the Smithsonian Institution, to exhibit his paintings. While the gallery was displayed in the Castle on the Mall, Stanley added a few paintings, including portraits of five Pueblo Indians who visited the capital in 1851.

Henry's support is significant, for throughout most of the 1850s the secretary strongly resisted every effort to make the Smithsonian a museum. He envisioned it as a community of scholars dedicated to scientific research. That Henry consented to exhibit Stanley's gallery suggests that his paintings were highly esteemed for their ethnological as well as artistic value.

Stanley evidently hoped that either the Smithsonian or the federal government would buy the gallery and thereby free him of the financial burden it entailed. Financial problems continually beset the artist, who went so far as to borrow twelve hundred dollars from Henry. An indication of his need to find other sources of funds was his decision to sign on as an illustrator with the Pacific Railroad Survey in Washington Territory. This survey, one of several authorized by the Congress to determine the best route for a transcontinental railroad, was led by Isaac I. Stevens, governor of Washington Territory. As artist, Stanley was to sketch the character and scenery of the country surveyed.

As before, Stanley carried his Daguerrean equipment with him, which he used to take portraits as well as landscapes. The Indians, according to his son, were amazed at his abilities with a paintbrush, but they were even more astounded by his photographic portraits produced with the aid of sunlight. In the expedition report, Stevens wrote: "Mr. Stanley . . . was busily occupied during our stay at Fort Union with his daguerreotype apparatus, and the Indians were greatly pleased with their daguerreotypes."[18] Stanley, who gave duplicate images to the Indians who posed for him, used the daguerreotypes to prepare finished oils in his studio.

The six months Stanley spent with the Stevens expedition were his last in the Far West. Upon his return to Washington, he married Alice C.

English and turned to other ways of earning a living, although he continued to paint Indian themes. A major source of income was the extensive reports of the railroad surveys that the government published. Stanley furnished illustrations for two volumes and is the artist most heavily represented in the set. He also painted two panoramas, one of western scenes and one of scenes from the Civil War, as well as portraits on commission and scenes of Indian life based on sketches and imagination.

Like Catlin, Stanley did not benefit materially from his gallery, which he valued at nineteen thousand dollars. Whether Dickerman, who had since dropped from view, was to share in the proceeds of a sale, is not known. Regardless, a sale never occurred, even though prospects were enhanced when Charles Bird King's collection was added in 1858. Together, according to Joseph Henry, the Stanley and King galleries formed "the most valuable collection in existence of illustrations of the features, costumes, and habits of the aborigines of this country."[19]

85. *John Mix Stanley,* Game of Chance, *ca. 1853, oil on canvas, 28¼ × 39⅜ in. The Thomas Gilcrease Institute of American History and Art, Tulsa, Oklahoma*

86. *John Mix Stanley,*
Gambling for the Buck,
1867,
oil on canvas, 20 × 15⅞ in.
Stark Museum of Art,
Orange, Texas

Several times over the next decade, Stanley petitioned both houses of Congress and the Smithsonian's board of regents to buy his gallery. The petitions did arouse some congressional support, but not enough to generate an appropriation. Eventually, Stanley tried elsewhere. The New-York Historical Society and the University of Michigan were interested, and he probably would have succeeded in completing a sale had fate not intervened. On 24 January 1865, fire destroyed the Smithsonian's art gallery, consuming all but five or six of Stanley's paintings and one or two of King's. As Henry later explained to Stanley, who was now living in Detroit, "an attempt was made to secure the pictures, but while one of the workmen of the Institution was on a ladder handing down some of the larger ones, the ceiling of the room gave way and precipitated the burning embers on the floor below; the attempt had therefore to be abandoned, all were consumed except the following: Indian Council, Hunter's Escape, Scalp Dance, Buffalo Hunt, Indian on Black Horse, Indian Chief on Horseback."[20]

Although Stanley never received a penny in compensation, his situation was not as dire as one would have imagined. Two years before the fire, he had moved to Detroit, where he finally found a home. The citizens of Detroit welcomed the artist, giving him several important commissions and helping make his final years both pleasant and prosperous. Besides painting the portraits of some of the city's leading figures, Stanley ventured into the field of chromolithography, using the process to publish copies of his most popular Indian paintings. He also did two monumental canvases in the years before his death, one of them being *The Trial of Red Jacket,* completed in 1868. Featuring 172 individuals, it reportedly grossed eight thousand dollars in admission fees during a tour of midwestern cities. Stanley evidently remained productive until his death in April 1872, at age fifty-eight.

Thanks to McKenney's *History of the Indian Tribes of North America,* we have a fairly complete record of King's Indian gallery. The same, unfortunately, cannot be said for Stanley's work. Despite the enormous loss, however, enough remains to secure his position in the history of western art. Julie Ann Schimmel, his major biographer, has located more than three hundred images by this prolific artist. Of these, twenty are Indian portraits and another fifty are scenes of tribal life.

Stanley's work is difficult to categorize. He had a wide range of styles, and his paintings present an uneven mixture of quality from mediocre to very good. Because of his gallery, most people acquainted with his work focus on the paintings he did in the 1840s and fail to realize these represent only the initial efforts of a thirty-year career during which he painted a number of historical topics and landscapes in addition to commissioned portraits. Throughout his active life, however, his major interest was documenting the American Indian.

According to the catalogue published by the Smithsonian in 1852, Stanley's gallery consisted of 152 paintings, all but 32 of them portraits. Stanley did most of his genre paintings in the 1850s and 1860s, after placing his gallery in the Smithsonian Institution, when he was far from the West and no longer able to document specific events or individuals. The majority of these scenes seem to have been of Indians at work or play and in harmony with themselves and nature. Although not a romanticist, Stanley did idealize his subjects, and his genre scenes, except for his hunts, are characterized by tranquillity and dignity. Although, like Catlin, he tended to paint Indians in their finest ceremonial clothing, his images otherwise are factual and simply stated. It is this quality, Schimmel believes, that led Eastman to prefer Stanley's work to Catlin's.[21]

One of the themes that attracted Stanley was gambling, a pastime that all North American tribes enjoyed. Of his surviving canvases, four are on this subject. *Game of Chance* (fig. 85), painted in the early 1850s, shows a group of Indians playing cards, one diversion of white civilization that Native Americans eagerly adopted. The second painting, *Blackfeet Card Players* (fig. 3), although done more than a decade later, is quite similar in mood and setting. Gambling is also the topic of the painting that critics consider Stanley's finest effort, *Gambling for the Buck* (fig. 86), which he completed in 1867. Interestingly, the atmosphere is virtually the same as in *The Disputed Shot* (fig. 87), which shows three white trappers—instead of three Indians—pondering the disposition to be made of a handsome buck that one of them has killed. By the time Stanley painted this canvas in 1858, fur trappers were already becoming American folk heroes.

Stanley may not have had Catlin's flair for showmanship, but he was his equal in virtually every other artistic respect. He even attempted to publish a portfolio of his paintings, perhaps hoping thereby to recreate and preserve his Indian gallery in published form, but his untimely death ended that project. Regardless, on the basis of his surviving paintings alone, it is obvious that he deserves the acclaim that only belatedly he has received as one of the premier artists of the American Indian.

Like Catlin and Stanley, Charles Wimar (fig. 88) developed as a young man a lifelong fascination with Indians.[22] He was a native of Germany and did not even come to the United States until he was about fifteen years old. Wimar was born in Siegburg near Bonn on 19 February 1828. After his father died seven years later, his mother married a man named Becker, who immigrated alone to St. Louis and eventually opened a tavern. Once the business was established, Becker sent for his family. Wimar arrived with his mother and stepbrother and step-sisters in 1842, but the transition to American life was difficult for the shy, introspective teenager. Because of his broken English, the boy much preferred the company of the Indians who frequently camped near his step-father's tavern when visiting St. Louis to trade furs and buy supplies.

Two years after his arrival, Wimar was apprenticed to Leon de Pomerade, a local house painter and folk artist. Wimar spent some six years with Pomerade. During this period, he traveled with his mentor up the Mississippi, caught his first glimpse of the western landscape, and became increasingly obsessed with sketching Indians and their way of life. Pomerade may have been an artist of limited ability, but he could recognize talent. He urged his young apprentice to get formal training and then devote himself "to that peculiar style of art" and preserve a record of the Indians for posterity before they would be "a race clean gone."[23]

Anticipating a bequest that never materialized, Wimar left for Germany in 1852 and entered the Düsseldorf Academy, where he studied first under Josef Fay and then under a fellow German American, Emanuel Leutze. Since the academy encouraged large-scale, dramatic paintings on heroic or historical themes, Wimar complied with scenes of Indian life taken from books by James Fenimore Cooper and other writers on American frontier themes. Always concerned with accuracy, the young artist assembled as many authoritative sources as possible, including prints and books by Catlin. He even prevailed upon his parents to send him an Indian costume and ornaments from St.

89. *Charles Wimar,*
The Captive Charger,
1854,
oil on canvas, 30 × 41 in.
The Saint Louis Art
Museum, Gift of Miss Lillie
B. Randell

Louis. Because of his black hair, dark complexion, high cheekbones, and his preoccupation with Indians, his fellow students thought he was one himself, which greatly amused Wimar. "Here they call me the Indian painter," he told his parents. "I laughed myself sick that many of them think I am a descendant of the Indians, and I had the greatest trouble to talk them out of that."[24] Even after his return to the United States, Wimar had

difficulty persuading people otherwise, especially since he favored buckskin clothing.

As he finished his paintings, Wimar would send them home to St. Louis for sale to raise money to continue his training. Among the paintings done in Düsseldorf were *The Captive Charger* (fig. 89) and *The Attack on an Emigrant Train* (fig. 90). *The Captive Charger,* completed in 1854 and one of his finest efforts, sold almost immediately for

three hundred dollars. "This pleases me very much," the elated artist wrote, "because it is the main thing to make money quickly. The pictures I am working on now will presumably bring more, because one is much larger than all the others and I might state much better. When I shall have the costumes and studies I shall make better things . . . [although] there are people who enjoy my things better than I do."[25]

Wimar painted two versions of *The Attack on an Emigrant Train*, an incident he read about in *Impressions de voyages et aventures dans le Mexique, la haute Californie et les régions de l'or* by Gabriel Ferry. The version illustrated here is believed to be the last major oil he did at Düsseldorf. "It represents," he told his parents, "a caravan of gold-diggers encamped on the prairie who are defending themselves in the camp against an attack by

90. *Charles Wimar,*
The Attack on an
Emigrant Train, *1856,*
oil on canvas, 55¼ × 79 in.
The University of Michigan
Museum of Art, Ann Arbor,
Bequest of Henry C. Lewis

an Indian band. You will already get the idea from the enclosed picture which I took after my first drawing."[26]

Upon returning to St. Louis in 1856, Wimar worked so energetically developing a study collection that one visitor described his studio as "a perfect museum of Indian curiosities."[27] Much of his source material he obtained by making extended trips up the Mississippi and Missouri rivers on board American Fur Company steamboats. These vessels went north each spring to bring supplies to their distant trading posts and to pick up furs and would, for a nominal sum, carry passengers, usually hunters and adventurers. Wimar on at least three occasions availed himself of such an opportunity to pursue his art while collecting firsthand information on the geography, wildlife, and tribes of the Upper Missouri region.

Wimar fully described his most extensive trip, made between May and November 1858, for a German newspaper.[28] He carried an ambrotype camera—purchased for one hundred dollars—that he used to capture portraits and scenes of Indian life. Wimar recalled that at a Yankton Sioux village about eleven hundred miles above St. Louis, a large group of gaudily dressed Indians paraded proudly on the shore alongside the boat until its steam calliope sent them fleeing in terror. Nonetheless, the artist managed to take several photographs, and later, when some of the chiefs came on board, he filled five pages of his notebook with detailed sketches of their clothing, weapons, and headdresses. Later in the trip, Gros Ventre warriors at Fort Berthold threatened to kill him when he attempted to take their pictures and forced him to put the camera away. The Gros Ventres believed that they would die of smallpox if they were photographed. Despite their fears and threats, their costumes were so picturesque that Wimar used subterfuge to get his pictures, standing behind a curtain and shooting through a hole.

Wimar left the steamboat at Fort Union, twenty-five hundred miles above St. Louis, and joined one of the parties going up the Yellowstone River to trade with the Crow Indians. On this excursion, the party shot sixty-four buffaloes for food, affording the artist a wonderful opportunity to make careful studies of their anatomy, hooves, and heads. He later put these sketches to good use for his masterpiece and largest canvas, *Buffalo Hunt* (fig. 91), which no less an authority than Buffalo Bill Cody declared to be accurate and true to life.[29]

Wimar's foreground placement of the action here and in *The Attack on an Emigrant Train,* combined with his meticulous draftsmanship, give these paintings great visual appeal. His virtuosity lends his art validity, even though we have seen their clichéd successors and banal imitators hundreds of times in prints and western movies. Wimar's paintings are the most dramatic of the five artists under discussion, but they are not sensational or melodramatic. Certainly, the narrative content of his genre scenes is less theatrical than that of his contemporary fellow artist of St. Louis, Charles Deas.

Unfortunately, as early as 1857 failing health began to keep Wimar from his easel. Sometimes he coughed "so badly" he could not work, a sign that he was already suffering from "consumption," the dreaded tuberculosis that was to take his life only six years after he returned from Germany.

During that short time, Wimar produced some forty-five paintings. Most were small, little more than finished sketches. *The Buffalo Dance* (fig. 1), completed in 1860, is one of the finest from this period. The subject is the same as Catlin's *Bull Dance* (fig. 80) but more handsomely executed. Wimar must have used the drawings by Catlin and Karl Bodmer as models for this impressive painting, however, because it is doubtful the remnant population of that once powerful and important tribe were performing the Bull Dance by the time Wimar visited the Mandan country.

Failing health may have slowed him down, but it did not keep him from falling in love. On 7 March 1861, Wimar married Anna von Senden of St. Louis. They had one child, named Winona, who died in 1864, less than two years after her father.

Despite his rising success as an artist, Wimar struggled financially and had to tackle a variety of tasks to make a living. In 1861 he received his most important public commission, decorating

the rotunda of the St. Louis Court House. Wimar painted four large panels as well as a number of associated portraits and allegorical figures. He asked five hundred dollars for this commission, but the city fathers were so pleased they paid him a thousand. Although one of Wimar's half-brothers assisted him in the mammoth project, the intense activity it demanded hastened his death. His health deteriorated rapidly, and workmen eventually had to carry the dying artist to his scaffold, as he insisted upon completing his commission. Finish it he did, but a letter from the last weeks of his life indicates how severe a trial it was for Wimar and his family: "I feel a little stronger," he wrote his brother, but "otherwise everything is the same, I can't talk at all and swallowing is not at its best, but improves daily. It is very bad that I can't get advice from my doctor, one loses all confidence."[30] He was only thirty-four when he died on 28 November 1862.

Had it not been for his premature death, which came just as he was realizing his artistic potential, Wimar's reputation today might well have eclipsed that of his fellow documentary artists. "He was the youngest of the first generation of Indian painters," wrote one historian, "yet none of them—Catlin, Eastman, Miller, or Stanley—are the equal of Wimar in the authenticity of their record, the command of their craft, nor in imaginative power."[31]

91. *Charles Wimar,*
Buffalo Hunt, *1861,*
oil on canvas, 36 × 61 in.
The Thomas Gilcrease
Institute of American History
and Art, Tulsa, Oklahoma

Seth Eastman (fig. 92) differs from Catlin, Stanley, and Wimar in several respects. A graduate of West Point, he was a career army officer to whom art was an avocation and not a means of livelihood. Eastman also had much more contact with Indians on the American frontier, some seven years in all, developing a deep respect for them as a people and a regard for their culture that was highly unusual for his day. In fact, he learned the language of the Santee Sioux and fathered a child by a Sioux mistress.[32] His regard for Indians and their lifeways is evident in his work, which is not romantic or sensational but almost reportorial in nature. His paintings are so carefully detailed— doubtless reflecting his experience as a topo- graphical engineer—that one could identify spe- cific objects, if they still existed.

Eastman must have had considerable innate ar- tistic ability because he received little formal training either before or after he entered West Point. Indeed, during his student years at the academy, the drawing master was Thomas Gambrede, of whom one critic wrote: "his utter want of skill or knowledge in the art [of drawing]

must have required uncommon talents . . . to teach that which he did not know."[33]

Born in 1808 at Brunswick, Maine, Eastman entered the academy in 1824. Upon graduating five years later, he served briefly at Fort Crawford and Fort Snelling in Michigan Territory and then returned to the academy as an assistant teacher of drawing, a position he held until 1840. He fol- lowed that assignment with a few months in Florida hunting the elusive Seminoles before being reassigned to Fort Snelling—today Minneapolis, but then the heartland of the Santee Sioux. He remained in Minnesota for seven years. There- after, until the Civil War, he was stationed at a variety of western outposts interspersed with as- signments in Washington, D.C. He saw no com- bat during the war, serving instead as a recruiting officer in Maine and as the military governor of Cincinnati. Although he was on the retired list after 1863, Eastman remained on active duty for several more years. In 1866, he attained the brevet rank of brigadier general and command of the Harrodsburg Military Asylum in Kentucky. He held that post only a short time before returning to Washington, where he died on 31 August 1875.

Throughout his military career, Eastman was never far from an easel or drawing board. His art sprang from interest and commitment, however, and not from a need to support himself and his growing family, which began in 1835 with his marriage to Mary Henderson. Nonetheless, he was remarkably successful in getting assignments that allowed him to practice art while on active duty, beginning with the post as drawing instructor at West Point. Later, in the 1850s, he served five years in Washington assigned to the Bureau of Indian Affairs as the primary illustrator for Henry Schoolcraft's six-volume *Indian Tribes of the United States,* for which he produced some three hundred plates. Following his retirement, he was called back to active duty by the Congress, which passed a joint resolution in 1867 authorizing him to paint pictures to decorate the Capitol and to paint scenes of Indian life for the room assigned to the House Committee on Indian Affairs. In 1870, he received a similar commission to paint seventeen pictures of forts for the House Committee on Military Affairs.

Although he was not a great artist, Eastman's work is very important ethnographically. What is particularly impressive about it is the depth and breadth of subject matter. By the time he left Fort Snelling, he had assembled a sizeable collection of sketches and paintings—some four hundred pieces. His linguistic abilities and personal relationships naturally gave him insights into Santee Sioux culture and access to ceremonies not available to other white men. Also, while other artists tended to focus on the sensational or colorful, Eastman concerned himself with the everyday life of the Indian. Warfare, for example, is represented in his oeuvre by just five paintings; games, hunting, ceremonies, and village life predominate. This emphasis makes his work especially significant today.

Like many other artists of his era, Eastman found the camera an invaluable tool. "If anything were wanting to complete our opportunities for gaining all [the] information that was of interest, we found it in the daguerreotype," wrote Mary Eastman. When her husband learned of a feast or ceremony that he wanted to record, he would prepare his Daguerrean apparatus ahead of time and then, when the Indians least expected it, "transferred the group to his plate." Upon seeing the pictures, their "awe, consternation, astonishment and admiration, surpassed description."[34]

Mary Eastman obviously shared her husband's sympathetic interest in Indians. Not only did she welcome them to her home and table, but she also tried to learn their language and songs. Before leaving Minnesota, in fact, she completed a manuscript about her experiences among the Indians and later published it under the title *Dahcotah; or, Life and Legends of the Sioux around Fort Snelling.* The book is conspicuously silent about her husband's Indian daughter and grandchildren.

Seth Eastman must have devoted a good portion of his military salary to his ethnographic interests because his wife later petitioned Congress—unsuccessfully—for a partial reimbursement. The basis for her claim was that Schoolcraft's history, which was an official government publication, benefited from the resource material they had collected. Her husband, she wrote, had been "obliged to purchase from the Indians their dresses and utensils, and to pay them also for the privilege of painting their customs and ceremonies from life." Because of this, all their "private means" were spent "in the collection of materials for his work—the purchase of dresses, utensils of war and domestic use,—of an instrument by which he took daguerreotype views of their dances, feasts, &c while they were celebrating them; and also to pay Indians who assisted him to persuade others to consent to the representation of customs they deemed sacred—to give them clothes, and often food for a considerable period of time, while he found their presence a necessity or assistance."[35]

Since the art buyers of Eastman's day seldom valued his genre paintings, it is fortunate that economics did not dictate the artist's taste in subject matter. Although he was not dependent on his art to support his family, which quickly boasted five children, he did welcome the additional income of an occasional sale. Eastman, for example, was especially pleased with a painting titled *Indian's Burial* (The Thomas Gilcrease Institute of Amer-

ican History and Art, Tulsa), completed in November 1847. He described the large canvas as "highly finished and painted from nature." Expecting it to fetch at least $500, he gave it to a friend who offered it for sale in St. Louis. No one wanted it. Eventually, the painting was sold in New York City, but Eastman netted only $120 after expenses. This seems to have been the rule rather than the exception whenever Eastman attempted to sell his work; the buying public did not share his appreciation for such mundane topics as skinning buffaloes and spearing muskrats in winter.

Eastman's paintings are excellent examples of both his artistic and ethnographic skills. *Medicine Dance* (1848; fig. 93), painted from life, depicts an episode in the ceremony by which a Sioux member is initiated into the Medicine Society. The clarity and comprehensiveness of the scene suggest that Eastman worked from one or more daguerreotype references.

Typical of his interest in recording ordinary activities of tribal life is *Sioux Indians* (fig. 94), a tranquil scene depicting a group of Sioux men and women about to embark on a canoe trip. Painted in Washington in 1850, it is one of his finest efforts.

Two of Eastman's paintings document the excitement and enthusiasm of lacrosse, a game popular with the Indians of the Upper Midwest and widely enjoyed today by youngsters across the country. According to Mary Eastman, the object of the game pictured in *Ballplay of the Sioux on the St. Peters River in Winter* (1848; fig. 95) was to succeed "in throwing the ball [a piece of baked clay covered with deer skin] into a space marked off. . . . The ball is not thrown by hand," but cast with "a long stick with a circular frame at the end of it; this they call a bat stick, and, simple as it looks, requires great skill to manage it."[36] Similar in concept is an especially fine painting titled *Lacrosse Playing Among the Sioux Indians* (1851; fig. 10).

Indians readily adapted to their own use the games carried west by the white men they encountered. We have already seen Stanley's paintings that show card playing by Native Americans. Eastman depicted a similar scene. *Chippewa Indians*

94. *Seth Eastman,*
Sioux Indians, *1850,*
oil on canvas,
26⅜ × 38½ in.
Joslyn Art Museum, Omaha,
Nebraska

Playing Checkers (1848; fig. 96) features two men studying the board, a hovering kibitzer looking over their shoulders. Eastman had ample opportunity to develop this painting, according to his wife, because the Chippewa players had spent considerable time in the guardhouse, where they passed the time away smoking and playing cards and checkers.

As an artist, Eastman is more akin to Catlin than to Wimar. His skills were not finely honed, and the primitivism evident in his paintings probably was due to lack of training rather than to deficiency of talent. But, in composition and characterization, *Chippewa Indians Playing Checkers* does not suffer in comparison with *The Checker Players* (1850; fig. 23) of George Caleb Bingham, a master of American genre painting. Eastman is a worthy member of that group of artists who sought to preserve for posterity a record of the Native Americans.

96. *Seth Eastman,*
Chippewa Indians Playing
Checkers, *1848,*
oil on canvas, 30 × 25 in.
The Regis Collection,
Minneapolis

Alfred Jacob Miller (fig. 97), probably the most gifted of the artists under discussion in this essay, differs from the others in that he went west, not from any burning desire to paint Indians but because he was commissioned to do so. Yet were it not for his western paintings, Miller would probably be unknown today. Born in 1810, the son of a prosperous Baltimore grocer, his talent was recognized at an early age, and he was encouraged to pursue an artistic career. He studied for a time with Thomas Sully before going abroad for the grand tour. Thanks to the American consul in Paris he was allowed to attend the prestigious École des Beaux Arts, where he was the only American student. He then went to Rome and studied for a time at the English Life School before returning to the United States. Miller was evidently so skilled that he had difficulty getting through customs because French officials thought his student copies were stolen originals.[37]

Despite his artistic talent, Miller's career did not have an auspicious beginning. He opened a studio in Baltimore that enjoyed only limited success.

He then relocated his studio to the French Quarter in New Orleans where, in the fall of 1836, he met Captain William Drummond Stewart, the Scottish nobleman who changed his life.

Heir to a fortune in Scotland and second in line to a title, the forty-two-year-old Stewart was already a legend in his own time. He had served with distinction in the British army during the Napoleonic Wars and now seemed driven by a relentless search for further adventure and excitement as an explorer and big game hunter. Already a veteran of several excursions to the American West, he was about to embark on still another one when he stumbled upon Miller's studio. Stewart liked what he saw and made Miller an offer the struggling artist could not refuse. The nobleman asked Miller to accompany him and "sketch the remarkable scenery and incidents of the journey" so that he could have a pictorial souvenir of the American West.[38]

Miller readily accepted and embarked upon a great adventure. Consisting of approximately one hundred white men and twenty Indian guides, the expedition, sent out by the American Fur Company to collect the annual harvest of furs obtained during the winter by its trappers, left from near present-day Kansas City and traveled west through Kansas to the North Fork of the Platte River. Along the way, Miller sketched Chimney Rock, Scott's Bluff, and Fort Laramie, the first drawings of what were to become major landmarks to pioneers along the Oregon Trail. At South Pass, the expedition crossed the Continental Divide in present-day Wyoming, where Stewart and Miller attended the annual rendezvous of the mountain men, held that year in the Green River Valley. Also at the gathering were more than three thousand Indians, among them Shoshones, Nez Perces, Flatheads, and Crows.

Miller appreciated the wonderful opportunity that had been presented to him and made the most of it, but he did not enjoy the life of a frontiersman. He could barely tolerate the camp routine and later grumbled that Stewart was something of "the military martinet & rigidly exacted from me all the duties of the Camp—said I had been spoiled at home." Since Miller could pay someone to take his turns at sentry duty, his only real obligation other than drawing was to tend his horse. Even this he considered an onerous chore. He especially resented having to catch it every morning, which entailed running "a considerable distance in moccasins."[39] A rheumatoid condition later in life he blamed on this excursion.

Despite his lack of enthusiasm for the outdoors, Miller did compile a remarkable visual record of his experiences. All told, he drew some two hundred sketches and watercolors and took voluminous notes. The sketches were later the basis for more finished watercolor (figs. 98, 99) and oil paintings (figs. 2, 100, 101). What makes his work especially significant is that he was the first white artist to record the life of the mountain man, already past its zenith. His drawings of the rendezvous are the only pictorial record of that annual

98. *Alfred Jacob Miller,*
Trappers, *1858–60,*
watercolor and gouache on
paper, 11¹⁵⁄₁₆ × 9⁷⁄₁₆ in.
Walters Art Gallery,
Baltimore

wilderness festival of trappers, traders, and Indians. Within three years of his visit to the 1837 rendezvous, this unique chapter in American history had closed.

At summer's end, Miller returned to his studio and began preparing the finished drawings for his eccentric patron, who had returned to Scotland to assume the duties of his baronetcy and attend to the estates he had recently inherited. Miller prepared a number of large oils, which he exhibited in Baltimore and New York, and then accepted Stewart's offer to visit Scotland and paint additional western scenes to decorate a hunting lodge. Miller left for Scotland in 1840 and returned to Baltimore two years later. There he remained until his death in 1874.

Typical of Miller's genre work are the four oils included here, three of which derive from his 1837 trip west. *Hunting Wild Horses* (fig. 2) depicts the Indian horse hunts Captain Stewart and Miller enjoyed watching on their trip. Miller was enthralled by the spectacle of the Indians using lassoes to capture the wild horse herds that roamed the plains. These scenes provided Miller the opportunity to sketch—and later paint—his favorite subject, the horse, in action. The horses are portrayed as wild and unpredictable, a characteristic Miller saw in the Indians as well.

The Lost Greenhorn (fig. 100) was one of Miller's favorite paintings, and he did several versions. Based on an actual incident, it shows Captain Stewart's English cook scanning the plains for a landmark that will guide him back to camp. The boastful cook, who had persuaded Stewart to let him go hunting alone, found buffaloes and gave chase. Within a short time he was hopelessly lost and had to spend a harrowing night on the prairie. All ended happily when searchers found the sheepish "greenhorn" alive and well the following morning.[40]

Trapper's Bride (fig. 101), considered by artist and critics alike to be one of Miller's best paintings, is also one of his best-known works. The large oil is based on an incident he witnessed at the rendezvous: an Indian warrior sold his daughter to a trapper for trade goods—guns, blankets, red flannel, tobacco, beads—worth six hundred dollars. Miller liked this painting so much that he made several copies in later life.

The fourth oil, *Buffalo Hunt* (fig. 102), lacks some of the authenticity of the other three. The Indians, while nobly rendered, are not easily

99. *Alfred Jacob Miller,* Trapping Beaver, *1858–60, watercolor on paper, 8⅞ × 13¾ in. Walters Art Gallery, Baltimore*

identifiable by tribe because Miller paid scant attention to details of dress, and their ponies look more like the Arabian chargers of the Old Masters than the rangy mustangs they would have been riding.

Although Miller painted some one hundred oils based on his western sojourn, they are for the most part drab and lacking in spontaneity. His watercolors are better, but his most significant artistic legacy is to be found in the original western sketches (fig. 103) on which both the oils and the watercolors were based.

One of the first historians to appreciate the importance of Miller's drawings was Bernard DeVoto. "With history's hindsight," DeVoto wrote, "it is easy to wish that he had kept his mind on what seems to be his proper business, that instead of preparing himself to cover an eventual half-acre of canvas with mementoes he had systematically set down every detail in a way

100. *Alfred Jacob Miller,*
The Lost Greenhorn, *n.d.,*
oil on canvas,
17⅞ × 23⅞ in.
Buffalo Bill Historical
Center, Cody, Wyoming

101. *Alfred Jacob Miller,*
The Trapper's Bride, *1845,*
oil on canvas, 36 × 28 in.
Harrison Eiteljorg Collection,
Indianapolis

of life which was already beginning to disappear." Nonetheless, Miller did record an "astonishing amount," DeVoto points out. "It is a pack saddle or a stirrup, a bag of possibles, the curve of an Indian cradle or pommel or arrow case, buffalo ribs roasting on a fire . . . small authentic matters recorded for our use, whose very commonplaceness makes them valuable."[41]

Taking the Hump Rib (fig. 103), an ink and wash sketch, is typical of Miller's field drawings as well as an excellent example of the ethnographic information these drawings often contain. This one shows the manner in which Indians butchered buffaloes. Instead of slitting their hides along the belly, they rolled the slain animals onto their stomachs and began the butchering process by slitting the hides along the backbone. The hides were then peeled off and stretched out on the ground to form a relatively dirt-free surface on which to lay the hunks of meat taken from the carcass.

Miller, an unlikely artist of the American frontier, spent only one season in the West, yet his record of Indian life and the fur trade was more complete than Catlin's or Stanley's. Moreover, although he arrived on the scene several years later than Catlin and Karl Bodmer, he penetrated farther west than either of them. He was one of the first white artists to sketch the Rocky Mountains and to record the mountain man.

If Miller was a legitimate documentary artist, he also harbored a romantic vision of the West.

102. *Alfred Jacob Miller,* Buffalo Hunt, *ca. 1850, oil on canvas, 30¼ × 50¼ in. Amon Carter Museum, Fort Worth*

In his notes he described more than one drawing as an Arcadian scene. Indeed, he lamented the fact that American artists did not share his feelings for the noble red man. How ironic that his colleagues would journey to Europe to study Greek and Roman sculpture and ignore the Indians, whom he judged, echoing Benjamin West, "equal in form and grace (if not superior) to the finest beau ideal ever dreamed of by the Greeks." As far as Miller could tell, "not a single sculptor has thought it worth his while to make a journey among these Indians, who are now sojourning on the western side of the Rocky Mountains, and are rapidly passing away."

However, his romantic vision apparently did not extend beyond the physical form of his sub-

103. *Alfred Jacob Miller,*
Taking the Hump Rib,
ca. 1837,
pen and ink, ink wash, and
graphite on paper,
8 × 10⅞ in.
Amon Carter Museum,
Fort Worth

ject; as to the Indians' character, Miller seems to have shared in the bigotry of the times: the Indian, he remarked, "uses every strategem, fair and foul, to preserve . . . [his] worthless life."[42]

Several themes common to the work of all five artists can be identified. The era in which they were active, about 1830 to 1860, was the heart of the Romantic Age in American thought and art. Their eccentric personalities and life stories are the very stuff of romance, even though their western adventures can be measured in months, compared to years or decades of studio painting and gallery promotion.

Landscape painting was less important to these artists than to some of their eastern counterparts. Though undoubtedly familiar with the well-established artistic convention of placing Indian figures in landscape paintings, Stanley, Eastman, and Miller had other aims. Their scenery is the visual setting for the real subjects of the paintings—the hunts, the games and amusements, the journeys, the rhythms of action and repose that constituted Indian camp life.

Although true landscapes are relatively few among them, these artists depicted—almost exclusively—an outdoor world. Interior scenes are remarkably rare. This skewed ratio may reflect actual conditions of Indian life; it may reflect the personal reserve or domestic modesty of Indians and/or artists. But not to be underestimated is the importance of one of the intellectual assumptions of the age, the Romantic appreciation of the Indian's close proximity to the state of nature. Painters were expected to see this idea demonstrated in Indian life in the West, and their patrons expected to see it portrayed in their art.

The assumption derives from Rousseau, and two significant Indian stereotypes are grounded in it—the Noble Savage and the Vanishing American. The relationship to these popular images of the five artists under discussion is complicated, for they both accepted and undermined the stereotypes. These artists appreciated Indian culture, admired elements in the Indian way of life, and conveyed in their portraits and genre scenes, if not nobility, surely great dignity and self-possession. Catlin could satirize—as he did in the comic

contrast of his well-known portrait of the Indian chief going to and coming home from Washington—but he never patronized.

Certainly Catlin and Miller were interested in the appearance and habits of Indian warriors. Martial decoration, attire, and accoutrements are depicted; feats of strength, skill, and daring are sketched; but ferocious savagery is not emphasized. Eastman's lack of interest in warfare has already been mentioned. The more balanced view and accurate ethnology of these artists condemns the sensational fantasy illustrations so common later in the nineteenth century and makes the characterization of the Indian even in Bingham's *The Concealed Enemy* (1845; fig. 12) seem contrived and false.

Interestingly, except for Wimar's *The Attack on an Emigrant Train* (fig. 90), these artists did not depict the enmity that marked many Indian-white interactions in the United States. White hostility toward Indians is conspicuously absent from their paintings, although the policy of removal of the tribes from the East was well under way, even as Catlin started up the Missouri. Most people who thought about it believed Indian lifeways were doomed to disappear; many fervently hoped so. The Indian's supposed state of nature was viewed with considerable ambivalence even by those most sympathetic to Native Americans (Thomas McKenney, for example, the first commissioner of Indian Affairs and a staunch friend of the Indians, was an earnest advocate of cultural assimilation). To capture in paint a race about to vanish was a conscious objective for these artists; to make a dollar by capitalizing on public interest in Indians was also a motivation. For most of them, however, painting Indians proved profitless. Yet they persisted, dressed up in buckskins and starving for their art. Their contemporaries surely considered them daft.

In retrospect, we can see that the Romantic notion of the Vanishing American was an exaggeration, that nostalgia for an innocent state of nature was more related to conflict and rapid change in white American society in the 1830s and 1840s than to understanding what was happening to Indians. The Indians faced and survived worse vicissitudes later in the nineteenth century, and in many respects Indian culture thrives today. In fact, greater genre scenes of Indian life now emanate from the hands and hearts of contemporary Indian artists.

This in no way should diminish our appreciation of the work of the artists discussed in this essay. In the three decades before the Civil War, changes were taking place in the social, economic, and political circumstances of Indians in the Far West. What a gap there would be in the visual record of these people had Catlin, Stanley, Wimar, Eastman, and Miller not chosen to document their appearance and customs. At the least we have a pictorial record of undeniable authenticity; at best we also have images of power and beauty.

NOTES

1. The most complete and authoritative study of George Catlin and his work is William H. Truettner, *The Natural Man Observed: A Study of Catlin's Indian Gallery* (Washington, D.C.: Smithsonian Institution Press, 1979). Unless otherwise cited, the basic facts about Catlin's life and travels are from this work.

2. William Dunlap, *History of the Rise and Progress of the Arts of Design in the United States* (New York: Benjamin Bloom, 1965), 3:172. Catlin's view is from *A Descriptive Catalogue of Catlin's Indian Gallery, Egyptian Hall* (London: C. and J. Adlard, 1840), p. 3.

3. For a complete history of Charles Bird King and the War Department gallery, see Herman J. Viola, *The Indian Legacy of Charles Bird King* (Washington, D.C.: Smithsonian Institution Press, 1976).

4. John C. Ewers, "George Catlin: Painter of Indians of the West," *Annual Report of the Smithsonian Institution for 1955* (Washington, D.C., 1956), p. 492.

5. John Francis McDermott, *Seth Eastman: A Pictorial Historian of the Indian* (Norman: University of Oklahoma Press, 1961), p. 105.

6. Because of the criticism, Catlin later published an entire volume of illustrations on this ceremony entitled *O-Kee-Pa: A Religious Ceremony and Other Customs of the Mandans* (London: Trübner and Company, 1867), which has been reprinted with an introduction by John C. Ewers by Yale University Press (New Haven, 1967).

7. Maria R. Audubon, *Audubon and His Journals* (New York: C. Scribner's Sons, 1897), 2:10. Miller quoted in Bernard DeVoto, *Across the Wide Missouri* (Boston: Houghton Mifflin Company, 1947), p. 409.

8. DeVoto, p. 392.

9. George Catlin, *Letters and Notes on the Manners, Customs, and Condition of the North American Indians* (London: author, 1841), 2:125–26. This was reprinted by Dover Publications (New York, 1973).

10. DeVoto, *Across the Wide Missouri,* p. 395.

11. Catlin quote and interpretation of fig. 82 from Truettner, *The Natural Man Observed,* p. 261. Observation of Catlin's artistic license from Ewers, "Catlin," p. 501.

12. Seth Eastman to John Mix Stanley, 28 January 1852, copy enclosed with "Memorial of John M. Stanley praying Congress to purchase his gallery of Indian paintings now deposited in the Smithsonian Institution," Committee of the Library, SEN34A-H10, RG 46, National Archives and Records Administration (hereafter cited as NARA).

13. The most authoritative study of Stanley and his work is Julie Ann Schimmel, "John Mix Stanley and Imagery of the West in Nineteenth-Century American

Art" (Ph.D. diss., Department of Fine Arts, New York University, 1983). Unless otherwise cited, the basic facts about Stanley's life and paintings are from this study.

14. See Viola, *King*, pp. 68–87.

15. Caleb Sumner Dickerman to secretary of war, 11 August 1842, Letters Received by the Secretary of War Relating to Indian Affairs, RG 75, NARA; commissioner of Indian Affairs to Dickerman, 17 August 1842, Commissioner of Indian Affairs, Letters Sent, RG 75, NARA.

16. *Louisville Daily Democrat*, 3 March 1846.

17. Quoted in Schimmel, "Stanley," p. 86.

18. *Reports of Explorations and Surveys, to Ascertain the Most Practicable and Economical Route for a Railroad from the Mississippi River to the Pacific Ocean*, vol. 12, bk. 1 (Washington, D.C.: A. O. P. Nicholson, 1860), p. 87.

19. *Annual Report of the Board of the Smithsonian Institution . . . 1858* (Washington, D.C., 1859), pp. 41–42.

20. Joseph Henry to Stanley, 11 March 1865, Letter-book 1, p. 108, Smithsonian Institution Archives.

21. Schimmel, "Stanley," p. 215.

22. Information about Wimar's life and work is meager. The best sources are Perry T. Rathbone, *Charles Wimar, 1828–1862: Painter of the Indian Frontier* (St. Louis: City Art Museum of St. Louis, 1946); and William Romaine Hodges, *Carl Wimar: A Biography* (Galveston: Charles Reymershoffer, 1908). Unless cited otherwise, the basic facts about Wimar and his work are from Rathbone.

23. Pomerade quoted in Rathbone, *Wimar*, p. 11.

24. Quoted in Rathbone, p. 16.

25. Rathbone, pp. 14–15.

26. Rathbone, p. 16.

27. Hodges, *Wimar*, p. 23.

28. The letter, which was originally published in Düsseldorf in the journal of the academy, is quoted verbatim in both Rathbone, *Wimar*, and Hodges, *Wimar*.

29. Hodges, pp. 16–17.

30. Wimar quoted in Rathbone, *Wimar*, p. 30.

31. Rathbone, p. 5.

32. Seth Eastman's Indian daughter, born out of wedlock, eventually married a Sioux warrior and had five children, one of them being Charles Eastman, the famous physician and author.

33. Dunlap, *Arts of Design,* 2:255. The best account of Eastman's life and work is McDermott, *Eastman*. Unless otherwise cited, the following information is taken from that work.

34. Mary H. Eastman, *Dahcotah; or, Life and Legends of the Sioux Around Fort Snelling* (New York: J. Wiley, 1849; reprint ed., Minneapolis: Ross & Haines, Inc., 1962), p. xiv.

35. Memorial of Seth Eastman to both Houses of Congress, 5 December 1859, and Mary Eastman to Chairman, House Committee on Military Affairs, February 1867, NARA.

36. Eastman, *Dahcotah,* p. 56.

37. The most recent and complete work on Alfred Jacob Miller and his western art is Ron Tyler, ed., with a Catalogue Raisonné by Karen Dewees Reynolds and William R. Johnston, *Alfred Jacob Miller: Artist on the Oregon Trail* (Fort Worth: Amon Carter Museum, 1982).

38. William Harvey Hunter, Jr., *Alfred Jacob Miller: Artist of Baltimore and the West,* Peale Museum Historical Series, no. 5 (January 1950), p. 4.

39. Quotes from Hunter, p. 5, and James Thomas Flexner, *That Wilder Image: The Painting of America's Native School from Thomas Cole to Winslow Homer* (Boston: Little, Brown & Company, 1962), p. 90.

40. John C. Ewers, *Artists of the Old West* (New York: Doubleday & Company, 1965), p. 124.

41. DeVoto, *Across the Wide Missouri,* p. 414.

42. Miller quotes from Ronnie C. Tyler, *Alfred Jacob Miller* (Fort Worth: Amon Carter Museum, 1972), pp. 7, 9.

THE PRINTS OF LIFE IN THE WEST, 1840–60

BERNARD REILLY, JR.

Most of the paintings included in this book were produced and shown for the first time in the United States during the 1840s and 1850s. They were part of a general flowering of genre painting in this country that was echoed in the graphic art of the period by a rise in the number of prints devoted to the portrayal of everyday life in America. Yet, far from simply imitating painting, the prints were produced according to traditions of their own, which governed the subjects they presented.

In the culture of antebellum America, printmaking played a different role from painting, providing a wider variety of images to a much broader audience. Unlike painting, printmaking was not a single, cohesive medium but a collection of media, including lithography, engraving, wood engraving, and other techniques. The very term *printmaking,* with its connotation of a single process, was unheard of in the nineteenth century. As an art form, the making of prints was further divided by various traditions and functions—an established documentary tradition, the popular illustrative tradition, and the tradition of reproducing original artworks. Prints of the American West before the Civil War reflect these divisions, and can be best understood with reference to them.

The image of the frontier in pre–Civil War America was largely conveyed to Easterners

through the published writings of travelers and, in visual terms, through documentary prints. Inexpensive lithographs and engravings were natural vehicles for intelligence from the West. New cities and settlements were advertised in prints; from the 1830s on, lithographs of settlements and scenery in the West were sent east, and portraits of explorers and Indians were circulated throughout the country.[1]

Though valuable to historians today, such documentary images conveyed little to contemporaries about the character of everyday life on the frontier. It was precisely this information that the genre prints provided and continue to provide. These appeared as popular prints, as book illustrations, and as reproductions of works by the painters of western scenes. Unlike documentary prints, genre prints were not conceived as objective records but instead self-consciously embodied the values and interests of their audience. They are an art form whose content was shaped as much by its audience as by its creators.

While documentary prints by men like George Catlin and Seth Eastman provided their audience a view of the West's diversity, genre prints moved toward typifying and summarizing their subjects. In the genre prints of the 1840s and 1850s one may trace the development of the shared image of the frontiersman, the pioneer, the trapper, and the Indian—figures who by this time had been ov-

Doney, after Bingham, The Jolly Flat Boat Men *(detail, see fig. 124)*

ertaken by history and progress. The popular iconographic function of the genre print is intimately bound up with the nature of printmaking in nineteenth-century America and is rooted in the century's beginning.

Before the 1820s, printed images were relatively rare in the United States. There were no print shops—or, at least, no shops devoted solely to prints—and most American books were devoid of illustrations. Comparison of the number of surviving prints published in England or France with the same period's yield in the United States dramatically demonstrates the relative poverty of images in this country. Thousands of British and French etchings and engravings survive from the first quarter of the nineteenth century, as compared with mere hundreds of American prints.

Granted the paucity of prints in general, portrait prints actually had considerable currency in the United States and were the first reproductions of American art to be widely distributed. Typically copies of paintings of American public figures, scientists, and authors, portrait prints were naturally newsworthy. They accompanied presidential elections, deaths, and important new books. Portraits of western figures were much rarer. William Strickland's *Merriweather Lewis* [sic], published in the *Analectic Magazine* in 1816, and James Otto Lewis's subscription portrait of Daniel Boone (fig. 104) were among the earliest. Lewis's stipple engraving, reproducing a painting by Chester Harding, was undertaken shortly after the famous pioneer's death in 1820. Advertisements appeared in St. Louis newspapers offering subscriptions, two hundred of which were sold at three dollars each—no small outlay for the average American of the time.

Despite the currency of portraits, prints did not reach anything like a mass audience in the United States until the 1820s, when two important developments occurred: the beginning of commercial lithography in America, and new interest in and patronage of engraving. Both developments were made possible by the enlarged literate middle class that was resulting from immigration, natural population growth, and prosperity.

104. *James Otto Lewis (1799–1858), after Chester Harding (1792–1866),* Col. Daniel Boone, *ca. 1820, stipple engraving, 11¾ × 8¹⁄₁₆ in. The Saint Louis Art Museum*

Lithography, the process of printing from drawings on stone, was invented at the end of the eighteenth century as a means of reproducing music scores. It rapidly became the workhorse of graphic media.[2] In the late 1820s and early 1830s, lithographic houses sprang up in many major American cities, supplying businesses with advertising trade cards, labels, calendars, and stationery, and producing portraits, political satires, renderings of current events, and political campaign banners. In the market that capitalized on public issues and concerns, timing was critical, and lithographers were responsive. Since a print could be drawn on stone and printed within twenty-four hours, the medium was well suited to subjects that came and went rapidly. Such subjects were the stock-in-trade of most of the early firms and remained their chief commodities until offset printing displaced lithography at the end of the century.

The production of the lithograph was largely the work of in-house draftsmen. In the United States a fairly strict division of labor was observed between the design of the original and the manual process of printmaking, that is, drawing the image on stone. Before the 1860s few American painters actually worked in the graphic medium themselves. Rembrandt Peale, Thomas Cole, and William Morris Hunt were a few of the exceptions. Thus what one sees in the prints is at best a collaboration between painter and professional draftsman, heavily influenced by the skill and judgment of the latter, who had only modest professional status and rarely achieved artistic distinction beyond his craft. His training was haphazard, obtained most often through some form of apprenticeship. With few exceptions, the lithographer was considered a craftsman, not an artist. The early career of Nathaniel Currier, a lithographer who began working in New York during the early 1830s, illustrates the usual pattern of activity. Currier resorted to all sorts of tasks, including designs for music covers, trade cards, renderings of buildings for architects, certificates, political campaign banners, and book illustrations for various printers and publishers or occasionally for publication over his own imprint.

Although western images appear in their work infrequently, the early lithographers did play a role in shaping the image of the frontier. Most often they featured Indians rather than pioneers—an Indian hunter or brave on a lithographed music cover for a song celebrating the American wilderness in a romantic vein inspired by Henry Wadsworth Longfellow or James Fenimore Cooper. Such images, designed merely to generate interest in the music, usually portrayed the Indian in the guise of exotic nobility or savage fierceness, as the occasion required. Advertising trade cards, another staple of the early lithographer, invoked the traditional association of the Indian with tobacco and other produce of the American land. During the 1850s, as eastern sophistication about the Native American grew, these images became less poetic and more realistic, sometimes employing authentic portraits derived from the paintings of George Catlin and Charles Bird King.

Before the rise of interest in genre in the 1840s there were few individual prints of frontier life. The theater had occasional western characters such as the wild backwoodsman Nimrod Wild-fire in James Kirke Paulding's play *The Lion of the West,* which opened in New York in 1831. The 1838 dramatization of Robert Montgomery Bird's novel *Nick of the Woods* introduced New Yorkers to the Kentucky half breed Jibbenainosay. On occasion, an enterprising sheet-music publisher would issue a lithographed portrait of a popular actor in the role of such a character.[3]

From time to time the frontiersman appeared in political cartoons, as a representative of the West. A Westerner in stovepipe hat and buckskins cheers for Andrew Jackson in David Claypoole Johnston's 1824 etching *The Foot-Race.* This figure became a fixture in political cartoons of the 1840s whenever the artist sought to convey in a few lines of heavily accented dialect the viewpoint of western America.

Book and magazine illustration was as important as individual lithographs in disseminating the image of the western frontier. The 1840s saw a dramatic surge in the number of illustrated books and magazines produced in the United States. From the class of cheap literature made possible by this growth sprang perhaps the best-known frontiersman of the first half of the nineteenth century, Davy Crockett. Crockett was a fictional character loosely based on the real-life Tennessee native and statesman, Colonel David Crockett. Starting in 1835, his exploits were recounted in inexpensive illustrated almanacs. The fictional Crockett was as wild as the Victorian Easterner expected in a product of less-civilized regions. In larger-than-life proportions, he also had the attitudes and prejudices popularly ascribed to the Westerner: a contempt for foreigners (chiefly the British), Indians, and blacks, balanced on the positive side by independence, resourcefulness, and prodigious strength.[4] Crockett almanacs were published in Boston and New York well into the 1850s. They were heavily illustrated with crude woodcut pictures of Crockett, his adventures, his foes, and the often fantastical creatures of the backwoods. The illustrations were designed and engraved by nameless craftsmen in the employ of commercial engraving firms, and were on the whole unsophisticated productions.

The Crockett almanacs reflected a growing popular interest in the frontier. The late 1830s and early 1840s brought a flood of tales and stories of the West written by authors like Henry Clay Lewis, Thomas Bangs Thorpe, and William T. Porter, a literature that reveals an appreciation for regional color and humor. The hardships and dangers of life in the West and the dialects and idiosyncrasies of its people offered American writers a wealth of potential for humor. This literary genre flourished in magazines like the *Spirit of the Times* (New York) and in the inexpensive paperbound books turned out by the publishing firms of Carey and Hart and of T. B. Peterson, both of Philadelphia. Many of the stories, which comprise a fund of character studies and yarns featuring names like "Simon Suggs" and "Stoke Stout," were illustrated by F.O.C. Darley early in his career.

In 1836 and again in 1840, the theme of the frontier emerged in presidential campaigns. Whig campaign strategists concocted for their candidate, William Henry ("Tippecanoe") Harrison, an image of a noble rustic citizen to play against the aristocratic style of his opponent, incumbent Martin Van Buren. This so-called Log Cabin campaign was waged in pamphlets, newspapers, and lithographed broadsides. Through these media, the candidate's home on the North Bend of the Ohio River, his career as an Indian fighter, and service as governor of the Indiana Territory were woven into a largely mythical picture of frontier life. Lithographs of log cabins in the wilderness and of the "North Bend Farmer" at his plough abounded. The stereotyped frontiersman in buckskins endorsed Harrison on campaign broadsides.

The evolution of the image of the frontier and frontiersman was complex, shifting from one election to the next, but the frontier ideal steadily figured in several subsequent presidential contests, even to Lincoln's Illinois "rail-splitter" campaign of 1860. In 1844 Henry Clay was given the rustic sobriquet "the mill boy"—during the campaign,

George Caleb Bingham produced a banner on this theme for the Boonville Clay Club. In 1856 John C. Frémont's heroic past as a western explorer was exploited on campaign posters and banners.

Illustrated books on the history of the West, on western lore, and on the Indians were turned out in quantity during the 1830s and 1840s. Authors like John Frost and James Hall, whose histories and travel accounts were rich in anecdotes, were issued and reissued.[5] They told the story of the opening and growth of the West in terms of personal experience, adventure, and trial. Such works lent themselves naturally to illustration in vivid and expressive terms. The mid-century American had available to him a wide range of literature on Indians, from Darley's romanticized treatment of the Native American in *Scenes in Indian Life* (1843) to George Catlin's colorful *North American Indian Portfolio* (1845) to serious ethnographic studies like H. R. Schoolcraft's encyclopedic *Historical and Statistical Information Respecting the History, Condition and Prospects of the Indian Tribes of the United States* (1851–57).

F.O.C. Darley was a remarkably talented self-taught artist from Philadelphia and the first American to achieve success and fame as an independent illustrator.[6] *Scenes in Indian Life* (figs. 105, 106) was his major work on the West before the Civil War. It consisted of a series of fifteen etchings on stone from outline drawings, which Darley had produced in 1842 intending to publish them himself. The scenes were etched on stone by Thomas Sinclair of Philadelphia and issued in five parts of three plates each by J. R. Colon, a publisher of magazines, novels, and maps. Darley may have been motivated in part by the favorable reception of George Catlin's twelve-volume *Letters and Notes* in 1841.

Unlike Seth Eastman's illustrations for Schoolcraft and Catlin's prints for *North American Indian Portfolio,* Darley's pictures of the Indians were not drawn from observation or scientific study, but were imaginative tableaus based on paintings by Catlin, Charles Bird King, Titian Ramsey Peale, and the other painters of the Indian. His book, which cost only one dollar for the complete set of fifteen lithographed plates, was smaller and

105. *Thomas S. Sinclair (ca. 1805–81), after Felix Octavius Carr Darley (1822–88),* Scenes in Indian Life, No. 10, *1843, lithograph, 7½ × 9⅜ in. Published by J. R. Colon. Amon Carter Museum, Fort Worth*

106. *Thomas S. Sinclair (ca. 1805–81), after Felix Octavius Carr Darley (1822–88),* Scenes in Indian Life, No. 7, *1843, lithograph, 7³⁄₁₆ × 8⁷⁄₁₆ in. Published by J. R. Colon. Amon Carter Museum, Fort Worth*

cheaper than the deluxe editions of Schoolcraft and Catlin.

The chief appeal of Darley's Indian prints lies in their exciting narrative qualities. In the 1840s Darley must have been a complete novelty. American illustration had as yet seen nothing to compare with his dynamic—and often extremely violent—compositions and his masterful handling of the human figure in action. In their portfolio format and dramatic force, Darley's *Scenes* anticipated the large heroic series of lithographed scenes from frontier history that were to appear in the 1850s—G. W. Fasel's *Heroic Deeds of Former Times* (fig. 107) and Karl Bodmer's *Annals of the United States Illustrated*. Later, in his small, wood-engraved illustrations for John Ludlum McConnel's book *Western Characters* (1853), Darley gave visual form to the different frontier types portrayed by the author in almost mythic terms.

In 1844, shortly after establishing his Indian gallery in London's Egyptian Hall, George Catlin produced a volume of thirty-one lithographs entitled *North American Indian Portfolio,* reproducing many of the scenes found in his gallery paintings.

The *Portfolio* followed an earlier work, published in London in 1841, entitled *Letters and Notes on the Manners, Customs, and Condition of the North American Indians,* Catlin's major study of the American Indian's history, culture, and way of life. The *Portfolio* included much less text than the earlier work, and provided more attractive and larger images than the woodcuts in *Letters and Notes.* The lithographs included portraits as well as scenes from Indian life. Of the hundreds of scenes portrayed in his gallery, Catlin chose mostly hunting subjects for the *Portfolio.* His experience with the gallery had taught him that the dramatic qualities of the struggle for survival and the excitement of the hunt appealed to European audiences. The volume provided Catlin a means of widening the audience for his advocacy of the American Indian; through it he reached far more people than was possible by means of his museum alone.

The *Portfolio* was not Catlin's initial venture into lithography. He had been one of the few American painters who experimented with the medium before 1850. In 1838 he produced and published a large lithographed portrait of the Seminole chief

107. *George Wilhelm Fasel (active 1829–65),* Heroic Deeds of Former Times—6—The Women of Bryant's Station Kentucky Supplying the Garrison with Water, *1851, toned lithograph (hand colored), 13⅞ × 15³⁄₁₆ in. Printed by Nagel & Weingaernter, Published by Emil Seitz. Print Collection, The New York Public Library, Astor, Lenox and Tilden Foundations*

108. *After George Catlin, No. 12. Buffalo Hunt, Chasing Back, 1845, color lithograph (hand colored), 13⁵⁄₁₆ × 18⁵⁄₁₆ in.* North American Indian Portfolio, *Published by James Ackerman.* Library of Congress (Rare Books Division), Washington, D.C.

Osceola. Wise to the value of pictures as persuasive tools on political issues, he used his noble *Osceola* as a part of his lobbying effort against the government's inhumane Indian policies.[7]

The first lithograph in the *Portfolio,* entitled *North American Indians,* was drawn on stone by Catlin himself. For the rest, Catlin enlisted an English lithographer by the name of McGahey, and the stones were printed by the prestigious London house of Day & Haghe in black and buff, the extra stone giving a considerable range of tonality to the drawing. They were extensively and carefully hand colored, a procedure that was in this case more than the superficial enhancement most popular prints received. For the Catlin prints, hand coloring was essential to achieving authenticity in the Indians' costume and paint and in the color of flora and fauna. Attention to the original paintings must have been very close and, judging by the standard of authenticity maintained in the work, Catlin himself may have been closely involved in production.

In 1845 James Ackerman published an American edition of the *North American Indian Portfolio* (fig. 108). A sign painter turned commercial lithographer, Ackerman was active in New York in the 1840s and 1850s. The *Portfolio* was his major achievement. Obviously impressed with the London edition of Catlin's *Portfolio,* he set out to prove that American lithography could do justice to such works of art. Although it is unclear just what role Catlin took in the production of the American portfolio (he was in England during this process), Ackerman vaguely suggests in his preface some form of collaboration between the author and publisher.

Within the space of a year Ackerman had twenty-five plates of the work redrawn and printed. These plates appear to have been copied from the English lithographs rather than from Catlin's own paintings. Like the English prints, they are printed in two colors: black and a single blue or olive tone, which customarily established the dominant coloring of sky or background. They were then extensively and carefully hand colored to approximate the original in all respects. Again, the coloring was not merely decorative, but an integral and highly demanding part of the artwork, so that each print is virtually a painting. Ackerman managed to better the English lithographers—his prints are drawn and colored with more clarity and vividness than their prototypes—and pro-

duced a work representative of the best reproductive lithography of the time. Ironically, he
failed to mention the name of the lithographic
artist who drew the prints on stone.

Schoolcraft's monumental *Historical and Statistical Information* was published in six volumes, with
several hundred illustrations, a daunting production appropriate to its scientific weight. It was an
undertaking so large that the publishers farmed
out production of the plates to ten different engravers and two lithographic firms. The illustrations included eighty-five scenes of Indian rituals,
sports, occupations, and other aspects of daily life
by the painter Seth Eastman. Many of these reproduced, with minor variations, paintings Eastman executed while stationed at Fort Snelling—
Ballplay of the Sioux on the St. Peters River in Winter
(fig. 95), for example, was engraved as *Ball Play
on the Ice* (fig. 109). Although ostensibly included

as scientific records, Eastman's prints presented a
more widely appealing and fascinating picture of
the human aspects of Indian existence. For this
reason the publishers reissued a number of the
plates in more popular form: *The Aboriginal Portfolio* of 1853 (not to be confused with that of 1835–
36), which incorporated a briefer commentary on
Indian life, and an 1854 book of poems and stories
by Mrs. Eastman entitled *Chicora and Other Regions
of the Conquerors and the Conquered*.[8]

While Catlin and Eastman produced extraordinarily accurate Indian depictions meant to convey an authentic picture of Indian life, Nathaniel
Currier's early prints of the 1840s, such as *The
Indian Warrior* (fig. 110) and *Indian Hunter* (fig.
111), depict generalized figures of no particular
tribe; the prints are decorative rather than instruc-
tive. In the light of the available sources and copious iconography of the American Indian in 1845,

Currier's generalized depictions are curiously outdated. Indeed, *Indian Hunter* is traceable to a source that was at least five years old; the same figure appeared on a bank note for the Bank of Pensacola, engraved by the firm of Rawdon, Wright, Hatch and Edson.[9]

Poorly designed as Currier's early western work was, the prints were well marketed, and, as time went on, Currier improved his product by assembling a stable of skillful foreign-born draftsmen like Otto Knirsch and Louis Maurer. He also acquired, in one way or another, the right to reproduce paintings by artists like Arthur Fitzwilliam Tait and George Catlin. In 1852–53 Currier produced and copyrighted two lithographs under arrangement with Tait, *The Prairie Hunter. "One Rubbed Out!"* (fig. 112; painting, fig. 69) and *A Check. "Keep Your Distance."* The second print is unsigned, but the first is signed by German-

American lithographer Otto Knirsch. Virtually the same size and format, the prints may have been companion pieces, designed to be framed and hung as a pair. Close similarity in handling of the lithographic crayon, in the overall tonal quality, and in the rendering of details suggests that both prints were the work of Knirsch. Printed in black and white, they were carefully and lavishly colored by hand with watercolor and gouache.

Tait had a fairly longstanding—and profitable—relationship with Currier & Ives. The firm produced four other western prints from his paintings, *The Last War-Whoop* (fig. 113; painting, fig. 74) and *The Pursuit* (fig. 114; painting, fig. 73) in 1856, and *Life on the Prairie. The Trapper's Defense, "Fire Fight Fire"* (fig. 76) and *Life on the Prairie. The Buffalo Hunt* in 1862. Like the earlier prints after Tait, *The Last War-Whoop* was issued in black and white with hand coloring. *The Pursuit* was

112. *Otto Knirsch (active 1853–60s), after Arthur F. Tait,* The Prairie Hunter. "One Rubbed Out!", *1852, lithograph (hand colored), 16¼ × 20⅝ in. Published by Nathaniel Currier. Library of Congress (Prints and Photographs Division), Washington, D.C.*

produced by chromolithography, a technique for reproducing paintings in color more cheaply and quickly than conventional lithography with its painstaking hand coloring.[10] *The Pursuit* chromolithograph lacks some of the nuances of coloring often achieved in hand-tinted lithographs. Both prints were drawn on stone by Louis Maurer, a draftsman who produced over a hundred works for Currier & Ives between 1853 and 1893. He was particularly good at rendering horses, and drew most of the firm's best racing scenes.

Aside from Currier's 1851 print of California prospectors, *The Gold Seekers,* and an undated view called *Prairie on Fire,* Tait's scenes were the earliest frontier images issued by the firm. These subjects must have appealed to Currier's sense of the contemporary market. Since his 1840 publishing success with a print of the Lexington steamboat disaster, Currier had exercised an impressive knack for reading the changing interests of the American public. The topics of sport and adventure were certainly a draw, and one can see Tait's western scenes in this context. Of the thirty-eight prints that Currier & Ives produced after Tait's paintings, all but four deal with hunting and rural sports or life in the West.[11] They reflected—

and fostered—a view of life in the West as perilous and hardy. Tait's scenes have a narrative, anecdotal emphasis characteristic of most of Currier & Ives's productions and valued by their largely middle-class audience.

Sometime in the 1850s Currier & Ives also published fifteen of George Catlin's *North American Indian Portfolio* scenes separately (figs. 115, 116). These were printed from the same stones as Ackerman's original edition, though, in some cases, an extra stone was added for enhanced color before the prints were carefully watercolored; the handwork adhered closely to the colors in the Ackerman version. The Catlin prints made an impressive addition to Currier's western stock and must have rendered his earlier Indian prints obsolete. In his imprint, Currier credited Catlin but made no reference to Ackerman, from whom he must have acquired the stones to produce the prints.

During the late 1840s, a number of European firms entered the American market in competition with American lithographers like Currier & Ives. The demand for decorative prints expanded with the growth of American cities. Both Goupil & Com-

113. *Louis Maurer*
(1832–1932),
after Arthur F. Tait,
The Last War-Whoop, *1856,*
lithograph (hand colored),
18³/₁₆ × 25⁹/₁₆ in.
Published by Currier & Ives.
The Harry T. Peters
Collection, Museum of the
City of New York

114. *Louis Maurer*
(1832–1932),
after Arthur F. Tait,
The Pursuit, *1856,*
toned lithograph (hand
colored), 19¹/₈ × 25⁹/₁₆ in.
Published by
Nathaniel Currier.
Amon Carter Museum,
Fort Worth

pany and M. Knoedler opened publishing offices in New York at this time and began building inventories of American subjects. They bought paintings or the right to reproduce them from American painters like George Caleb Bingham, Richard Caton Woodville, and William Sidney Mount. These firms achieved a high level of quality in the draftsmanship and printing of stones. The place of lithography as a fine art was firmly established in France, and her lithographers and

115. *After George Catlin,*
Buffalo Bull, Chasing
Back. "Turn About Is Fair
Play," *ca. 1850s,*
toned lithograph,
12⁷⁄₁₆ × 18³⁄₁₆ in.
Published by Currier & Ives.
Colgate Collection, Division
of Graphic Arts,
National Museum of
American History,
Smithsonian Institution,
Washington, D.C.

116. *After George Catlin,*
Indians Attacking the
Grizzly Bear. The Most
Savage and Ferocious
Animal of North America,
ca. 1850s,
lithograph (hand colored),
12¼ × 17⅞ in.
Published by Currier & Ives.
The Harry T. Peters
Collection, Museum of the
City of New York

patrons maintained a much higher standard than those in the United States. Two of Bingham's paintings, *Canvassing for a Vote* (fig. 24; lithograph, fig. 117) and *The Emigration of Daniel Boone*, were sent to Paris by M. Knoedler where, in 1852, they were drawn on stone by Claude Regnier. These prints were more subtly drawn and adeptly printed than such domestic work as Currier & Ives's lithographs after Tait. Bingham no doubt realized that the quality of French lithography was unri-

117. *Claude Regnier (active 1847–53), after George Caleb Bingham,* Canvassing for a Vote, *1852–53, toned lithograph, 17⅛ × 20⁵⁄₁₆ in. Published by M. Knoedler. Amon Carter Museum, Fort Worth*

valed in the United States—a fact acknowledged by the American lithographers' habit of pirating French work.

Possibly in an attempt to close the gap between American and Continental lithography, United States firms began to hire a number of lithographic draftsmen from Europe during the 1840s. Foreign-trained artists like Leopold Grozelier, Francis D'Avignon, and D. C. Fabronius helped Amer-

ican printers gain ground on the best French and English work. They created some outstanding individual prints. Grozelier produced two extremely beautiful lithographs after western genre paintings, *On the Prairie* (fig. 118), published by J. E. Tilton in 1860, and *Western Life—The Trapper* (fig. 119), published in about 1855 by M. Knoedler. Both were printed by the firm of J. H. Bufford. Grozelier was arguably the finest lithographic

118. *Leopold Grozelier*
(1830–65),
after Charles Wimar,
On the Prairie, *1860,*
lithograph (hand colored),
22 × 29¾ in. (sheet).
Printed by J. H. Bufford,
Published by J. E. Tilton & Co.
The Thomas Gilcrease
Institute of American History
and Art, Tulsa, Oklahoma

draftsman working in the United States during the 1850s. Born in Paris in 1825, he studied under the distinguished painter-lithographer Bernard Romain Julien. He brought with him to the United States the high standards of French draftsmanship and technique.

Grozelier worked for several lithographic houses in New York and Boston, but his prints for Bufford are his best work. Bufford was an established Boston firm with a record of fine printing. The company had printed lithographs by artists like Winslow Homer, and Fitz Hugh Lane and was equal to the task of printing Gro-

zelier's drawings as few American firms were. Bufford's work was considerably better than that of Currier & Ives, which was oriented to the mass market. However, *On the Prairie*, which reproduced Charles Wimar's 1856 painting *The Attack on an Emigrant Train* (fig. 90), was probably targeted for the popular audience served by Currier & Ives, as the print offered the same sort of drama as some of the latter firm's frontier scenes.

Grozelier's *Western Life—The Trapper*, his print after Charles Deas's *Long Jakes* (fig. 34), must have had a slightly different appeal. M. Knoedler, also the publisher of Bingham's *Canvassing for a Vote*,

issued the print in an expensive *chine collé* edition in folio size. It is a masterpiece of American lithographic portraiture. It is also at once graphically beautiful and faithful to the original, differing from Deas's painting in no detail but in rendering technique; all of the tonal and textural values are equivalent to the original but are conveyed in terms of the lithographic crayon, drawn in a distinctly graphic rather than painterly way.

Both prints were drawn on stone with sensitivity and a masterful handling of the crayon. They were produced with considerably more care than most lithographs of the time and are superior

examples of what black and white lithography could achieve in the interpretation of painting. In a sense, they can be considered the swan song of the medium, which went into an artistic eclipse before being revived as an original art form by Whistler and his followers later in the century. By the 1850s the process of chromolithography was already highly developed and finding widespread use in the United States as the chief means of reproducing paintings. A chromolithograph (fig. 120) after Alfred Jacob Miller's *The Lost Greenhorn* (fig. 100), produced by New York publisher H. Ward in 1851, illustrates the lengths to which printers went to replicate the original in every respect. It was possible through chromolithography to imitate the actual look of oil paint and the texture of brushstrokes and canvas. This was the logical outcome of the trend toward making art universally available and of the development of the high-quality reproductive aspects of lithography.

While the quality of lithography was being refined, a different class of prints was being produced by engraving. When George Caleb Bingham had his painting *The County Election* (fig. 22; engraving, fig. 121) engraved by John Sartain in 1854, he was following an artistic practice begun in Renaissance Europe. Since the time of Dürer

and Raphael, many artists had sought to broaden the audience for their works through engraved copies. In eighteenth-century Britain and France, side by side with documentary printmaking, an industry of reproductive engraving grew up in response to public interest in painting.[12] The tradition was preserved in the United States. Here, since the beginning of the nineteenth century, engraving had been used to publicize the early efforts of American portrait, historical, and genre painters. Genre scenes had a special popularity, appealing to the American sense of national character and fondness for moral instruction.

It was John Lewis Krimmel (1786–1821), called "the American Hogarth," who launched Amer-

120. *After Alfred Jacob Miller,*
The Lost Greenhorn, *1851,*
chromolithograph,
19 × 24 in. (sheet).
Published by H. Ward, Jr.
Buffalo Bill Historical
Center, Cody, Wyoming

ican genre painting and forged its initial alliance with printmaking. During his brief career (ended by his drowning death at the age of thirty-five), Krimmel depicted middle-class society with remarkable accuracy. Krimmel and the publishers of his day recognized the broad appeal of such work and saw to it that a number of his paintings were engraved and published. Alexander Lawson's engraving of his *Election Day at the State House* (1815–20) set an important precedent in

American printmaking by detailing the characters and incidental color of a political event. The print thus anticipates Sartain's engraving of Bingham's *The County Election*.

During the four decades that separate Krimmel's and Bingham's work, gift books and polite magazines sustained the genre tradition and prepared the ground for the western genre prints of mid century. By acquainting the American public with the work of American painters, they also antici-

121. *John Sartain (1808–97), after George Caleb Bingham,* The County Election, *1854, mezzotint, engraving, stipple, and etching (hand colored), 22³/₁₆ × 30³/₁₆ in. Printed by Jas. Irwin, Published by Goupil & Co. Amon Carter Museum, Fort Worth*

pated the art-unions of the 1840s, which were responsible for perhaps the earliest organized support for native engravers and artists. Gift books were collections of poems, stories, and engraved plates issued annually in elegantly printed and bound editions. Periodicals like *Sartain's Magazine* and the *New York Illustrated Magazine* offered similar content on a monthly basis. Both kinds of publications appealed to a genteel, educated, and affluent class, and illustrations were central to this appeal. Often reproductions of paintings or drawings by American artists, they were not mere illustrations, since they often inspired the book or magazine's text.[13] It was in such a context that Charles Deas's *Long Jakes* was published in 1846. The July issue of the *New York Illustrated Magazine,* a monthly journal of literature and art, carried an engraving of Deas's painting done by W. G. Jackman (fig. 122). The print appeared along with an essay commenting on the virtues of the original and the lore of the trapper.

Little is known of Jackman aside from the fact of his being a New York reproductive engraver who supplied the magazine with a number of plates over the course of several years. His *Long Jakes* was "executed in the first style of the art" from the original painting, according to the editor, who expressed in his announcement of the work great eagerness to do "full justice" to the original.[14] Jackman's engraving faithfully reproduces the original, scrupulously preserving the details of costume and accessories. The engraver somewhat generalized the background detail, and in his rendering of the clothing gave the subject a more ragged look than the original. Still, his aim was fidelity to the original—finally an impossible task since the engraving is very different in scale from the painting. Instead of the monumentality achieved in the original, the engraved image has the gemlike, precious quality characteristic of the small gift-book-style plates.

An ancillary branch of engraving important to the history of genre prints was bank-note engraving, the business of producing images and decorative details for currency, stock certificates, bonds, and other types of securities. Before 1861 it was not the federal government but state banks

and private banks that issued paper money in the United States. The "security engraving" industry became a major source of patronage, employing on a regular basis hundreds of artists and engravers, and spawning dozens of engraving firms. Bank-note engraving comprised an important fund of popular imagery, with genre subjects figuring prominently in its repertoire. Moreover, the art was extraordinarily pervasive and democratic in exposure. During the first half of the nineteenth century, thousands of individual images were designed to decorate bank notes, and these thousands were printed in millions of impressions. Once in circulation, they passed through the hands of countless Americans. It is hard to imagine an adult of those times who would not have handled paper currency regularly. Bank-note engraving was an art that reached the people as no other visual medium could.

The subject matter of these engravings was heavily symbolic. Even the genre scenes were laden with associative values. In representing banks, states, and other civic or commercial organizations, the designs had to convey the economic and social values shared by these institutions and their constituents, including themes of industry, agriculture, commerce, and progress. Such themes were expressed through abstract symbols or through more literal portrayals of representative characters or activities. During the 1840s and 1850s, genre subjects became common, with images of the American farmer and pioneer representing agriculture and progress, mainstays of the American economy. Images chosen for engraving on bank notes were generally conservative in style, and their subjects of lasting rather than strictly contemporary significance. In circulation, they had to survive the test of time and use, and this encouraged a kind of classicism in their illustrations, wherein costume and appointments were generalized and the figures were established types.

Western subjects were incorporated into the stock of bank-note imagery during the 1840s, although the Indian appeared well before this, usually as the Indian Queen personifying America or symbolizing the untamed frontier. But during the

1840s, Indians began to be portrayed more commonly in the context of daily activities—as hunters, braves, or trackers. However, these were generalized Indians, of no distinguishable tribe, who represented the vast unmolested potential of the territories beyond the frontier. Newly available works on Indian life, such as Catlin's *North American Indian Portfolio,* may have stimulated this interest and certainly served as sources for the scores of buffalo hunts that appeared on notes in the 1850s.

Other frontier subjects ranged from pioneers,

farmers, and trappers, to families protecting their homesteads, to flatboatmen similar to those by Bingham. These motifs were most frequently found on currency issued by the less heavily settled western and southern states, such as Mississippi, Florida, Kentucky, Michigan, and Nebraska. Ironically, the scenes were all created by eastern firms like Toppan Carpenter & Company of Philadelphia, Rawdon Wright and Hatch of New York, and the American Bank Note Company, also of New York.

The designs for bank-note illustrations originated in several ways. Most often an artist was specially commissioned to furnish a drawing on a specified subject or theme. Many of these scenes were produced by illustrators, like Charles Parsons, Charles Shearman, and F.O.C. Darley, the consummate book illustrator who excelled in this kind of work as well. Darley's bank-note illustrations succeed in being at once generalized and dramatic. While details of costume and tribe-specific accoutrements are suppressed, the Indians are vivid and convincing.

In addition to specific commissions, it was also common practice for an engraver to copy a well-known painting or a published print for a bank-note vignette. Some were derived from Seth Eastman's illustrations in Schoolcraft or were loosely based on plates from Catlin's *North American Indian Portfolio,* or Darley's *Scenes in Indian Life*. It is doubtful that permission was obtained from either the artists or their publishers to put their works to this new use. As in the rest of the printmaking industry, this sort of plagiarism was rampant, suggesting that copyright on designs was either incompletely understood or inadequately enforced.

Documentation of the sources and authors of bank-note vignettes is scarce, but certain quotations can be traced. Some of Darley's original drawings of frontier scenes and Indians done specifically for bank-note vignettes still exist. The American Bank Note Company's *Westward Ho* features a frontier scout lifted from Emanuel Leutze's 1861 mural *Westward the Course of Empire,* in the United States Capitol.

Despite piracy and free quotation from originals, bank-note engravers and designers maintained a high level of quality and craftsmanship. Through their work they provided an avenue by which American genre scenes—especially those of frontier life—reached an extremely wide audience.

Owing to the combined patronage of gift-book publishers and bank-note firms, the engraving industry was in a healthy state during the 1840s and helped create a climate of interest for the major western prints, the genre plates after Bingham, Ranney, and other western painters. These prints, more ambitious and expensive than the western

123. *Alfred Jones (1819–1900), after Richard Caton Woodville (1825–56),* Mexican News, *1853, engraving, etching, and stipple (hand colored), 23 × 18⁹/₁₆ in. Printed by J. Dalton. Amon Carter Museum, Fort Worth*

prints produced before them, were produced by engravers who, unlike their counterparts in lithography and book illustration, were distinguished members of the art world. Painters like Asher B. Durand and John Kensett had emerged from the ranks of copperplate engravers. There was a general respect for the profession. Recognition came in the form of high fees—engravers were usually paid more than the artists who designed the originals—and membership in such prestigious organizations as the National Academy of Design and the Pennsylvania Academy of the Fine Arts. Master engravers were sought after by publishers and entrusted with commissions for large-plate works that involved commitments of large amounts of time and money.

The American Art-Union and, before it, the Apollo Association were among several organizations founded during the 1840s to promote the fine arts in the United States. Their aim was to create a sound base of public support for art by raising the level of public taste through exposure to fine American works. Through membership fees and lotteries, they established a feasible means of funding exhibitions and a regular series of en-

124. *Thomas Doney (active 1844–49), after George Caleb Bingham, The Jolly Flat Boat Men, 1847–48, mezzotint, engraving, stipple, and etching (hand colored), 18¹³/₁₆ × 24 in. Printed by Powell & Co., Published by the American Art-Union. Amon Carter Museum, Fort Worth*

gravings after contemporary American paintings. The art-unions were an important force in the patronage of engraving.[15]

In their selection of works to reproduce, art-unions preserved traditional preferences for historical scenes and genre subjects. Beginning with William Sidney Mount's *Farmers Nooning* in 1843 and ending with Richard Caton Woodville's *Mexican News* (fig. 123) in 1853 (both engraved

by Alfred Jones), the American Art-Union showed a bias toward images of American regional scenes, as a means of broadcasting the best efforts of American artists. Thomas Doney's mezzotint *The Jolly Flat Boat Men* (fig. 124), produced from Bingham's painting (fig. 13) under the American Art-Union's aegis in 1848, and T. Dwight Booth's engraving (fig. 125) after Ranney's *The Trapper's Last Shot* (fig. 55), produced by the Western Art-Union in 1850, are prime examples.

The Jolly Flat Boat Men was Bingham's first genre work to be reproduced as a print. The painting was purchased by the American Art-Union in late 1846 and earmarked for engraving in December when the Art-Union contracted Thomas Doney to make two plates from it. The first, a small etching, was published in the Union's *Transactions* for 1846 to announce publication of the second, larger plate, scheduled for 1847 but actually finished in February 1848.

For Bingham, such recognition was impressive and had a lasting effect on his career. However, the arrangement was short on immediate financial reward; Bingham was paid $290 for his painting and nothing for permission to reproduce it. Indeed, the American Art-Union, like other publishers, often entirely skirted the expensive issue of reproduction fees by using paintings from private or public collections whenever possible. Artists were rarely paid for the use of their works and had no control over the reuse of their original or of the resultant plate after the original was sold. The steel plate for Bingham's *The Jolly Flat Boat Men* was eventually auctioned and a new edition pulled from it by a commercial publisher in 1860. Hence the reproduction of one's work was rarely a significant means of support for American artists of the time.

Thomas Doney was an accomplished mezzotint artist. During the 1830s, mezzotint, a technique that had passed out of vogue at the end of the eighteenth century, made a comeback in the United States. John Sartain pioneered this revival in his portraits and in the plates for gift books and magazines, reproducing paintings by American artists. Mezzotint is quite different from line engraving in both aesthetic and technical characteristics. In it, the artist works primarily in tones rather than line. With its capacity for increased subtlety of modeling and light effects, it could more closely approximate the continuous tones of painting, and, as an intaglio process, it could also realize deeper blacks and more striking contrasts than lithography. This made it an ideal reproductive medium.

For preparing and supervising the printing of the two plates for *The Jolly Flat Boat Men* Doney was paid $3,374.70, more than ten times the amount Bingham received for his original painting. The large plate was printed in an edition of close to 10,000, to accommodate the 9,666 members of the Art-Union in 1847. This was a substantial edition and was completed only with great difficulty. It took nine months just to pull the impressions,[16] and careful attention had to be paid to the plate since mezzotints are particularly subject to wear. Once in circulation, Bingham's print was copied and imitated by magazines and by printmakers such as Currier & Ives, with and without credit to the artist.

Of Bingham's later genre prints, only two, *The County Election* (1854) and *Martial Law* (1872), were engraved in the United States. *The County Election* (fig. 22; engraving, fig. 121) was engraved by John Sartain under Bingham's close supervision. Considered the finest mezzotint engraver of his time, Sartain was contracted by the artist himself and the undertaking financed by advance subscription. The plate took eighteen months to complete. In contrast to *The Jolly Flat Boat Men* print, Bingham initiated the *County Election* project himself and sold publishing rights to Goupil & Company only when the work was complete. As Bingham himself lacked the distribution network of an American Art-Union, he needed a large publisher like Goupil to market the print widely.

William T. Ranney's painting, *The Trapper's Last Shot* (fig. 55; engraving, fig. 125), was reproduced by Cincinnati's Western Art-Union in 1850. The engraver, T. Dwight Booth, is known to have worked at various times in Cincinnati, New York, and Chicago. Among his major projects was an engraving of *The Committee of Congress Drafting the Declaration of Independence,* after Peter F. Rothermel's 1851 canvas. In his version of *The Trapper's Last Shot,* Booth seems to have followed the customary painstaking procedure for engraving large plates. Normally the composition was built up in layers, incorporating light sketching on the plate of the general design elements and figures, and then a heavier working up of the

125. *T. Dwight Booth
(active 1830–57), after
William Tylee Ranney,*
The Trapper's Last Shot,
*1850, engraving,
17¾ × 23⅝ in. (sheet).
Published by J. M. Emerson
& Co.
Bancroft Library, University
of California at Berkeley*

landscape or surroundings. The figures were filled in last, sometimes by the hand of a different engraver, beginning with the clothing and ending with the faces, hands, and other significant details. Often different stages of a single engraving would involve etching, roulette work, burin-engraving, and rocker-work (that is, mezzotint). The completed work was often a marvel of subtlety and nuance, its finish deceptively machined-looking.

Booth's rendering of the painting reproduced the original faithfully. The details of the forms and landscape are attentively drawn, the figure very carefully translated into line, with some stipple used on the face, hands, and bedroll. It is interesting to note that Booth's print was the exact size of the original painting and, unlike Jackman's *Long Jakes,* preserved the monumental quality of Ranney's main figure.

The plate of Booth's print was later reissued by the New York publisher, J. M. Emerson. Ranney received credit but no remuneration. Another New York publishing house, Currier & Ives, published a clumsy lithographic copy of the print (fig. 126) sometime after 1855—with no attribution to the artist.

Engraving projects of this magnitude were not undertaken casually. A large plate, on the scale of Sartain's *County Election* or Booth's *The Trapper's Last Shot,* could consume a year or more of work. The plate for *The County Election* was begun in November 1852 and was not completed until May 1854. Some plates absorbed even more time and the labor of several engravers.

Unlike many of the lithographs discussed earlier, these large engravings were produced not for the masses but for a discerning audience. The 9,666 members of the American Art-Union who received impressions of Bingham's *The Jolly Flat Boat Men* were expressly interested in American art. Engravings after Bingham's *County Election* and *Stump Speaking* (fig. 25; engraving, fig. 127) were produced and distributed by the publishing house of Goupil, an international fine-arts firm that catered to an affluent clientele. Moreover, the engraver's technical refinement was recognized and appreciated by American connoisseurs. For example, John Sartain's mezzotint after Bingham's *The County Election* incorporates aquatint, roulette, and burin-work, and was issued in various states, including signed proofs before letters—that is, artist's proofs—and proofs on fine india paper.

The large engravings and lithographs after American western paintings, Doney's *The Jolly Flat Boat Men,* Grozelier's *Western Life—The Trapper,* Booth's *The Trapper's Last Shot,* and others stand apart from the popular and documentary prints of their era, which served their function, lost their topical edge, and were sup-

126. *After William Tylee Ranney,* The Trapper's Last Shot, *after 1855, lithograph (hand colored), 11 × 15⁹⁄₁₆ in. Published by Currier & Ives. The Harry T. Peters Collection, Museum of the City of New York*

planted by newer prints. Documentary views of the West and portraits of its Indians became obsolete with changes wrought by history. The prints after Bingham, Ranney, Tait, and Wimar escaped this ephemerality and proved timeless. The permanent importance of the paintings reproduced and distributed through these prints was no doubt clear to the engravers, printers, and publishers who brought them about. For to commit a painting to such form was to express confidence in its quality as art and in the universal, abiding interest of its subject. Judging by the time and labor devoted to their reproduction, the paintings by Bingham, Tait, Ranney, and Wimar were considered statements of enduring worth about the American frontier. Given their expense, these images tended to reflect a conservative vision and established values. But they also summarized for their time the historical essence of the American West. One might even consider their survival today an affirmation of this confidence on the part of their audience and collectors.

127. *Louis-Adolphe Gautier (active 1847–76), after George Caleb Bingham,* Stump Speaking, *1856, aquatint, mezzotint, rouletting, and engraving (hand colored), 22⁵/₁₆ × 30¼ in. Printed and published by Goupil & Co. Amon Carter Museum, Fort Worth*

NOTES

1. See John W. Reps, *Cities on Stone: Nineteenth Century Lithograph Images of the Urban West* (Fort Worth: Amon Carter Museum, 1976).

2. For an account of the early development of lithography, see Michael Twyman, *Lithography, 1800–1850: The Techniques of Drawing on Stone in England and France and Their Application in Works of Topography* (London: Oxford University Press, 1970).

3. Edward Williams Clay's 1831 portrait lithograph of "Mr. Hackett as Nimrod Wild-fire" is in the collection of the New-York Historical Society. An unsigned lithograph of "Jibbenainosay," possibly by Nathaniel Currier, is in the collections of the Prints and Photographs Division, the Library of Congress.

4. Franklin Julius Meine, *The Crockett Almanacks* (Chicago: The Caxton Club, 1955).

5. See, for example, James Hall, *Sketches of History, Life and Manners in the West* (Philadelphia: H. Hall, 1835); and John Frost, *Thrilling Adventures among the Indians . . .* (Philadelphia: J. W. Bradley, 1849).

6. The most thorough study of Darley's work to date is contained in Christine Anne Hahler's essay in the exhibition catalogue ". . . *Illustrated by Darley": An Exhibition of Original Drawings by the American Book Illustrator Felix Octavius Carr Darley (1822–1888)* (Wilmington: Delaware Art Museum, 1978).

7. William Truettner, *The Natural Man Observed: A Study of Catlin's Indian Gallery* (Washington, D.C.: Smithsonian Institution Press, 1979).

8. For the history of the Schoolcraft volumes, see John Francis McDermott, *Seth Eastman: Pictorial Historian of the Indian* (Norman: University of Oklahoma Press, 1961), pp. 79–96.

9. The Pensacola bank note is reproduced in Grover C. Criswell, *North American Currency* (Iola, Kan.: Krause Publishing Company, 1965), p. 185.

10. See Peter C. Marzio, *The Democratic Art: Pictures for a 19th-Century America* (Boston: David R. Godine, 1979), pp. 26–31.

11. Media Projects, Inc., *Currier & Ives, A Catalogue Raisonné,* 2 vol. (Detroit: Gale Research Company, 1983), lists forty-six prints after Tait published by Currier & Ives. When one eliminates the prints that are merely different editions, versions, and details of the same Tait work one is left with thirty-eight prints.

12. Richard Godfrey chronicles the early development of reproductive engraving in eighteenth-century England in his *Printmaking in Britain: A General History from Its Beginning to the Present Day* (New York: New York University Press, 1978), pp. 31–65.

13. On the gift books and literary magazines and their engravings, see Ralph Thompson, *American Literary Annuals and Gifts Books, 1825–1865* (New York: H. W. Wilson, 1933), pp. 31–65.

14. The editor's announcement of the upcoming publication of Jackman's plate of *Long Jakes* appeared in the editor's note section of the *New York Illustrated Magazine,* June 1846, p. 128. Henry William Herbert's extended essay on the western hunter appeared along with the plate in the following issue (July 1846, pp. 169–74).

15. See Jay Cantor's "Prints and the American Art-Union" in *Prints in and of America to 1850,* edited by John D. Morse (Charlottesville: University Press of Virginia, 1970), pp. 297–326; and John Francis McDermott, "George Caleb Bingham and the American Art-Union," *New-York Historical Society Quarterly* 42 (January 1958): 60–69.

16. John Francis McDermott, "Jolly Flatboatmen: Bingham and His Imitators," *Antiques* 73 (March 1958): 266–69. Still the most thorough documentation of Bingham's print oeuvre is found in E. Maurice Bloch, *George Caleb Bingham: The Evolution of an Artist* (Berkeley and Los Angeles: University of California Press, 1967).

EXHIBITION CHECKLIST

PAINTINGS

GEORGE CALEB BINGHAM (1811–1879)

Raftsmen Playing Cards, 1847
oil on canvas, 28 × 38 in.
Lent by The Saint Louis Art Museum:
Ezra H. Linley Fund

The Checker Players (Playing Chequers), 1850
oil on canvas, 25 × 30 in.
Detroit Institute of Arts, Gift of Dexter M. Ferry, Jr.

The Squatters, 1850
oil on canvas, 25 × 30 in.
Museum of Fine Arts, Boston, Bequest of Henry L.
Shattuck in memory of the late Ralph W. Gray
(Amon Carter Museum and Pennsylvania Academy
of the Fine Arts only)

The County Election, 1851–1852
oil on canvas, 35⁷⁄₁₆ × 48¾ in.
Lent by The Saint Louis Art Museum
(Amon Carter Museum only)

Canvassing for a Vote, 1852
oil on canvas, 25⅛ × 30¼ in.
The Nelson-Atkins Museum of Art, Kansas City,
Missouri (Nelson Fund)

Wood-Boatmen on a River (Western Boatmen Ashore by Night), 1854
oil on canvas, 29 × 36¼ in.
Amon Carter Museum, Fort Worth

The Jolly Flatboatmen in Port, 1857
oil on canvas, 47¹⁄₁₆ × 69¹⁰⁄₁₆ in.
Lent by The Saint Louis Art Museum

CHARLES DEAS (1818–1867)

Winnebagos Playing Checkers, 1842
oil on canvas, 12⁷⁄₁₆ × 14¾ in.
Thyssen-Bornemisza Collection, Lugano, Switzerland

Long Jakes (Long Jakes, The Rocky Mountain Man), 1844
oil on canvas, 30 × 25 in.
Vose Galleries of Boston, Inc.

A Group of Sioux, 1845
oil on canvas, 14⅛ × 16½ in.
Amon Carter Museum, Fort Worth

The Death Struggle, ca. 1845
oil on canvas, 30 × 25 in.
The Shelburne Museum, Shelburne, Vermont

The Voyageurs, 1845
oil on canvas, 24 × 29½ in.
Rokeby Collection, New York

The Voyageurs, 1846
oil on canvas, 13 × 20½ in.
Museum of Fine Arts, Boston, M. and M. Karolik
Collection

Prairie Fire, 1847
oil on canvas, 28⅞ × 36¹⁄₁₆ in.
The Brooklyn Museum,
Gift of Mr. and Mrs. Alastair Bradley Martin

WILLIAM TYLEE RANNEY (1813–1857)

Hunting Wild Horses (The Lasso), 1846
oil on canvas, 36 × 54½ in.
Enron Art Foundation/Joslyn Art Museum, Omaha

Prairie Burial, 1848
oil on canvas, 28½ × 41 in.
Private Collection

The Retreat, 1850
oil on canvas, 30½ × 48½ in.
Private Collection

The Trapper's Last Shot, 1850
oil on canvas, 18 × 24 in.
Vose Galleries of Boston, Inc.

The Scouting Party, ca. 1851
oil on canvas, 30 × 40 in.
Private Collection

Advice on the Prairie, 1853
oil on canvas, 40 × 54 in.
Private Collection

The Trappers, 1856
oil on canvas, 23½ × 36 in.
Enron Art Foundation/Joslyn Art Museum, Omaha

ARTHUR F. TAIT (1819–1905)

Trappers at Fault, Looking for the Trail, 1852
oil on canvas, 36 × 50 in.
Helen Dill Collection at The Denver Art Museum

The Prairie Hunter—One Rubbed Out!, 1852
oil on canvas, 14 × 20 in.
Enron Foundation/Joslyn Art Museum, Omaha

*American Frontier Life
(Trapper Retreating Over River),* 1852
oil on canvas, 24⅜ × 36¼ in.
Yale University Art Gallery,
Whitney Collections of Sporting Art, given in
memory of Harry Payne Whitney, B.A. 1894, and
Payne Whitney, B.A. 1898, by Francis P. Garvan,
B.A. 1897, M.A. (Hon.) 1922

The Check, 1854
oil on canvas, 30 × 44 in.
The Thomas Gilcrease Institute of American History
and Art, Tulsa, Oklahoma

The Last War Whoop, 1855
oil on canvas, 30 × 44 in.
Milwaukee Art Museum Collection, Gift of Edward
S. Tallmadge as a Memorial to the Men Who Loyally
and Selflessly Gave Their Lives for Our Country in
World War II

Buffalo Hunt, 1861
oil on canvas, 24½ × 36½ in.
Private Collection

GEORGE CATLIN (1796–1872)

Bull Dance, Mandan O-Kee-Pa Ceremony, 1832
oil on canvas, 23¼ × 28 in.
The Anschutz Collection, Denver

Buffalo Chase, Mouth of the Yellowstone, 1832–1833
oil on canvas mounted on aluminum, 24 × 29 in.
National Museum of American Art, Smithsonian
Institution, Gift of Mrs. Joseph Harrison, Jr.

Buffalo Chase in Winter, Indians on Snowshoes,
1832–1833
oil on canvas mounted on aluminum, 24 × 29 in.
National Museum of American Art, Smithsonian
Institution, Gift of Mrs. Joseph Harrison, Jr.

JOHN MIX STANLEY (1814–1872)

Game of Chance, ca. 1853
oil on canvas, 28¼ × 39⅜ in.
The Thomas Gilcrease Institute of American History
and Art, Tulsa, Oklahoma

The Disputed Shot, 1858
oil on canvas, 36 × 29 in.
Corcoran Gallery of Art, Washington, D.C.; Gift
of William Wilson Corcoran, 1869

Blackfeet Card Players, 1869
oil on canvas, 20 × 42 in.
John F. Eulich Collection,
Dallas
(Buffalo Bill Historical Center and Amon Carter
Museum only)

CHARLES WIMAR (1828–1862)

The Captive Charger, 1854
oil on canvas, 30 × 41 in.
Lent by The Saint Louis Art Museum:
Gift of Miss Lillie B. Randell

The Attack on an Emigrant Train, 1856
oil on canvas, 55¼ × 79 in.
The University of Michigan Museum of Art,
Ann Arbor, Bequest of Henry C. Lewis

The Buffalo Dance, 1860
oil on canvas, 24⅞ × 49⅝ in.
Lent by The Saint Louis Art Museum:
Gift of Mrs. John T. Davis

Buffalo Hunt, 1861
oil on canvas, 36 × 61 in.
The Thomas Gilcrease Institute of American History
and Art, Tulsa, Oklahoma

SETH EASTMAN (1808–1875)

Chippewa Indians Playing Checkers, 1848
oil on canvas, 30 × 25 in.
The Regis Collection, Minneapolis

Ballplay of the Sioux on the St. Peters River in Winter,
1848
oil on canvas, 25¾ × 35¼ in.
Amon Carter Museum, Fort Worth

Medicine Dance, 1848
oil on canvas, 25½ × 35¼ in.
Private Collection, on loan to the
Buffalo Bill Historical Center, Cody, Wyoming

Sioux Indians, 1850
oil on canvas, 26⅜ × 38½ in.
Joslyn Art Museum, Omaha

Lacrosse Playing Among the Sioux Indians, 1851
oil on canvas, 28³⁄₁₆ × 40¾ in.
Corcoran Gallery of Art, Washington, D.C.; Gift of
William Wilson Corcoran, 1869

ALFRED JACOB MILLER (1810–1874)

The Trapper's Bride, 1845
oil on canvas, 36 × 28 in.
Harrison Eiteljorg Collection, Indianapolis

Buffalo Hunt, ca. 1850
oil on canvas, 30¼ × 50¼ in.
Amon Carter Museum, Fort Worth

The Lost Greenhorn, n.d.
oil on canvas, 17⅞ × 23⅞ in.
Buffalo Bill Historical Center, Cody, Wyoming

PRINTS

Dimensions listed indicate the image size, except for
those followed by an asterisk, which include the image
and accompanying imprint, and those followed by a
double asterisk, which reflect the print's sheet size.

NATHANIEL CURRIER (1813–1888)

Indian Hunter, 1845
lithograph (hand colored), 12⁹⁄₁₆ × 8½ in.*
Library of Congress (Prints and Photographs Division)
(Amon Carter Museum and Pennsylvania Academy
of the Fine Arts only)
Colgate Collection, Division of Graphic Arts,
National Museum of American History,
Smithsonian Institution
(Buffalo Bill Historical Center only)

The Indian Warrior, 1845
lithograph (hand colored), 12⅝ × 8⁹⁄₁₆ in.*
Library of Congress (Prints and Photographs Division)
(Amon Carter Museum and Pennsylvania Academy
of the Fine Arts only)

Indian Family, n.d.
lithograph (hand colored), 12¾ × 8⁹⁄₁₆ in.
Colgate Collection, Division of Graphic Arts,
National Museum of American History, Smithsonian
Institution
(Buffalo Bill Historical Center only)

AFTER FELIX OCTAVIUS CARR DARLEY (1822–1888)

Thomas S. Sinclair (ca. 1805–1881)
Scenes in Indian Life, No. 10, 1843
lithograph, 7½ × 9⅜ in.*
Published by J. R. Colon
Amon Carter Museum, Fort Worth

Thomas S. Sinclair (ca. 1805–1881)
Scenes in Indian Life, No. 7, 1843
lithograph, 7³⁄₁₆ × 8⁷⁄₁₆ in.*
Published by J. R. Colon
Amon Carter Museum, Fort Worth

AFTER GEORGE CALEB BINGHAM (1811–1879)

Thomas Doney (active 1844–1849)
The Jolly Flat Boat Men, 1847–1848
mezzotint, engraving, stipple, and
etching (hand colored), 18¹³⁄₁₆ × 24 in.
Printed by Powell & Co., Published by the American
Art-Union
Amon Carter Museum, Fort Worth

Claude Regnier (active 1847–1853)
Canvassing for a Vote, 1852–1853
toned lithograph, 17⅛ × 20⁵⁄₁₆ in.*
Published by M. Knoedler
Amon Carter Museum, Fort Worth

John Sartain (1808–1897)
The County Election, 1854
mezzotint, engraving, stipple, and
etching (hand colored), 22³⁄₁₆ × 30³⁄₁₆ in.
Printed by Jas. Irwin, Published by Goupil & Co.
Amon Carter Museum, Fort Worth

Louis-Adolphe Gautier (active 1847–1876)
Stump Speaking, 1856
aquatint, mezzotint, rouletting, and
engraving (hand colored), 22⁵⁄₁₆ × 30¼ in.
Printed and published by Goupil & Co.
Amon Carter Museum, Fort Worth

AFTER CHARLES DEAS (1818–1867)

Leopold Grozelier (1830–1865)
Western Life—The Trapper, ca. 1855
lithograph (proof), 20 × 18¼ in.
Printed by J. H. Bufford, Published by M. Knoedler
Amon Carter Museum, Fort Worth

William G. Jackman (active 1841–1860s)
Long Jakes, 1846
engraving, 4¾ × 5¾ in.
Published in *New York Illustrated Magazine of
Literature and Art*
The New-York Historical Society, New York City

AFTER WILLIAM TYLEE RANNEY (1813–1857)

T. Dwight Booth (active 1830–1857)
The Trapper's Last Shot, 1850
engraving, 17¾ × 23⅝ in.**
Published by J. M. Emerson & Co.
Bancroft Library, University of California at Berkeley

Lithographer unknown
The Trapper's Last Shot, after 1855
lithograph (hand colored), 11 × 15⁹⁄₁₆ in.
Published by Currier & Ives
The Harry T. Peters Collection,
Museum of the City of New York

AFTER ARTHUR F. TAIT (1819–1905)

Otto Knirsch (active 1853–1860s)
The Prairie Hunter. "One Rubbed Out!", 1852
lithograph (hand colored), 16¼ × 20⅝ in.*
Published by Nathaniel Currier
Library of Congress (Prints and Photographs Division)
(Amon Carter Museum and Pennsylvania Academy
of the Fine Arts only)
Colgate Collection, Division of Graphic Arts,
National Museum of American History,
Smithsonian Institution
(Buffalo Bill Historical Center only)

Louis Maurer (1832–1932)
The Pursuit, 1856
toned lithograph (hand colored), 19⅛ × 25⁹⁄₁₆ in.*
Published by Nathaniel Currier
Amon Carter Museum, Fort Worth

Louis Maurer (1832–1932)
The Last War-Whoop, 1856
lithograph (hand colored), 18³⁄₁₆ × 25⁹⁄₁₆ in.
Published by Currier & Ives
The Harry T. Peters Collection,
Museum of the City of New York

Lithographer unknown
*Life on the Prairie. The Trapper's Defense,
"Fire Fight Fire.",* 1862
toned lithograph (hand colored), 19⅞ × 27³⁄₁₆ in.*
Published by Currier & Ives
Amon Carter Museum, Fort Worth

AFTER GEORGE CATLIN (1796–1872)

Lithographer unknown
North American Indian Portfolio, 1845
color lithograph (hand colored), 13⁵⁄₁₆ × 18⁵⁄₁₆ in.
Published by James Ackerman
Library of Congress (Rare Books Division)

Lithographer unknown
Buffalo Bull, Chasing Back. "Turn About Is Fair Play,"
probably 1850s
toned lithograph, 12⁷⁄₁₆ × 18³⁄₁₆ in.
Published by Currier & Ives
Colgate Collection, Division of Graphic Arts,
National Museum of American History,
Smithsonian Institution

Lithographer unknown
*Indians Attacking the Grizzly Bear. The Most Savage
and Ferocious Animal of North America,* probably 1850s
lithograph (hand colored), 12¼ × 17⅞ in.
Published by Currier & Ives
The Harry T. Peters Collection,
Museum of the City of New York

AFTER CHARLES WIMAR (1828–1862)

Leopold Grozelier (1830–1865)
On the Prairie, 1860
lithograph (hand colored), 22 × 29¾ in.**
Printed by J. H. Bufford
Published by J. E. Tilton & Co.
The Thomas Gilcrease Institute of American History
and Art, Tulsa, Oklahoma

AFTER ALFRED JACOB MILLER (1810–1874)

Lithographer unknown
The Lost Greenhorn, 1851
chromolithograph, 19 × 24 in.**
Published by H. Ward, Jr.
Buffalo Bill Historical Center, Cody, Wyoming

INDEX

PHOTO CREDITS

All photographic material was obtained from the collections indicated in the captions, except for the following—Hillel Burger: fig. 28; Geoffrey Clements, Inc.: fig. 41; Helga Photo Studio, Inc.: fig. 35; Linda Lorenz: figs. 17, 36, 95, 102, 103, 105, 106, 109, 114, 117, 119, 121, 123, 124, 127; James A. Milmoe: figs. 50, 63, 67, 80; Clive Russ: figs. 34, 40; Taylor & Dull, Inc. (courtesy Kennedy Galleries, Inc.): fig. 2.